DAUGHTERS
OF AQUARIUS

CultureAmerica

ERIKA DOSS

PHILIP J. DELORIA

Series Editors

KARAL ANN MARLING

Editor Emerita

DAUGHTERS OF AQUARIUS

WOMEN OF THE SIXTIES COUNTERCULTURE

GRETCHEN LEMKE-SANTANGELO

 UNIVERSITY PRESS OF KANSAS

Published by the

University Press of Kansas

(Lawrence, Kansas 66045),

which was organized by the

Kansas Board of Regents and

is operated and funded by

Emporia State University,

Fort Hays State University,

Kansas State University,

Pittsburg State University,

the University of Kansas, and

Wichita State University

Library of Congress Cataloging-in-Publication Data

Lemke-Santangelo, Gretchen
    Daughters of Aquarius : women of the sixties
counterculture / Gretchen Lemke-Santangelo
        p. cm — (CultureAmerica)
    Includes bibliographical references and index.
    ISBN 978-0-7006-1633-6 (cloth : alk. paper)
    1. Counterculture—United States—History—
20th century. 2. Hippies—United States History—
20th century. 3. Young women—United States
History—20th century. 4. United States—Social life
ad culture—1945–1970. 5. Ninteen sixties. I. Title.
HQ799.7.L45 2009
305.48'969097309046—dc22

                                        2008048044

British Library Cataloguing-in-Publication Data
is available.

Printed in the United States of America

10   9   8   7   6   5   4   3   2   1

The paper used in this publication is recycled and
contains 30 percent postconsumer waste. It is acid
free and meets the minimum requirements of the
American National Standard for Permanence of
Paper for Printed Library Materials Z39.48–1992.

Permissions are on page 235.

For Anthony and Elizabeth

CONTENTS

 ACKNOWLEDGMENTS

It gives me great pleasure to acknowledge that this project was a collaborative endeavor. Back in 2001, when the book was just an idea, Nancy Scott Jackson, Virginia Scharff, and Nan Enstad convinced me and the University Press of Kansas to run with it. As the project moved forward, I incurred an enormous debt to the women who entrusted me and others with their stories. Their generosity and candor made the book possible. I am also indebted to Timothy Miller, Professor of Religious Studies at the University of Kansas. He, Deborah Altus, and several other scholars conducted more than 500 interviews with former and current commune members. During November of 2006, Tim granted me access to the 60s Communes Project collection, referred me to other critical sources and contacts, and helped me feel entirely at home and welcome in Lawrence, Kansas. After finishing the first draft, I was immeasurably grateful for the advice that I received from Kalyani Fernando, Erika Doss, Nan Enstad, Martha Jane Brazy, Carl Guarneri, Myrna Santiago, Paul Flemer, Brother Charles Hilken, Kathy Roper, and Micah Muscolino. Their insightful, concise, and often brilliant suggestions significantly enhanced the quality of the manuscript. I would also like to thank production and copy editors Jennifer Dropkin and Libby Barstow for their careful attention to detail and style. Saint Mary's College not only granted me a sabbatical midway through the project but also provided a generous endowment that covered my research expenses. Lisa Law, the Estate of Irwin Klein, Ida Griffin, Mark Weiman, the Estate of Allen Cohen, and Bernadette Cummings of Rhino Entertainment Company supplied the stunningly beautiful photographs and art that accompany the text. Brad Boca, of Looking Glass Photo, applied his formidable artistic talents to retouching and modifying the graphics for publication. Friends, family and old colleagues also offered much support. Anthony Santangelo, my beloved life-companion, protected my privacy, sheltered me from outside distractions, and listened patiently as I attempted to make sense of my sources and clarify my arguments. Anna Marie Daniels, my sister, offered up her story and provided plenty of encouragement to stay on task. She, like many other former hippie women, has a very strong work ethic. My good friends Margaret Marie, Philippe (hippie guy) Habib, Heidi Cartan, Steve Woolpert, and Virginia Logan also sustained and enlivened my spirits. Finally, I am deeply grateful to William Chafe and Robert Cherny. From the start of my professional career they encouraged me to take creative risks and mine history's margins for hidden gems.

Gretchen Lemke-Santangelo

DAUGHTERS OF AQUARIUS

enise Kaufman's parents, Hank and Golda, married in 1944 when Hank was still in the service. After the war ended, they settled in San Francisco's Richmond district and welcomed baby Denise. Born in the fall of 1946, she entered a world alive with song. Home life, vacations, gatherings with family friends, and summer camp were filled with "magical musical experiences." As a child, she not only wrote poetry; she also studied piano at the San Francisco Conservatory of Music and performed with the San Francisco Children's Opera. At fourteen, Denise took up guitar and joined the Bay Area's lively folk music scene. Although "pretty out of sync" with her high school peers, she fit right in with the bohemian folk subculture. Then, in 1965, she met psychedelic pioneer Ken Kesey and discovered a world that offered even more creative possibilities. "Within weeks I quit school, moved to La Honda, became Mary Microgram and got on the Bus." After a year and a half of "exploring and stretching the boundaries . . . of consciousness" as a Merry Prankster and playing music that expressed the emerging counterculture sensibility, she moved back to San Francisco.[1]

By that time the Haight Ashbury was hippie central, a swirling, colorful, all-hours hub of youthful yearning. It wasn't long before Denise hooked up with four other young, female musicians and formed The Ace of Cups. Unlike many of the male artists who eventually eclipsed them, they composed and performed music that emphasized the values of the counterculture. Denise, as a fellow band member recalled, wrote "song jewels," lyrics that expressed a generation's longing for intimacy, community, spiritual transcendence, and self-transformation. After they disbanded, Denise became a woman of the New Age, studying yoga, Sanskrit, Indian philosophy, and meditation and creating a new profession as a teacher, healer, and organic farmer. She, like countless hippie women, not only helped shape the counterculture but also carved out a sphere of influence in the social, cultural, and political movements of the 1970s and 1980s.[2]

In the mid-1960s, Denise and her fellow band members, while fully committed to creating a new social order, occupied the margins of a male-dominated landscape. The early counterculture, for all of its exuberant, visionary idealism, was the "territory of men."[3] To many of her male peers, Denise was a mere "chick," an imposter and interloper. How dare she and other women be the authors rather than the subjects of the unfolding countercultural drama? Indeed, while hippies challenged many of their elder's values by embracing antimaterialism, communal living, sexual liberation, voluntary poverty, cooperative social and economic relations, and a romantic attachment to nature, their gender constructs were essentialist, heteronormative, and—at least initially—hierarchical.

While seemingly confined to conventional roles, women were in fact launching a subtle rebellion against prevailing class and gender norms. Rejecting the suburban domesticity of their mothers, hippie women revived an older, agrarian ideal that assigned greater value and visibility to female productive labor. They also cast off the privatized nuclear family structure in favor of communal living arrangements that, like large extended families of the past, permitted women to share chores, conversation, advice, and practical knowledge. Within "tribes," women's work was not only more varied, creative, and challenging; it was performed in the service of broader countercultural ideals. Women therefore assigned political significance to their labor. Indeed, their arduous efforts, in contrast to men's often transitory contributions, sustained many of hippiedom's grand social experiments. Women's expanding sense of their own importance was further enhanced by the counterculture's emphasis on cooperation, reciprocity, interdependence, closeness to nature, physical and emotional expressiveness, egalitarianism, and nonaggression—traits that women, within an essentialist gender framework, "naturally" possessed. Slowly but surely they began to articulate a feminist vision that emphasized the dignity, if not superiority, of traditional "feminine" values and labor. Thus, in contrast to most women's historians, I argue that feminism did not bypass the counterculture. Indeed, cultural feminism, typically regarded as an outgrowth of lesbian disaffection with new left-derived feminist theory and practice, emerged simultaneously and with equal force among hippie women of all sexual orientations.[4]

By the late 1960s and early 1970s, women translated their new-found skills, confidence, and the very notion of female difference into a source of power and authority within their own families and communities. And by the 1980s, their influence extended into the wider culture, transforming middle-class attitudes toward food, the environment, health, birth, child rearing, and spirituality. Like their nineteenth-century counterparts who parlayed "feminine" virtue into positions of authority in social reform movements, hippie women—as coarchitects of cultural feminism—used their "innate" qualities and talents to move counterculture values and practices into the mainstream. In the process they profoundly altered the social, political, economic, and cultural landscape of the United States.

In recent years, historians have produced a rich body of literature on women's political activism during the 1960s, detailing women's contributions to the decade's social struggles, how sexism within the New Left and civil rights movements precipitated the resurgence of feminism, and how second-wave feminists transformed contemporary political and social relations. To date, however, no similar study has been done on women of the counterculture. Indeed, for decades now, the experience and contributions of counterculture women such as Denise have been shrouded in popular misconceptions and stereotypes—stereotypes that I examine more closely in Chapter 1. Those of us who teach courses on women of the 1960s must therefore rely on a handful of memoirs, scattered and often ambiguous primary sources, and extrapolation from personal experience to fill in their story. In the meantime, studies on the counterculture proliferate. Its origins, art, music, literature, sexual mores, philosophical and spiritual tenets, pharmacopoeia, and legacy have all received scholarly attention. It is disappointing that none focus on hippie women. This work is intended to spark interest in recovering their stories and filling this gap.

Chapter 1, opening with a general introduction to the counterculture, focuses on mainstream and counterculture representations of women and how these images have obscured the complexity, agency, and creativity of their subjects. Hippie women, I maintain, sometimes played with and manipulated stereotypes to their advantage but mostly experienced them as degrading obstacles that interfered with their efforts to reinvent themselves and society.

Chapter 2, after establishing the white, middle-class origins of counterculture youth, moves directly to "real" women: their family backgrounds, sources of dissatisfaction with mainstream culture, early expressions of nonconformity and rebellion, and initial contacts with the counterculture. Many women, I assert, developed counterculture identities as children and adolescents. For them, finding hippiedom was like finding a home. As Marla Hanson, a member of The Ace of Cups, recalled, "I hated L.A. and was ready to do anything but stay there. When my friend Joel Beverly showed up at my door one day and asked me if I wanted to go to San Francisco, I said yes. I packed a bunch of stuff in a laundry bag (I was insane by then) and Joel and I took a bus to SF. When I saw the first sign on the SF freeway that said, 'Go back you are going the wrong way' my face broke into a huge smile and I knew I was where I wanted to be."[5] In leaving home, women like Marla not only transgressed class and racial boundaries; they abandoned prevailing gender norms for an as yet undefined alternative.

Chapter 3 details hippie gender constructs, the sexual revolution, and the extent to which their proscriptions confined or liberated counterculture women. I examine the latter question in relationship to women's sexuality, body image, intimate partnerships, and reproductive roles, concluding that freedom and constraint were not mutually exclusive. Indeed, hippie sexual constructs, while essentialist and heteronormative, were formulated and enacted outside of the confines of suburbia, the nuclear family, and middle-class moral and sexual strictures, rendering them somewhat flexible, fluid, and open to reexamination and reinterpretation. Sexual liberation, I argue, ultimately translated into a wider range of options, including lesbian partnerships.

Chapter 4 examines gender constructs and the theme of constraint versus freedom in relation to women's various economic survival strategies and quest for "right livelihood." The counterculture's division of labor, I maintain, confined most women to domestic roles. Their actual tasks, the arena in which they labored, and the sense of mission and purpose that informed their work, however, made it all appear novel, challenging, and exhilarating. Many, particularly those who had moved back to the land, had the additional satisfaction of mastering new skills such as composting, gardening, animal husbandry, canning, brewing, cheese making, quilting, midwifery, and alternative medicine. Their roles, departing sharply from the nuclear family-based suburban domesticity of the 1950s, more closely resembled those of their pioneer grandmothers and great grandmothers. Finally, most eventually realized that they provided a disproportionate share of the labor needed to sustain counterculture families and communities—a realization that contributed to the development of a woman-identified feminist consciousness.

Women's longing for spiritual enlightenment and self-actualization was, as Chapter 5 explains, at the core of their counterculture experience. Drug experimentation, chiefly with psychedelics, was but one expression of their longing. Women also explored a wide range of spiritual alternatives and therapies and ventured across the United States and abroad in search of personal growth and enlightenment. It was here, I argue, that women experienced the unfettered, no-holds-barred freedom normally reserved for men. Moreover, many of the spiritual alternatives and therapies affirmed women's "innate" gifts and talents, reinforcing their emerging cultural feminist consciousness. Their experimentation with alternate spiritual traditions certainly had some historical precedents, but their drug use and largely unsupervised travels were completely out of the ordinary. Never before had such large numbers of young, middle-class women taken their search for self-realization in such radical directions.

Chapter 6 focuses on the experience of "little sisters," the runaways and girl children of hippie parents who were the youngest members of the counterculture. Runaways, often cast as vulnerable, potential victims, were remarkably resilient, resourceful, and determined to secure and maintain their freedom and autonomy. In contrast, girls who were born into the counterculture often faced too many choices and longed for "normal" parents, limits, and boundaries. As hippie parents matured, settled down, and established their own behavioral limits, they achieved a better balance between freedom and restraint. Indeed, many of their child-rearing practices are now considered "mainstream."

Chapter 7 chronicles women's journey from the margins of hippiedom to the center of the New Age. Their feminist awakening, growing out of the convergence of counterculture gender constructs and hippie ideals, was absolutely crucial to this transition. In the 1970s, I maintain, most hippie women spurned feminist critiques of essentialism in favor of a difference-based, women-identified claim to power. Inherently peaceful, cooperative, and nurturing and in tune with their emotions, bodies, and nature, they cast themselves at the true representatives of Aquarian ideals. This assertion, backed up by their concrete, economically tangible contributions to counterculture experiments, allowed them to demand authority within their own families and communities and to extend their influence into post-1960s New Age movements. If they lacked pull and respect during the 1960s, they most certainly made up the deficit in the 1970s and 1980s.

In writing this account, I relied heavily on women's personal recollections of the 1960s counterculture. My choice was dictated partly by necessity (the paucity of other sources) and partly by commitment to a participatory model of scholarship. Given that women's experience has been so seriously distorted and ignored, I felt ethically compelled to place their stories at the center of the narrative. Oral history, however, is notably unreliable. As a product of memory it is easily warped by the all-too-human tendency to selectively recall or embroider past events. Above all, memory is mediated by or filtered through present interpretations of the past. I was aware, for example, that women were very, very young during the 1960s—young, spirited, romantic, relatively privileged, self-absorbed, and caught up in the seemingly unlimited possibilities of the time. As older adults, I predicted, they would quite understandably look back on the 1960s—their youth—with nostalgia. To my surprise, the much greater problem was that women feared my judgment and were all too willing to engage in self-censorship. Years of neoconservative critiques of 1960s "hedonism," coupled with popular culture stereotypes of air-brained, spaced-out hippie chicks, left many women mistrustful and guarded. Some, I suspected, not only censored their memories to avoid unflattering labels or assumptions about their character but also actually forgot or edited out entire chunks of their experience. I found it incredibly sad, for example, that women felt so defensive about their past that they could not—at least initially—bring themselves around to discussing the fun, playful, sensual, and yes, frankly hedonistic, aspects of the counterculture. When they relaxed, however, it often seemed as if a dam had burst. The fullness and complexity of their experience, and the pleasure of "owning" it, happily came forth.

To compensate for the caprice of memory and self-censorship, I drew on a wide array of primary sources including sociological, anthropological, epidemiological, psychological, and criminological profiles of counter-culture youth, underground and mainstream press coverage, and rare, but revealing, real-time interviews with hippie women. I also took care to present the differences as well as similarities in women's experience. Still, significant gaps remain, particularly in regard to women's travels, drug use, and expressions of sexuality and desire. Like many ventures into uncharted historical terrain, this study undoubtedly raises more questions than it answers. In describing the rough contours of women's experience, I fervently hope that other scholars will flesh out and revise my broad, exploratory findings. The topic richly deserves additional treatment.

In the interest of making this work accessible to a wide audience, including the women who so generously shared their stories, I deliberately avoided disciplinary jargon and the professorial voice. In counterculture-speak, I attempted to "get down" with the material and relate it in a transparent, minimally intrusive fashion. I also, on occasion, used counterculture language in my analysis and commentary. I hope that terms such as *straight* or *shit jobs* are comprehensible to readers. Also, the word *hippie* appears throughout the text, a word that was often used to disparage the counterculture. For stylistic reasons, mainly to avoid tiresome repetition, I used *hippie* and *counterculture* interchangeably. Given the passage of time, I am reasonably confident that this won't cause offense. Finally, I must be honest about my struggle to remain dispassionate. On one hand, I have a long standing affection for the counterculture. I share many of its values and have enjoyed teaching its exceptionally bright, curious, and engaged children. On the other hand, I have deep reservations about difference-based claims to power. They are, in my estimation, not only scientifically specious; they are strategically flawed. I am also, along with sociologist Robert Bellah, concerned that the counterculture's preoccupation with self-realization—especially in its New Age manifestation—did not always translate into a broader commitment to social justice and the common good. This said, I hope I have achieved something of a balance.

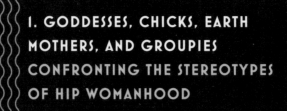

I. GODDESSES, CHICKS, EARTH MOTHERS, AND GROUPIES CONFRONTING THE STEREOTYPES OF HIP WOMANHOOD

he 1960s counterculture was a youth rebellion against the priorities, values, and conventions of mainstream U.S. society. The established order, according to hippie rebels and as summarized by social critic Philip Slater, gave "preference to property rights over personal rights, technological requirements over human needs, competition over cooperation, violence over sexuality, concentration over distribution, the product over the consumer, means over ends, secrecy over openness, social forms over personal expression, striving over gratification, oedipal love over communal love." Youth, however, did more than reject these preferences. In an often disorganized but highly creative and idealistic manner, they set out to fashion an alternative culture. Their ideal, in contrast to the old order, was nonhierarchical, nonviolent, cooperative, antimaterialistic, spontaneous, playful, tolerant, emotionally and physically expressive, and respectful of nature. Above all, they sought to create a society that prioritized the individual quest for transcendence, self-actualization, and intimate community.[1]

These ideals and the desire to enact them were hardly without precedent. During the nineteenth century, U.S. reformers such as Robert Owen and John Humphrey Noyes launched utopian experiments in response to social and economic dislocations associated with rapid industrial expansion. The transcendentalists' concerns and ideals even more closely paralleled those of the 1960s counterculture. Indeed, Henry David Thoreau, with his emphasis on pacifism, voluntary simplicity, communion with nature, and search for inner truth, became somewhat of a hippie idol. During the next century, successive generations of bohemians openly rejected middle-class moral conventions, cultural tastes, and patterns of consumption. Then, during the 1950s, as many soon-to-be hippies were entering adolescence, the Beats launched a vigorous attack against postwar militarism, consumerism, cultural and social conformity, racism, cold war demagoguery, and moral conservatism. The counterculture, as several scholars of the 1960s have noted, inherited and built upon their critique.

Moreover, hippie youth weren't the only members of their generation to voice discontent with U.S. values and policies. Their African American peers, later joined by other young people of color, mounted a formidable campaign for civil rights, political power, economic justice, and cultural pride. Some of these activists, especially those within the nonviolent civil rights movement, attempted to model a new social order— one based on universal brotherhood and the transforming power of love, cooperation, and nonhierarchical, highly democratic decisionmaking structures. A vibrant student left was even more closely aligned with the counterculture, sharing its disdain of consumer culture, militarism, authoritarian and impersonal institutions, and "uptight" morality. Indeed, hippies and student activists not only came from the same white, middle-class demographic; they often blurred the distinctions between their movements by moving from one to the other or exchanging values, tastes, and practices. For example, both shared the same music, experimented with drugs, embraced communal living, and advocated sexual liberation. Hippies engaged in political activism, and die-hard radicals "dropped out." And at least two groups—the yippies and Diggers— defied categorization altogether.

Despite this slippage, there were some clear distinctions between the counterculture and the student left, at least among the purists on either end of the hippie-politico continuum. Hippies, to an even greater extent than the student left, believed that social change depended upon a shift in human consciousness. Overreliance on reason or rational thought, they maintained, had severed the ties between man and nature, mind and body, intellect and spirit. The result was a wasteland of loneliness, alienation, fear, and sublimated desire that expressed itself through frenzied consumption and aggression toward nonconforming others. In their estimation, said Timothy Leary, the New Left was "repeating the same dreary quarrels and conflicts for power of the thirties and forties," instead of challenging the structural deficiencies of Western culture— primarily, according to Timothy Miller, the "supremacy of reason, the notion that material prosperity is the supreme goal of society, the

sanctity of economic growth, or the belief that spiritual values constituted an opiate, or at least were important." Margot Adler, who moved
from the student left into the counterculture, echoed this sentiment,
observing that the left "did not really understand the human need for
the juice and mystery of ecstatic experience; it did not realize that one
can enter the flow of the mysterious, the non-ordinary reality known
to all artists, poets, and indigenous people." At times the relationship
between the two groups even bordered on antagonism. Many activists
branded hippies as naive, impractical, apolitical, self-absorbed, and hedonistic, while many hippies viewed the New Left as myopic, reformist,
boring, and "in a limited place."[2]

There were, in fact, elements of truth in the New Left critique of hippiedom. Despite the counterculture's rejection of mainstream materialism, hippie men and women enjoyed material comforts, especially those
that delighted and awakened the senses without extracting too high a
cost in terms of delayed gratification. The boundaries between ecstatic,
transcendent experience and outright self-indulgence were similarly
flimsy indeed. Perhaps the fairest, most impartial assessment is that
both groups were in a "limited place," awash in youthful idealism (and
hormones); disconnected from mainstream culture, values, and politics; and searching—without the benefit of much worldly experience—
for satisfying alternatives. Both groups, we would do well to remember,
were also painfully, heartbreakingly young. Most hippies and student
activists were in their late teens and early twenties.

Recognized as a distinct movement, the counterculture has received
a substantial amount of scholarly attention. Coverage of its women is
wholly inadequate, however, limited to a few autobiographies or sub-
sumed under general discussions of hippie gender roles and families.
Women's actual experience—who they were, why they joined, how they
lived, and what they valued—remains a mystery, hidden beneath lay-
ers of popular misconceptions, myths, and stereotypes that emerged
during the 1960s and still persist, largely unchallenged. Many of the
stereotypes were generated by the mainstream media and 1960s social
critics. Some originated with young feminists who came out of the New
Left. Still others were produced by the male hippies who dominated
underground art, publishing, music, and broadcasting enterprises. A
few women, mainly groupies and rock and roll artists, seemingly had a
hand in crafting images of hip womanhood, but their projections were

often orchestrated by managers and agents or reconfigured by their audiences. The vast majority of hippie women experienced little control
over their own image and were often too preoccupied with creating an
alternative culture or personal identity to offer a correction.

Older, middle-class Americans were appalled by the counterculture,
viewing it as an affront to their values and as a slap in the face for the
sacrifices they had made on behalf of their children. Most simply could
not comprehend why a generation that had everything — every imagin-
able convenience, comfort, and opportunity — would exchange its bright
future for illicit drugs, sexual promiscuity, and the squalor of crash pads
and communes. In their minds, something had gone horribly wrong
with their children. Their incomprehension and anxiety loomed even
larger when it came to their daughters. Hippie women and girls not only
betrayed their class and race but also stepped outside of prevailing gender constructs. To be a girl, even in the context of 1950s "permissive"
childrearing practices, was to be neat, clean, well-mannered, obedient,
helpful, domestically inclined, timid, and sexually pure. In contrast,
boys were expected, if not actually encouraged, to be adventurous, free-
spirited, and rebellious.

Parents, a host of adult experts, and the mainstream media frequently
attributed male rebellion to permissive parenting or wrote it off as an adolescent, boys-will-be-boys rite of passage. Female transgression, given
the lack of supporting gender conventions and its unprecedented scale,
was more difficult to explain. Uncomfortable with the notion of female
agency, straight adults characterized some hippie women as wayward
or deviant and others — the majority — as unwitting victims. The media,
in particular, played up the victim angle, portraying young women as
naive, trusting innocents who were either lured into the counterculture
by predatory males or ignorant of its dangers.

The message to parents was clear: they needed to recognize behavioral changes associated with the downward spiral into hippiedom and
take proactive steps to avert disaster. In 1967, for example, the *New York
Times* ran a four-part series on Linda Rae Fitzpatrick, an eighteen-year-
old hippie from an affluent suburban family who was murdered in an
East Village basement. Journalist J. Anthony Lukas juxtaposed Linda's
"two worlds" — safe, white, comfortable Greenwich, Connecticut, and
the squalid, ethnically diverse, drug-infested Greenwich Village — and
documented her sad, lonely slide from one to the other. Her parents, the

story suggested, could have prevented the tragedy had they been more attentive and vigilant. This, and dozens of similar articles, both fueled and relieved parental anxieties. Young women, they suggested, had not actually rejected middle-class values and conventions; they had simply been led astray.[3]

Television producers, recognizing a potential gold mine in adult fears, helped solidify the unwitting victim image in a series of prime-time programs that aired between 1968 and 1970. In them, young women were lured into "psychedelic purgatory" or "hallucinogenic debauchery" by older, guru-type males, drug pushers, or seemingly innocent boy-next-door figures. The lucky ones were rescued by concerned parents or cops, but others, high on drugs, attempted to fly out windows, ended up in psychiatric wards, or slipped into prostitution. Such images evoked alarm, but also dismay and anger at the apparent ignorance and naivete of the girls. How could they be so easily misled, so empty-headed, so stupid?[4]

At the same time the media pandered to adult fears, they adopted programming geared toward a younger, more hip audience. But here, too, counterculture women were represented in stereotypical fashion. For example, the *Smothers Brothers* comedic hippie character, Goldie O'Keefe, while spoofing mainstream anxieties about sex and drugs, was just as naive and air-brained as the girl victim. Although Goldie wasn't "lured" into the counterculture, she had clearly joined for superficial reasons and was perhaps too stupid to know better. She liked the sex, drugs, and rock and roll and was most definitely "into" having fun. In time, characters such as Goldie coalesced into the wide-eyed, air-brained hippie chick who, after a few tokes of marijuana or a hit of lysergic acid diethylamide (LSD), could be talked into doing just about anything.

By 1970, television audiences were treated to additional images of hippie women—images that had already taken root within the counterculture: the maternal, nurturing earth mother, and the foxy, sophisticated, ultrafeminine chick with almost supernatural intuitive powers. These representations, emerging after hippie hysteria had run its course and certain aspects of the counterculture had been co-opted and commercialized, were comfortingly tame and domestic. Hippie women, they communicated, were still women. Indeed, some, such as Julie Barnes of the *Mod Squad*, were even on the side of law and order.[5]

In contrast to television, several Hollywood producers and actors

Girl with Green Hair, *concert poster, 1966, by Stanley Mouse and Alton Kelley. © Estate of Chester L. Helms, Jr., images © Family Dog Productions, under exclusive license with Rhino Entertainment Company, a division of Warner Music Group.*

Sunset Angel, *concert poster, 1967, by Stanley Mouse and Alton Kelley.*
© *Estate of Chester L. Helms, Jr., images* © *Family Dog Productions,*
under exclusive license with Rhino Entertainment Company, a division of
Warner Music Group.

Gloria Swanson, *concert poster, 1966, by Stanley Mouse and Alton Kelley.*
© Estate of Chester L. Helms, Jr., images © Family Dog Productions,
under exclusive license with Rhino Entertainment Company, a division of
Warner Music Group.

Snake Lady, *Concert Poster*, 1967, by Stanley Mouse and Alton Kelley.
© *Estate of Chester L. Helms, Jr., images © Family Dog Productions,*
under exclusive license with Rhino Entertainment Company, a division of
Warner Music Group.

Aquarian Woman, *graphic*, San Francisco Oracle *1, no. 6, 1967,*
by Ida Griffin. Reprinted with the permission of Regent Press, CD-ROM
Digital Edition of The San Francisco Oracle; The Original Oracle Newspaper;
and the Estate of Allen Cohen.

Six Women, *graphic*, San Francisco Oracle 1, *no. 7, 1967.*
Reprinted with the permission of Regent Press, CD-ROM Digital Edition
of The San Francisco Oracle; The Original Oracle Newspaper; and the
Estate of Allen Cohen.

Naked Woman on Grass, *graphic*, San Francisco Oracle *vol. 1, no. 12, 1968, photograph by Thomas Weir, design by Bob Schnepf. Reprinted with the permission of Regent Press, CD-ROM Digital Edition of The San Francisco Oracle; The Original Oracle Newspaper; and the Estate of Allen Cohen.*

Madonna, *graphic*, San Francisco Oracle *1, no. 12, 1968, photograph by Michael Hilsenrad. Reprinted with the permission of Regent Press, CD-ROM Digital Edition of The San Francisco Oracle; The Original Oracle Newspaper; and the Estate of Allen Cohen.*

espoused counterculture values. Their representations of hippie women did little to disrupt emerging stereotypes, however. Indeed, films such as *Easy Rider, Psych Out, The Wild Angels, Wild in the Streets, The Trip, Head, The Graduate,* and *Zabriskie Point* foregrounded male rebellion and nonconformity. Women, often quite literally, were along for the ride as sexy, accommodating, and alternately wide-eyed and streetwise hand-maidens to men's quest for on-the-road freedom. A few films, such as *The Love-Ins,* used female victims to highlight the perils of hippiedom. Produced in 1967 by Sam Katzman, the film depicted a diabolical, gu-rulike professor who encouraged his students to experiment with drugs. Lured into taking LSD, a young woman descends into a nightmarish, frighteningly distorted world inhabited by *Alice in Wonderland* char-acters. If the more sympathetic films depicted women as peripheral, lightweight actors on the counterculture stage, *The Love-Ins* portrayed them as hapless victims. Either way, women subjects lacked substance and agency.[6]

Outside of the mainstream media, social critics reinforced these im-ages and added new ones. Joan Didion, in her essay *Slouching toward Bethlehem,* created a uniformly unflattering portrait of hippie women. The young, innocent victim; the brainless, superficial, hopelessly naive chick; and various combinations of the two occupy her center stage. To the side, she introduced new figures: the drug-obsessed, self-absorbed, neglectful mother and the unenlightened domestic drudge who was seemingly oblivious of the emerging women's liberation movement. The drudge, far from eliciting our sympathy, appeared intransigent— un-willing, for some inexplicable reason, to acknowledge her oppression.

Tom Wolfe, in *Electric Kool-Aid Acid Test,* relegated women to sup-porting roles as comely, hip consorts of influential men such as Ken Kesey or as sexually uninhibited, wide-eyed hippie chicks. Almost glee-fully, Wolfe described a series of women who lacked the sense or will to steer clear of predatory males and mind-altering substances. Prank-ster Mike Hagan, for example, was celebrated for having built a "screw shack" on Kesey's La Honda property for the sole purpose of bedding a succession of young women. One of his conquests, nicknamed "Stark Naked," accompanied the Pranksters on their cross-country bus tour, overindulged in drugs, and flipped out as they drove through Texas. Predictably, like the foolish victims on television, she was picked up by the police and institutionalized. In similarly gleeful, boys-will-be-boys terms, Wolfe described another young woman who, sky high on psyche-delics, was gang-banged by a horde of Hell's Angels. Although repre-sented as a willing participant, she was clearly incapacitated by drugs.[7]

Women of the New Left, who embraced feminism earlier than their counterculture peers, were largely responsible for the sexually exploited, domestic drudge image that appeared in Didion's essay. Having liber-ated themselves from menial roles and sexual objectification within their own movements by casting gender as a social construct, they were angry and puzzled by hippie women's apparent satisfaction with the counter-culture's essentialist gender roles—roles that seemingly confined them to cooking, cleaning, child rearing, and providing sexual services for men. Valerie Solanas's Society for Cutting Up Men (SCUM) Manifesto, for example, characterized the hippie male as a manipulative predator who, "excited by the thoughts of having lots of women accessible to him, rebels against the harshness of the Breadwinner's life and the monotony of one woman." Communes, she maintained, were nothing more than "an extended violation of females' rights, privacy and sanity" and ex-isted wholly to satisfy male needs. Vivian Estellachild's assessment was strikingly similar. After visiting two hippie communes, she concluded that "the fact is that the roles women can play are so very limited. There are two possibilities: sexual plaything and the madonna and child chew-ing at the breast. If you object then you are not natural, not grooving with nature, not doing things as they are supposed to be."

Robin Morgan went one step further in *Goodbye to All That,* a mani-festo published in underground newspapers across the United States and widely read and studied by New Left women. In it she bid "goodbye to Hip Culture and the so-called Sexual Revolution, which has functioned toward women's freedom as did Reconstruction toward former slaves—reinstituted oppression by another name." Moreover, she lashed out at women who chose "male approval" over the feminist awakening. From the outside looking in, it did appear that hippie women fell into this category; they were either too beaten down or too brainwashed to join the unfolding revolution. What this assessment failed to grasp, however, was that counterculture women were in the process of constructing an alternative identity that was very much in opposition to the prevailing gender norm of nuclear family-focused, suburban domesticity.[8]

Many of the feminists who came out of the New Left later joined the academy and quite determinedly and bravely carved out new fields in women's history and studies. Conducting research from their own frame of reference, they unintentionally perpetuated the sexually exploited, domestic drudge image and the notion that feminism entirely bypassed hippiedom. Indeed, this is still the standard historical interpretation. Sara Evans, for example, penned the earliest study of the radical feminist movement, placing its origins squarely within the civil rights movement and New Left. The counterculture, she argued, was not only on the sidelines of women's liberation; it "demanded that women accept sex with anyone, anytime, or admit that they were 'uptight' and 'unliberated.'" Almost twenty years later, in *Born for Liberty*, Evans reached the same conclusion. Although acknowledging that the counterculture's emphasis on "feminine values" was promising, she emphasized that "its focus on drugs and sex was often extremely exploitative of women." Ruth Rosen, in *The World Split Open*, similarly maintained that feminism swept past hippiedom. Her only mention of the counterculture is in reference to its

> ambiguous legacy for young feminists. On the one hand it legitimized all kinds of informal and unconventional behavior. It offered young women a sense of liberation, much of which revolved around drugs and sex. At the same time, the hippie culture tended to glorify women as barefoot and pregnant. Many young women rejected suburban materialism, grew and prepared their own food, sewed their own clothes, and lived off the land. Hippie women were not concerned about discrimination; they didn't want jobs. But to politically engaged women, who were just carving out a new identity, what did it mean to 'turn on, tune in, or drop out?' They had just begun to drop in and take themselves seriously. They had little inclination to drop out.[9]

In reality, as later chapters reveal, hippie women were very busy carving out new roles and identities, taking themselves seriously, and crafting—along with New Left and counterculture lesbians—an alternative feminism that emphasized difference rather than the social construction of gender and championed the development of a woman-centered and identified culture. The 1960s, then, gave rise to multiple feminisms—all with a different analysis of the problem and different strategies for change.

Mainstream stereotypes—especially the victim; the brainless, hedonistic chick; and the drugged out, self-absorbed, negligent mother—also endured well beyond the 1960s. Indeed, they became the stock figures in 1980s neoconservative attempts to blame the counterculture for the moral breakdown of society. The resulting stigma, as mentioned in the Introduction, led many counterculture women to doubt or deny their own experience, especially in relationship to drugs and sexual liberation.[10]

As these stereotypes emerged and took root, the counterculture generated its own images through male-dominated publications, art, and music — images that were just as shallow and distorted as those produced by external observers. By the late 1960s, hundreds of underground newspapers, with a readership in the millions, circulated throughout the nation. A majority were "bridge" publications, carrying content that appealed to both counterculture and New Left readers. A few, like the *San Francisco Oracle*, the *East Village Other* (EVO), Boston's *Avatar*, Chicago's *Seed*, and the *San Francisco Express Times*, were more strongly identified with hippiedom. All were dominated, however, by male editors and staff writers and geared toward a young, white, middle-class male readership. Although women and men joined the counterculture in equal numbers and for equally serious reasons, hippiedom's print record leaves the impression that women were peripheral to the movement and little more than decorative sex objects. Aside from contributing articles on food preparation and gardening, women mostly appeared as erotic subjects in male-produced poetry, short stories, news features, manifestos, editorials, and graphics. Viewed in isolation from other sources, the underground press certainly reinforced mainstream images of the brainless, sexually promiscuous hippie chick and the clueless, accommodating domestic drudge. More significantly, it placed women outside of the cultural revolution, completely ignoring their thoughtful and very deliberate commitment to counterculture ideals.[11]

Graphic art, for all of its swirling, visually rich, psychedelic glory, especially marginalized and demeaned women. Naked nymphs fill the pages of underground papers, serving as symbols of male liberation from conventional moral constraints and responsibilities. At times they appeared as young, wide-eyed but nonetheless eager innocents. At other times they exuded confident, even aggressive, sexuality. The virgin and the vamp, both products of male fantasy, also made regular appearances in press photography. For example, EVO ran a photograph of a semiclad, provocatively posed woman from the neighborhood as its own hip version of the pinup girl. Her apparent degree of experience and sexual sophistication varied from week to week, but the message was always the same: counterculture women willingly pandered to male desire. Many papers also ran sex ads to boost their revenue, claiming that the often graphic copy was consistent with the counterculture's oppositional stance toward mainstream moral strictures. Such ads reinforced the notion that women provided sex on demand. Other images, less demeaning but equally superficial, graced the pages of the underground press: the bewitchingly beautiful, intuitive, cosmic love goddess and the nurturing earth mother. They, like the virgin and the vamp, were young and sexually alluring, but their otherworldly and maternal qualities marked them as tantalizingly unattainable. Still, all four were products of the male imagination rather than "real" flesh and blood, self-determining women.[12]

Poster and album cover art reinforced all four images, especially the vamp, virgin, and love goddess. The most graphic representation of a young innocent appeared on the cover of the 1969 *Blind Faith* album. A girl, naked from the waist up and seemingly on the cusp of adolescence, cradles a miniature silver airplane in her hands and gazes out at the viewer with a vacant expression. She is her body. On the one hand, the image can be read as a counterculture corrective to the ills of advanced industrial society. Reduced in scale, and in the hands of a naked girl who is posed against a natural landscape, the plane—and technology more generally—is in its proper place. On the other hand, from a different and probably more common interpretive perspective, she is simply another little hippie chick ready for a romp in the grass. Either way, she is still an empty female vessel, stripped of agency and ready to be filled with someone else's agenda.

The vamp and love goddess, largely thanks to the creative genius of pioneer psychedelic artists Stanley Mouse and Alton Kelley, became stock images on concert posters and hand bills. Heavily influenced by art nouveau artists such as Alphonse Mucha, they produced some of the decade's most refined, visually striking representations of women. *Girl with Green Hair* (1966) depicts an ethereal beauty with flowing hair and a sensual expression who, as a beneficent love goddess, invites the viewer to participate in an otherworldly happening. *Sunset Angel* (1967) presents an even more unattainable goddess-like figure: a voluptuous, winged woman, who, despite her complete nudity, is too pure, good, and gentle for sex. In contrast, *Snake Lady* (1967) and *Gloria Swanson* (1966) wear seductive, almost sinister expressions that advertise much more than transcendent experience or cheerful, wide-eyed sexual accommodation. As vamps, they simultaneously entice and threaten to devour their prospective partners.

Underground comix contained the most denigrating female stereotypes. Like underground press graphics and poster art, comix production was a mostly male enterprise. Some women, including Trina Robbins, Nancy Kalish, Willy Mendes, Lee Marrs, and Kay Rudin, tried to break in but with limited success. Trina Robbins, for example, waged an on-going struggle for credibility with male cartoonists and editorial staff. Unable to make a decent living as an artist, she opened a boutique on Manhattan's lower east side where she traded "clothes to the editor and staff of *The East Village Other (EVO)* in return for them running free ads by me for my boutique in their paper. The ads were really comic strips and were so low-key that most people didn't even know they were ads. So in a way, I was sponsoring my own comic strip." In contrast to her strips, men's cartoons were "loaded down with . . . graphic rape scenes and every other degradation toward women that the writers/artists could think of. Entrails, usually female, were scattered over the landscape in a phenomenon of violence to women that I believe has never been equaled in any other medium."

In this world, seemingly ruled by male fantasy, there were no unattainable goddesses, only excessively naive or air-brained hippie chicks; drug-stupefied, masochistic drudges; and seductive, sadistic vamps—all with exaggerated anatomical features and sexual appetites. Nothing, including violence, was off limits. Male cartoonists pulled all stops, depicting men having sex with underage girls, women having sex with animals, gang rape, group sex (usually one man and several women), and women being penetrated in every conceivable orifice. All the while, male artists, editorial staff, and readers maintained that these images were revolutionary, intended to offend and challenge mainstream moral sensibilities.

By the late 1960s, New Left women, such as Robin Morgan, were no longer accepting that line. As marginalized staffers at the *Rat, Great Speckled Bird, Argus,* and other activist-dominated papers, they redefined these "liberatory" images as demeaning, exploitative expressions of male chauvinism and misogyny. As Aniko Bodroghkozy put it, while the more "politico" papers could "not entirely overlook the uprising in feminist politics among movement women," the even more male dominated "counterculture papers did their best to ignore the whole thing." Hippie women, having dropped out of mainstream and activist circles to forge an alternative culture, were absent from the mounting debate over representation and power. This, in turn, reinforced feminist convictions that hippiedom and its women were backward and unenlightened.[13]

Underground radio, like the underground press, was a male-dominated institution that played to young men between the ages of eighteen and thirty-four. Its programming and lack of an on-air female presence thus reinforced the notion that women were peripheral or marginal to the counterculture. San Francisco's leading hippie station, KMPX, the only one in town with any female staff, hired women solely because one of the male DJs, who wanted to work with his girlfriend, "cagily suggested to" the manager "that the station hire some female engineers rather than those ugly old male engineers." WNEW New York was even more unusual in that it had a female DJ. Alison Steele, who called herself "Nightbird." Staffing the midnight to 6:oo A.M. shift, she attempted to elevate content above sex, drugs, and rock and roll by opening with poetry and then playing music that supported her readings' theme. She eventually secured a more desirable 10:00 P.M. to 2:00 A.M. shift, but according to Gillian Gaar, she "had a terrible time with the guys. . . . They resented it mightily that a woman would be in that position, and they would certainly try to ignore my advice." She went on to explain, "I'll give you an idea of how they treated 'women in rock.' I complained to the station manager that I wanted a requisition to buy a step stool because I couldn't reach the record rows on top. And he said, 'Tell you what we'll do. We'll get a taller person.'"[14]

Counterculture music, composed largely by and for young men, not only relegated women to its physical margins, it replicated the superficial images and stereotypes contained in graphic and print media. According to music historian Sheila Whiteley, "the musical ethos of the period undermined the role of women, positioning them as either romanticized fantasy figures, subservient earth mothers or easy lays." Aside from a few tentative celebrations of female freedom and autonomy, such as It's A Beautiful Day's "White Bird" and Crosby, Stills,

Nash, and Young's "Suite Judy Blue-Eyes," most bands and lyrics fell into the male-focused love or sex school.

The ethereal, otherworldly beauty (Aquarian goddess) and the receptive, nurturing, supportive earth mother or Madonna occupied the less degrading end of the spectrum but still functioned primarily to satisfy male needs and desires. The goddess served as a dream lover, embodying male longing for untarnished, virtuous, transcendent Woman, while the earth mother promised more immediate gratification in the form of unconditional emotional and physical nurture. In contrast, young nymphs and vamps, both sexually available and insatiable, promised pleasure and trouble. The chicks, seemingly innocent and pure, were always ready to be shown a good time. But they were also potential jail bait or pesky hangers-on. The witchy vamps, like flesh-and-blood rock and roll groupies, were capable of fulfilling almost any sexual fantasy but could also devour men's souls, deplete male energy, and destroy lives and careers in demonic acts of vengeance.[15]

Female performers not only had to make music that appealed to male audiences, they had to look like goddesses, earth mothers, wild young chicks, or sultry, seductive vamps. The ideal, personified by Jefferson Airplane's Grace Slick, was a heady, unforgettable combination of radiant, unobtainable beauty and raw sexual energy. At once the Aquarian love goddess and the dangerous, exotic Salome, she mesmerized male fans with unadulterated female power. For example, during an outdoor concert on a rainy day, she removed her blouse and performed topless, explaining to the audience that she didn't want to be confined by wet clothing. At another concert, in Fort Wayne, Indiana, Ariel Swartly relates that "she raised the microphone and the crowd looked up expectantly. Jefferson Airplane was San Francisco's pioneering psychedelic band, so she might be going to tell them about flowing with the changes or beginning to see the light. Instead, her question cracked like a whip above their heads: 'Which one of you has the biggest cock?'"

Janice Joplin, another counterculture headliner, had more talent, but lacked the *look*. To achieve success, she submitted to several image changes, sang like she was "fucking," and tried to hold her own with the guys when it came to sex, drugs, and swearing. The contortions paid off in the short term but took a heavy toll on her physical and emotional health. She died of a drug overdose, but according to Gillian Gaar, Country Joe, Joplin's former lover, maintained that "sexism killed her.

Everybody wanted this sexy chick who sang really sexy and had a lot of energy . . . and people just kept saying one of the things about her was that she was just 'one of the guys.' . . . That's a real sexist bullshit trip, 'cause that was fuckin' her head around . . . she was one of the women. She was a strong, groovy woman."[16]

For female rock artists, success also hinged on performing with men. By the summer of 1967, solo women or all-female bands rarely received serious attention from male audiences, promoters, recording studios, and critics. During the early years of hippiedom, before the psychedelic sound gained broad commercial appeal, however, it had looked as if women might gain a foothold in its music scene. Indeed, beginning in 1965, women such as Ellen Harmon and Luria Castell (founding members of San Francisco's Family Dog commune) helped organize and promote weekly psychedelic concerts and happenings that introduced audiences to both LSD and the new sound. Not yet dominated by business-savvy impresarios such as Bill Graham and male rockers, the stage was still somewhat open to women promoters, sound technicians, multimedia artists, and musicians.

The Ace of Cups, one of the era's more successful girl groups, came together in 1966 as the Haight Ashbury district was emerging as hippiedom's primary cultural center. Like most counterculture women, its members were completely sold on and committed to the movement's ideals. Their intelligent, soulful lyrics, focusing on cooperation, love, peace, transcendent experience, and the beauty of nature—along with their exceptional talent—should have secured them a place among the psychedelic greats. Their message, lacking broader appeal to commercially targeted male youth audiences, was soon usurped, however, by the male sex-love school. They continued to enjoy success, but in a back-up position to Crosby, Stills, Nash, and Young, Jefferson Airplane, Quicksilver Messenger Service, Big Brother and the Holding Company, Sons of Champlin, and The Band.

June Millington and her sister Jean arrived on the music scene a bit later and encountered similar obstacles. Forming the band Fanny,

we were just trying to do it as women. And I suppose the act itself was very political. If you had set me down and asked me what I thought about politics, I'd have told you I distrusted the establishment, I distrusted the newspapers, I distrusted the politicians. All I wanted to do was really just get off. And not be what society told me that a girl was supposed to be. To get married and to go live in the 'burbs and raise kids—that to me would have been death.

Like The Ace of Cups, Fanny and its more substantive counterculture message were buried under an avalanche of sexism. June and Jean, half Filipino, also waged an on-going struggle against racial stereotypes. Following a tour across the United States and Europe, June suffered a nervous breakdown. The pressure of "ignoring the fact that we were just regarded as chicks," combined with efforts "to pull off the straightjacket of racism and so forth," took its toll. Moving to Woodstock, New York, June focused on Buddhist practice and song writing, joined the emerging women's music movement with Chris Williamson and Holly Near, and founded the Institute for Musical Arts, a nonprofit organization that helps women—especially women of color—establish careers in music. During the 1960s, she recalled, "there was no place for me to learn anything. I always wanted to ask the guys—and there was always a little of that, you know, 'What does she really want? Does she want to learn the licks, or does she want to learn THE licks?'"[17]

Outside of the male-dominated world of rock and roll, female performers faced fewer obstacles. Their success also hinged, however, on conforming to hippie and New Left gender ideals. Joan Baez, Mimi Farina, and Judy Collins, for example, owed their counterculture appeal, at least during the 1960s, to their romantic ballads and sweetly "feminine" personas. As Avital H. Bloch noted, "part of Baez' success may be attributed to the 'feminine' image she presented to her audience. Her early persona blended such traditional, and stereotypical traits as sensitivity, sentimentality, gentleness, and innocence, which her hallmark songs, the love ballads, transmitted." Her voice, "which conformed to traditional ideals of women's beauty and 'purity,'" underscored and highlighted her Madonna-like qualities. It would not be until the early 1970s that another group of female artists—Joni Mitchell, Carole King, Bonnie Raitt, and Linda Ronstadt—were able to break out of such rigid molds and enjoy commercial success on the basis of their fresh lyrics and unique musical styles.[18]

Forced to conform to male-generated images or to play second fiddle to the guys, female artists had little impact on prevailing stereotypes—except to reinforce them. The same was true of group-ies, rock and roll camp followers who, at least in popular imagination, gave form and substance to standard representations of hippie women. Indeed, they built what might be considered careers by serving as love goddesses, nurturing earth mothers, wild chicks, and seductive vamps. Sexual availability was just one—albeit the most central, controversial, and sensational—component of their job description. They also acted as critics, co-composers, muses, confidantes, housemothers, amateur psychologists, informal managers and promoters, and arbiters of coun-terculture taste and fashion. In the process, many reaped substantial benefits: celebrity, the vicarious pleasure of cultivating or associating with creative genius, close friendships with other rock and roll women, and the exhilaration of transgressing sexual conventions and experienc-ing the on-the-road freedom normally reserved for males. Some even parlayed their groupie role into artistic sidelines. For example, the Chi-cago Plaster Casters created a media splash by making plaster casts of rock stars' penises or "rigs." Similarly, the GTOs (Girls Together Outrageously) gained notoriety as Frank Zappa's back-up girl group. While they and other camp followers undoubtedly shook up traditional gender conventions because of their sexual independence and bravado, they were still constrained, as Ann Powers put it, by "rock's basic gen-der division: male stars and female worshipers."[19]

By the early 1970s, groupies, like hippie women more generally, were condemned by many New Left feminists "as slavish hangers-on in a boy's club," part of "a long parade of slags, scrubbers, and band molls." Their critique, along with mainstream and counterculture-generated stereotypes, obscured the complexity, idealism, intention, creativity, and outright courage that undergirded most women's lives. Moreover, these images were a constant irritation, embarrassment, and diversion from the serious task of creating an alternative culture. As Constance Trouble recalled,

I risked everything—education, career, parental approval—all be-cause I wanted a life that affirmed nature, intimacy, creativity, co-operation, peace, justice and spirituality. And it bothered me to be written off as a "chick" or ungrateful, crazy daughter. Believe me, it took a lot of strength to stand up and say, "I was a hippie, and thoroughly benefited from the experience. I wasn't exploited, brain-washed, duped or oppressed. I was on a personal and collective mission of liberation and I loved almost every minute of it."

Similarly, Mary Gannon of The Ace of Cups reflected,

What we did and what we experienced was a wonderful world of culture shocked activity. . . . However, with my own family and in my educational career, I find myself defending over and over again the concepts which we were examining as a Braver New World. A really brave new world where people share, and you do love your brother, and things equal out and truth should be shouted from the rooftops.

Kathleen Taylor echoed this sentiment, observing that

it took a lot of courage to move against the tide, to forge deeper, more intimate relationships with our partners and children, to seek meaningful work or right livelihood, to live simply and within ecological boundaries and constraints. It wasn't about sex, drugs and rock and roll, it wasn't some woo-woo spiritual fantasy, it was real women creating and sustaining viable alternatives to the unimaginative, militarist, consumption-oriented status quo.[20]

There were, however, kernels of truth behind many of the stereotypes. Although many women were wholly committed to counterculture ideals, others were in it for the thrill and excitement of breaking cultural taboos and the sensual pleasures of sex, drugs, and rock and roll. Nor were commitment and pleasure mutually exclusive. Despite women's reluctance to admit it, the counterculture would never have attracted its youth following if it hadn't been fun. Indeed, trying on and playing around with different images must have been very pleasurable. Despite their antimaterialist philosophy, hippie women and men enjoyed dressing up—covering themselves in beads; lush, richly colored fabrics; and exotic scents and plumage. They looked, for all practical purposes, like love goddesses and Edwardian princes. Even in the most rustic communal settings, women made, salvaged, bartered, and lovingly maintained gorgeous outfits and accessories. Moreover, although many women resisted the stereotypes or conducted their daily lives outside of their more superficial renditions, they often manipulated images to their advantage. Beyond groupie appropriations of the libertine chick and vamp personas, hippie women obtained concrete benefits by "play-ing" the Aquarian goddess and earth mother. These two images, while emerging out of the counterculture, were consistent with mainstream constructs of ideal womanhood: soft, nurturing, receptive, life-giving, intuitive, generous, spiritual, and mysterious. They also embodied the very qualities championed by hippiedom. In time, many women, claim-ing to possess these very attributes by virtue of being female, cast them-selves as the true vanguard of the New Age. Discussed later in greater detail, this assertion of difference became a central feature of hippie women's feminist identity.

In the meantime, thousands of seemingly ordinary girls and women turned their backs on their families and set out to create a "brave new world." As Constance Trouble suggested, many "risked everything." They not only betrayed their class, they betrayed prevailing notions of respectable female behavior. The counterculture, Barbara Ehrenreich asserted, was much more threatening and jarring to conventional val-ues than the student left. In contrast to hippies, a majority of student activists were at least engaged in familiar forms of protest, connected and committed to reforming existing institutions, and physically recog-nizable to their parents. While some counterculture women grew up in bohemian, eccentric families that were more accepting of their daugh-ters' forays into hippiedom, most came from straitlaced, middle- and upper-middle-class backgrounds. But even the most iconoclastic par-ents, including those connected to the old left, were rattled and shaken by the sex, drugs, communal living arrangements, antimaterialism, and spiritual experimentation of their girl children. It was as if their darlings had run off and joined the circus. [21]

For example, Marylyn Motherbear Scott's mother, a vivacious, po-etry- and music-loving widow who encouraged her daughter's interest in theater, could never understand or accept Marylyn's decision to join the counterculture, characterizing it as a waste of her education and potential. Her disappointment, and perhaps sense of betrayal, created an enduring rift in their relationship—a rupture that Marylyn repeat-edly and fruitlessly tried to heal. Constance Trouble's struggle with her parents—particularly with her father—was similarly painful and last-ing. "His disappointment was always palpable. We were supposed to do better than our parents—professionally and materially—and he just couldn't fathom why I would 'throw it all away.'" For some women, like

Gina Stillman, it was even worse. "From a well-to-do California family," she was "ostracized by them" when she began living with Ramon Sender Barayon, an experimental artist, counterculture pioneer, and cofounder of the Morning Star commune. There was comfort in numbers, however. As Roberta Price, who also contended with parental disapproval, recalled,

> We're leaving our bewildered nuclear families to become part of a tribe that's forming. Bob Dylan's our script writer. *He not busy being born is busy dying . . . To live outside the law you must be honest . . . She's got everything she needs, she's an artist, she don't look back.* We hear irresistible messages in the rock and roll melodies uniting us, though our parents hear nothing but noise. They remember reading "The Pied Piper" to us when we were little. Now we're Children of the Sixties, although we're legal adults. A decade has taken our parents' place.[22]

Their rebellion, seemingly occurring overnight, was often a long time in the making. Although taking many parents by surprise, women's disenchantment with mainstream culture began in childhood and adolescence. Indeed, many reflected that they were always "countercultural." Hippiedom was simply the place where they found the freedom to "be themselves"—selves that were far more complex, dynamic, and interesting than the stereotypes and images suggest.

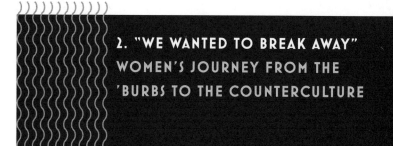

ost counterculture women were born between the mid-1940s and mid-1950s. Raised in relative affluence and during an era of cultural conservatism, they were scarcely groomed for rebellion. Many, however, displayed a surprising degree of independence, restlessness, and creativity at a young age. Many also recalled feeling alienated from their families and peers—even as children. When they reached adolescence and young adulthood, their alienation and restlessness produced an even greater degree of nonconformity and prompted their search for alternatives. As already mentioned, most described finding the counterculture as "coming home."

Scholars have long noted the class and ethnic homogeneity of the counterculture. Indeed, hippies of both genders were by and large children of prosperity. Well more than half came from middleclass families, and fewer than 3 percent were nonwhite. The counterculture's rejection of materialism, the work ethic, mainstream moral values, and militarism limited its appeal among working-class whites who were struggling to move up the economic ladder and were sending a disproportionate number of their sons into war.

The counterculture's voluntary poverty held even fewer attractions for economically disadvantaged minorities. Indeed, the hippie presence in ethnic enclaves often bred hostility. For example, in New York's East Village, one resident remarked, according to Peter Braunstein and Michael Doyle, that "the hippies really bug us, because we know they can come down here and play their game for a while and then escape. And we can't man." In a similar fashion, in rural New Mexico, home to many counterculture communal experiments, Elia Katz noted that the "Chicanos . . . deeply resent the money and leisure of the hippies" and regard them as "amoral and atheistic." Just as significantly, the counterculture, while amorphously committed to "brotherhood," couldn't compete with the vibrant, focused, and well-organized ethnic power movements of the same period in which activists of color engaged in their own struggles to transform the broader culture, strengthen their communities, and create alternative institutions.[1]

Moreover, the counterculture, while priding itself on inclusiveness, inherited some peculiar racial baggage from previous generations of youth dissidents, including a fascination with supposedly more authentic, unrepressed others. Young white women, as Wini Breines has suggested, were far from immune to romanticizing difference. By embracing the ethnic other or outsider, girls were rejecting more than middle-class racial phobias and notions of propriety and "orderliness"; they were expressing "their dissatisfaction with domesticity and suburbanism. . . . These were the boys they could not marry." As Breines went on to note, "Their stultifying environments made rebellious white girls more responsive to and interested in people outside it." More important, they sensed that their confinement was nearly as oppressive as others' exclusion. "'Throwing away' their reputations, these privileged young women opted for escape from the boundaries that confined their class, sex and race. That escape involved a longing for a different, more 'genuine' life; and in some cases a real effort to listen and learn."[2]

The counterculture's attraction to mysterious, more authentic others was particularly evident in its romanticization of American Indian and African American males. The former, regarded as repositories of ancient wisdom and warrior traditions, supposedly held the key to a more genuine spirituality. Black males, having ostensibly withstood and resisted centuries of white oppression, were seen as models of pure, unrepressed, instinctual masculinity. It is interesting that a few men of color and numerous fake Indians found that these stereotypes worked to their advantage. Hippies, eager to learn new ways of being and to cast off the racism of mainstream culture, sometimes afforded these cultural brokers special treatment, respect, and deference. For example, Wheeler's Ranch, a northern California commune, welcomed several African American men, including O. B. Ray, whom Bill Wheeler described as "a font of wisdom and mellowness at all times, a great sage and a much beloved tribal elder." Another man, also described by Wheeler, was "a jive-hustler inside a labyrinth of lies, with a jungle instinct for survival and a charming but deadly smile which hissed through a gap in his front teeth." Even after he raped several women and stole property, residents could not bring themselves to ask him to leave. They, like Bill, saw a "beautiful person struggling to emerge" out from under his "anger" and "rage." Similarly, this combination of guilt and romanticization allowed some Indian and Latino men to find empowerment by ministering to the longings and desires of white "wannabe" warriors and medicine men.[3]

Hippiedom held few such attractions for women of color. Its emphasis on sexual liberation, coupled with its exoticization of female others deterred women who had long been stereotyped as sexually promiscuous, enigmatic, and sensual beings. Unlike their male counterparts, who were viewed as the embodiment of "self-confident masculinity" or as repositories of ancient wisdom, women were identified almost entirely with their bodies, cast as ultranatural earth mothers or exotic love goddesses. These images were uncomfortably similar to those undergirding centuries of sexual exploitation. In the Wheeler's Ranch chronicles, "Home Free Home," there is only one account of a black woman, and it focuses entirely on the physical act of giving birth: "The most together birth I witnessed was by a black mother. She did not let out one sound, and the labor lasted only about four hours, unusual for a first birth. The expression on her face was business like and confident. If she felt any pain, she did not show it, and her baby was as fine and healthy as any born on the Ridge." Stereotypes of earthy primitivism and self-possession among women of color were not limited to Wheeler's residents. R. Crumb, who captured and caricatured male hippies' sexual fantasies in his underground comix, hyperexaggerated the physical anatomy and sexual appetites of women of color and endowed them with stereotypical cunning, steeliness, and street smarts.[4]

Thus, counterculture women and men were disproportionately white and middle class. Female hippies, to an even greater extent than their male peers, however, came from middle- or upper-middle-class families, headed by college-educated, professional or white-collar fathers. This difference points to some possible class variations in child-rearing practices. Girls from more affluent families may have been granted more autonomy and physical independence than their working-class counterparts. Indeed, girls needed a certain degree of physical freedom and mobility to locate and explore the hippie subculture and an even greater measure of emotional independence to actually join it. Working-class girls, as 1950s researchers observed, were more tightly controlled by their families than at least some of their brothers and more affluent female peers. Their parents, particularly those aspiring to middle-class status, were often more concerned about preventing moral lapses among their daughters than in fostering girls' independence and freedom. Rosaline Santangelo, for example, was fascinated by the few hippies that she observed on television but never encountered in her tightly knit, Italian American working-class neighborhood. Less than 2 miles away, down by the Staten Island ferry terminal, the hippie staff of the *East Village Other* had established a sprawling commune in an old warehouse, but Rosaline, and other girls in her community, were so closely supervised by parents and watchful neighbors that they were oblivious to its presence. Indeed, her parents would never have tolerated anything beyond her innocent efforts to emulate the tamer elements of hippie fashion—a string of love beads or a pair of flower power sandals. Actual contact with hippie kids was strictly forbidden.[5]

Although hippie women came from a narrower range of class backgrounds than their male peers, counterculture gender ratios were evenly balanced. What, then, prompted so many relatively affluent young women and girls to defy parental authority, embrace alternative lifestyles, and seek the kind of on-the-road freedom that had previously been the sole province of young men? As Barbara Ehrenreich noted, "A student left was at least comprehensible, but everything about the counterculture—the easy nudity, the drugs, the disdain for careers, the casual approach to dress and personal hygiene—was an affront to middle class values." Thus, it required considerable courage or motivation to break with convention.[6]

During the 1950s and 1960s psychologists and sociologists compiled an impressive body of research on "alienated" or "nonconforming" youth. Although much of this literature focuses on young men and boys, it provides—along with more contemporary material—insight into the sources of girls' discontent. In the popular imagination, the white, middle-class family of the 1950s consisted of a breadwinner father, homemaker mother, and a flock of well-loved children, all comfortably situated in a clean, safe, attractive suburban home. A burgeoning postwar economy ensured a steadily rising standard of living: a car in every garage, one or more televisions, family vacations, a bevy of laborsaving appliances, and plenty of presents for the holidays. Mothers, liberated from domestic drudgery, happily turned their energy to emotional housekeeping. With the help of new child development experts such as Dr. Benjamin Spock, they adopted a more "permissive" style of parenting that fostered spontaneity, creativity, curiosity, and independence in their young. Everyone, according to this myth, was content, happy, and well adjusted.

In reality, however, many postwar middle- and upper-middle-class families seethed with tension—particularly the families of "alienated" youth. Fathers, who may have dreamed of pursuing unconventional, intellectually stimulating careers in their youth, settled for stable, white-collar jobs that demanded conformity and stifled their creative ambitions. Wives, too, wanted something different and more expansive but were forced by convention into domestic routines that were less varied, creative, and visibly productive than those of their mothers. Even wives who worked outside of the home—as millions did during the postwar years—found little in the way of challenge and stimulation. Relegated to low-paying, pink-collar jobs, women identified more strongly with their roles as wives and mothers.[7]

According to Kenneth Keniston, in *The Uncommitted,* both parents, unable to sustain their youthful ambitions in the face of prevailing gender norms, "the pressures of supporting a family, and their desires for material success," often turned on each other. Men sought refuge in their jobs, retreating emotionally and physically from the home. Women, even those with outside jobs, channeled their frustration and disappointment into child rearing, keeping up the facade of a happy marriage, and shoring up class standing through consumption, entertaining, and maintaining a clean, orderly, and tasteful home environment. Nevertheless, the tension between couples was often palpable and oppressive to children. In *Young Radicals,* Keniston goes on to say that "alienated" male youth portrayed their fathers as distant, disappointed, and embittered and as having capitulated to "pressures for social success and recognition." They viewed their mothers in more ambiguous terms, characterizing them as intelligent, energetic women who "gave up promise and fulfillment for marriage" and aggressively transferred their own ambitions onto their sons.[8]

Maternal ambition and permissiveness, however, did not carry over to daughters, at least not to the same extent. Middle-class parents not only placed more restrictions on girls' physical mobility but also expected their daughters to do a better job of containing their emotions, bodily functions, and sexual urges. The sexual double standard, as examined in greater detail in the next chapter, was particularly burdensome to girls and young women. Most families also observed a strict division of labor, with girls assigned chores in keeping with traditional gender expectations. Educational aspirations also diverged according to gender. Middle-class mothers expected their sons to attend college but were relatively unambitious for their daughters. Although many girls found refuge and a sense of self-esteem in educational pursuits, they received little support from their parents. Making matters worse, when they reached their teens many faced outright ostracism for being too brainy. Anna Marie Daniels, for example, excelled in math and science and worshipped Marie Curie. Her mother, perplexingly unsupportive and disinterested in Anna Marie's ambitions, encouraged her to think of something more practical, such as a career as a librarian. When Anna Marie entered her teens, her male and female peers viewed her intelligence as an oddity or abnormality. Thus, soon-to-be alienated girls were less likely to view their mothers in sympathetic terms. Instead, they portrayed them as controlling, frustrated, and determined to prepare their daughters for a life as barren and unfulfilling as their own. Both parents, many girls eventually judged, had traded their youthful dreams for material security, status, and the appearance of contentment and satisfaction.[9]

Maintaining appearances was, in fact, a major preoccupation of 1950s middle-class households. Mothers, fathers, and children all faced enormous pressure to conform to an ideal that had been cooked up by the media and advertising executives. Image and appearance, secured through consumption and adherence to middle-class behavioral norms, held the key to respectability and status. One's place, one's status was far from secure, however. Families in the 1950s were threatened from within by marital discord, conflicts over assigned roles, domestic violence, sexual abuse, alcoholism, tranquilizer addiction, and rising teen pregnancy and divorce rates. Stephanie Coontz, in *The Way We Never Were*, related Bernita Eisler's dawning awareness of suburbia's contradictions:

As college classmates became close friends, I heard sagas of life at home that were Gothic horror stories. Behind the hedges and driveways of upper-middle-class suburbia were tragedies of madness, suicide, and—most prevalent of all—chronic and severe alcoholism. . . . The real revelation for me was the role played by children in . . . keeping up appearances. Many of my new friends had been pressed into service early as happy smiling fronts, emissaries of family normalcy, cheerful proof that "nothing was wrong" at the Joneses.[10]

Moreover, they were threatened from without, plagued by anxiety and uncertainty about the nature and location of external enemies. Families of the 1950s were constituted by policymakers as the first line of defense against political and social deviance, including communism, homosexuality, and juvenile delinquency—a designation that heightened pressures toward conformity, vigilance, and normalcy. Then there was "the bomb"—a threat that completely demolished one's sense of permanence and security. At the same time, ethnic minorities, largely locked out of the burgeoning postwar economy and completely excluded from suburban communities, were applying pressure against customary boundaries and insisting on economic, political, and social equality. Finally, the "other America," a full 25 percent of the population that fell below the poverty line, served as a constant reminder that affluence and economic security were far from assured or permanent.[11]

There is some indication that counterculture women—as youngsters—were more aware and questioning of these tensions, constraints, and contradictions than their female peers. Not only did they describe themselves as odd, different, and nonconforming; they emphasized their creativity, restlessness, idealism, noncompetitiveness, and a strong desire to be "open and free"—self-concepts that were likely to place them at odds with their families. Hippie women's narratives further indicate a predisposition to nonconformity. Many girls, such as Jan Camp, Virginia Logan, Constance Trouble, and Nancy Jean, felt constrained by class-based status anxieties and notions of propriety, claustrophobic and conflict-ridden households, and traditional gender roles that confined mothers and daughters to the home. Jan Camp, for example, was born in 1946 to Italian American parents and raised in Westfield, Massachusetts. Her parents, both first-generation Americans from working-class backgrounds, were highly religious and hard working. They not only "raised six children for God"; they achieved middle-class economic status. "But they didn't really know what they were doing. We used to sit down on Friday nights and watch the line up of *Leave It To Beaver* and *Father Knows Best,* and it was a mandatory date; we all had to be there and learn how to become a middle class family. And my mother wanted it more than any of us. My father was more out in the world, but my mother was really stuck in the home."

Her parents, Jan noted, had a traditional division of labor. "There was an understanding that he'd go out and earn the money, and she'd do everything else. He was the warm, loving parent, but my mother did all the work." This bred frustration and resentment on her mother's part. "What we really hated was the fact that my mother was really volatile and unpredictable, and her punishments never really fit the crime, and that my father did nothing about it." She went on to observe that "it was a very bizarre household. Our cousins would come over and think we were the perfect family. But that was only when company came. The whole energy—the feeling of Tina and Tony—was making us look like *Father Knows Best.* But there was no *Father Knows Best.*" The emotional volatility, and constant pressure to conform to a middle-class ideal led to early fantasies of escape. "From the time I was a very small child, I never felt that I belonged in that family. My brother and I ran away when we were very little, and we used to fantasize that our parents would die in a car crash and we'd be free." She also recalled feeling kinship with "all the oddball relatives," particularly an alcoholic uncle who "was the most interesting person of the bunch." Part of his appeal, no doubt, was his unwillingness to conform to middle-class notions of propriety.[12]

Virginia Logan, from a solid, very proper and politically conservative family, also felt trapped and confined. The oldest of three daughters, Virginia was born in England in 1946 to a British mother and an American military father. When she was a little over two, they came to the United States and after several moves settled in Appleton, Wisconsin. Her bright, outgoing mother, confined to the home with three small children and separated from her family and friends in England, had a violent and unpredictable temper. Like Jan's mother, she took it out on her children. Virginia's father, who spent a good part of every month on the road as an insurance claims adjuster, rarely intervened. To the outside world, they looked like a happy, *Father Knows Best* family, but from within it felt like a pressure cooker. Virginia found refuge in books and school: "Reading was what broadened my interest in a wider world and was also a way of being left alone. If I was reading, my mother wouldn't bother me." She also learned, at a very young age, to take care of her own emotional and physical needs—something that her overstressed mother strongly encouraged. But although this translated into considerable autonomy, it also generated feelings of not being wanted or belonging. "I always felt different, that I had to hide who I really was, that I couldn't be myself or express my needs and still be liked."[13]

Constance Trouble's home life was similarly stressful. Her parents divorced shortly after her birth, and she recalled feeling that "I somehow carried a taint or stain that might rub off on other families." She also felt adrift in her own family. "My mother was a very creative sensitive woman who never quite found her match. We all grew up feeling that we had held her back—father included. And she was always trying to better us, it just never let up—especially the pressure on us girls to behave properly and show good taste." Her brother, by virtue of "his boy status, got to go places we couldn't, and pursued interests that my mother couldn't control." Constance found comfort and refuge in nature and literature. "In nature there was no judgement, no self-consciousness, just complete acceptance. In books I found that truth and beauty were on the other side of the looking glass, beyond mere appearances."[14]

The pressure of keeping up appearances created even greater difficulties for Nancy Jean, who was raised in an upper-middle-class family by "an alcoholic businessman and a bright, unfulfilled, perfect-on-the-surface, but distant and aloof mother." Nancy, who was subjected to sexual abuse as a child, knew that speaking up would constitute an unforgivable betrayal of her family's proper image. Instead, she found refuge in nature and "acted out" in an unladylike fashion. She thus became the odd, "bad kid" in the family. Her story is similar to that of Marilyn Van Derbur. In *The Way We Never Were*, Stephanie Coontz tells us that Van Derbur, born just a few years earlier than Nancy Jean and crowned Miss America in 1958, "had been sexually violated by her father from the time she was five until she was eighteen, when she moved away to college."[15]

Other girls, such as Carolyn Adams, Charlotte Todd, Marylyn Motherbear Scott, and Kathleen Taylor, reported happier home lives but felt restricted by traditional gender norms and the overall climate of cultural conservatism and conformity. Sometimes these forces intersected; girls, more so than boys, were expected to be docile, obedient, and passive. Carolyn Adams (Garcia), born in 1946, was raised in an upper-middle-class, highly intellectual, old stock American family in Hyde Park, New York. Her entomologist father and botanist/schoolteacher mother provided her with plenty of intellectual stimulation and encouragement. She recalled spending hours exploring her parents' collections of "bugs and plants" as well as the great outdoors. She, like many other counterculture women, developed a strong connection with nature—"imagining myself running long distance over the old Mohawk trail or hunting deer or making clothes and foods of the Indians." Still, she had less physical autonomy than her brothers. "Girls didn't have as much personal freedom as boys did. I was jealous of the freedom the boys seemed to have and I was always angling for another little slice of freedom. Independence. That was my big goal as a child. Complete Independence." Although her home environment was relatively harmonious, school was another matter. Cast as a misfit because of her intelligence and athleticism, Carolyn experienced school as "an inner battleground. Daydreaming took me out the windows and into fresh, limitless landscapes and away from the tension of never quite fitting in, of the feeling of being odd and too smart."[16]

Charlotte Todd, raised by Catholic parents in New Orleans, felt similarly confined by gender expectations. Her math professor father, presiding over a boisterous family of ten children, sent his daughters to parochial grammar school and a private Catholic girls' academy. She recalled a happy childhood, but noted, "like we were teenagers and kids, but you have to be a lady too. And there's the heavy responsibility of acting like a lady."[17]

Marylyn Motherbear Scott and Kathleen Taylor enjoyed more physical autonomy but felt odd and out of place because of their intellectual independence and creativity. Marylyn was raised by her grandparents after her father was killed in World War II. Her mother cared for her during the summer and took her on outings, including the theater, throughout the year. A creative, imaginative, and precocious child, she cultivated friendships with children from varied ethnic and class backgrounds and explored different churches and neighborhoods in her community. Pushing the boundaries made her different: "There's a family or tribe of people who say about their youth, 'I was different. I don't know why. I wasn't the same as my family. My path took me another way—more independent, more out there, more somewhere else than. . . . ' I was one of those."

Kathleen Taylor, also from an unconventional family, was raised by a single mother and grandmother in New York City. With the encouragement of her grandmother, she spent most of her childhood in libraries and museums, cultivating "a life of the mind." She also attended an experimental grammar school, run on the Dewey model. More well read and intellectually worldly than her peers, she recalled feeling "different. I hadn't yet learned to trust my own critical capacities, but I at least learned to be suspicious of authority. That alone was enough to make me feel out of place," especially when she briefly attended a Catholic girls' school.[18]

When they reached adolescence and young adulthood, many of these odd, sensitive girls pushed even harder against the confines of their families and culture. With a surprising degree of ferocity, they quite consciously turned against middle-class notions of proper, ladylike behavior. Although female disaffection with gender conventions was widespread during the 1950s, most girls chose forms of rebellion that were normal for their larger youth cohort. They may have fantasized about running around with delinquents, beatniks, and darker "others" or having affairs with older men and experimenting with drugs, but they rarely went "all the way." To engage in overt rebellion, to do more than dream of freedom and transgression, carried too heavy a price. But for girls who were already alienated from adult and peer culture, acting out was the next logical step.[19]

Jan Camp's older sister had been "hell on wheels," and as a consequence her parents "really put a lid on me." Although appearing as the "good, trouble-free" daughter, Jan ran "with the dangerous kids" in high school. Attracted to adventure and risk, she especially loved "ridge running, driving around mountain curves as fast as possible with the really wild boys. What I really wanted was to have a band of Merry Men. I really liked the Zorro movies; that's where I got my sense of adventure." Cynthia Robins describes Carolyn Adams: rejected by her peers as too "brainy," she embraced an outsider image as "a beatnik" and "went to war" with her overly authoritarian gym teacher, who engineered Carolyn's expulsion from high school just before graduation. After receiving her diploma by mail, she worked briefly as a waitress and then accepted a ride out to California with her younger brother. This was not something that seventeen-year-old girls with her family's pedigree did.[20]

Virginia Logan, on the other hand, kept her rebellion under wraps.

Tired of rejection by her peers for being too smart and academic, she "focused on being liked and popular which didn't include focusing on school. And I made it, figured out what I needed to do to get into the popular girl group." Her apparent social adjustment and still excellent grades ensured that she was "always able to get away with a lot because my mother trusted me and left me alone. So I snuck out at night, and hung out drinking with friends." Her intelligence and intellectual sophistication still intimidated boys, however. At sixteen, in complete secrecy, she initiated an affair with her favorite teacher's husband. "It was like I was living a double life, especially when my teacher would invite me over or take me to various social functions."

Constance Trouble began sneaking out, cutting school, and associating with local college students whom she found more interesting than her peers and teachers. "You could have real conversations about big issues and ideas, and they totally related to my disaffection with class pretensions and conventional morality." But, she noted, "I completely ran amok. My older sister kept telling me to be cool, to be sneakier, but I threw all caution to the wind. I was inventing a new self, one that I didn't want to hide, and one that was, quite pleasurably, a thorn in my mother's side."[21]

Nancy Jean, who had already established a reputation as her family's "bad kid," got pregnant in high school "in order to leave home." Still a teenager, she married, moved into an apartment with her husband, and had three more children in quick succession. Charlotte Todd, while acting like a good Catholic girl at home, explored the New Orleans folk music scene, smoked marijuana, and — no doubt inspired by the Beats — began delving into Eastern religious philosophy. In a similar fashion, Marylyn Motherbear Scott ventured even further afield of her mostly white neighborhood than she had as a girl. There she encountered exotic "others" and began dating boys who were older and of different ethnic backgrounds, including her "first love," a Nicaraguan singer, artist, and poet. Her grandparents, "who weren't good at setting limits," sent her to live with an aunt and uncle, but they, too, failed to contain Marylyn's attraction to other, more interesting worlds.[22]

Pam Tent, raised in suburban Detroit, received a car from her parents as a sixteenth birthday present "so I'd never have to rely on a boy just to have a ride." Beginning in her junior year at a Catholic girls' college preparatory school, she used the car to play hooky and sneak out to downtown Detroit, where she and her friends frequented jazz clubs and coffee houses. Similarly, Jodi Mitchell couldn't be tied down. Starting at age fourteen, "I would save up my lunch money until I had $28, the exact amount for a Greyhound ticket from Chas., W. V. A. to New York City. I'd tell my mother I'd be late that evening. I was going to the library to study after school. I'd ride the little bus over the Kanawha River to downtown, walk to the depot, purchase a ticket and hop aboard through the long dark night." Once at her destination, she would stay with her grandmother in Brooklyn, who would "send me out with a pocketful of tokens for the subway, and some fresh fruit. I was free to explore."[23]

Eventually, these and thousands of other rebel girls found the counterculture. Some women, however, actually helped create it. Most hippie foremothers, such as Lenore Kandel, Diane Di Prima, Carolyn Adams, Marylyn Motherbear Scott, and Rain Jacopetti, were attached either to the Beat subculture or its allied avant garde literary and artistic circles during the 1950s and early 1960s. More experimental, idealistic, and playful than many of the Beats, they moved fluidly across the boundaries of bohemia to lay the foundation of a new counterculture. In most cases, psychedelic drugs played a pivotal role in their transition. Lenore Kandel, born in 1932 in New York City, spent most of her early childhood in rural Pennsylvania. When her parents separated she moved with her mother to Los Angeles, where she became a self-described "juvenile delinquent" who divided her time between drinking and driving around with friends and delving into Eastern mysticism, including Buddhism. Bright and intellectually precocious, she attended Los Angeles City College at sixteen and then moved on to New York's School for Social Research to study psychology. Living in bohemian Greenwich Village, she supported herself as a barmaid, cocktail waitress, and belly dancer.

In 1960 she moved to San Francisco and joined the tail end of the Beat movement. There she sang with folk groups and began reading and publishing her poetry. Although romantically involved with poet Gary Snyder and immortalized as "Ramona Swartz" in Jack Kerouac's *Big Sur*, Kandel never strongly identified with the Beats. By the early 1960s she was not only studying Zen but also dabbling in yoga, extrasensory perception, and psychedelic drugs. It was as a founding member of the Haight Ashbury scene that she discovered her "tribal" identity with an eccentric assortment of like-minded individuals intent on creating a counterculture. Her new tribe included the Diggers, an anarchist hippie collective that distributed free food, ran free stores, and organized a series of "happenings" or street pageants designed to challenge capitalist mode of production and consumption. Lenore and her fellow Diggers came very close to Jan Camp's vision of a band of "Merry Men." In 1966, Kandel's *Love Book*, a poetic ode to free love, was banned as obscene. This cemented her iconic status as the counterculture's reigning love goddess.

Lenore's friend, Diane Di Prima, also bridged the Beat generation and hippiedom. Born in Brooklyn, New York, in 1934, Diane went on to attend Swarthmore College and establish herself as a gifted young poet in the Beat enclave of Greenwich Village. Once in her new digs, Di Prima could love whom she pleased (including other women), produce art, and live in "light and freedom, air and laughter, the outside world," as she described it in her memoirs. Like Lenore, she eventually made her way out to the West Coast and became a core member of the Diggers and a staunch advocate of sexual freedom.[24]

The very precocious and much younger Carolyn Adams arrived in San Francisco during the summer of 1963 and found a job working at Stanford University's organic chemistry lab. Staffing the night shift, she sampled some of the psychedelic compounds the lab was analyzing. "I had a little 'spill' and got really high. I kind of nodded out. It was definitely a mild psychedelic experience with a lot of long, complex dreams, mostly about ancient ruined cities—Mayan—and jaguars. When I came to, my boss was shaking me by the shoulder. The machine was down. I had f___d up the sample and had taken the thing out of commission for a day." She lost the job but found another as a Merry Prankster. Sitting in a Palo Alto café, Carolyn was approached by Beat icon Neal Cassady and his friend Bradley and invited for a ride. They ended up at Ken Kesey's house in La Honda, which Carolyn recalled was like finding home. "I was on the hunt for compatible people. It's like one of those things you do in your early adulthood. When I met Ken Kesey and the Pranksters, I had that understanding immediately—that these guys were going to be my friends for a very long time."

As Kesey's lover and close confidant, Carolyn (a.k.a. Mountain Girl) was integrally involved in the Pranksters' efforts to forge an alternative culture—efforts that included a series of multimedia "acid tests" in which participants ingested LSD in an environment saturated with

psychedelic sound and color. By 1966 these "happenings" had contributed to the rise of a vibrant hip scene in San Francisco's Haight Ashbury
district, where Adams, ready for yet another adventure, joined her new
lover, Jerry Garcia, at the Grateful Dead's 710 Ashbury Street commune. There, at one of the city's first and most famous counterculture
communes, she kept the household running smoothly. Rock Scully, the
Dead's manager, recalled that "I never met a woman with quite as much
machismo as that girl had. . . . She spoke her mind and was quite tolerant except for anything that approached ignorance. If you were stupid,
she'd tell you. If you were behaving badly, she'd tell you that, too. She
wasn't a judgmental kind of person, she was just brutally frank. She was
judge and jury in those days." And she made it possible for the band to
focus on creating a new psychedelic sound.[25]

Marylyn Motherbear Scott, born in 1937, attended Boston University
and Bennington College, married, performed in local dance companies,
and launched the Boston Little Theater, which "did playwrights like
Lorca and Brecht." As part of the city's bohemian community, she and
her husband enjoyed a rich social life with other "intelligentsia." "We
used to smoke pot, drink, play bridge, and talk politics with friends
all weekend." Then, in the early 1960s, her husband and a "chemist
friend" cooked up some mescaline in their basement, and "this put us
on the cutting edge of psychedelia." They, like Lenore, Diane, and Carolyn, "were searching. We were looking for paths, we were looking for
significance in our lives, and so the group that we did that with were all
kind of explorers, seekers, thinkers."

Psychedelic drugs transformed Marylyn's bohemian circle into Boston's first counterculture community. "And it was through this . . . that
we started talking about communal living. Everyone living together. We
talked about love, we talked about how much we loved each other." In
the mid-1960s a friend returned from a trip out west and "told us that
California was really an amazing place. He said that the doors were open,
that people didn't have to lock their doors like they have to on the East
Coast . . . and it was just easy to live, and people loved each other, and it
was just a wonderful place." In 1967, after having helped create Boston's
counterculture, she, her husband, and their two children loaded their
possessions into a Volkswagen bus and "just moved into the West Coast
psychedelic scene."[26]

Rain Jacopetti, like Marylyn Motherbear Scott, started out as a bohemian experimental artist. In 1965, she and her husband, Ben, were running the Open Theater, a Berkeley performance space where they staged multimedia productions that combined slides, film, multiple sound tracks, projected images, props, and readings. With titles such as "Revelations," "The God Box," and "Congress of Wonders," their productions exhorted the audience to acknowledge that "the nature of the world around us has changed" and to embrace a new sensuality, ritual, and spiritual growth. In essence, they introduced viewers to what eventually became staple themes of the counterculture. In 1966, after staging a production at the psychedelic rock extravaganza called "The Trips Festival," the Jacopettis moved with some friends to Lou Gottlieb's (of Limelighters fame) property in Sonoma County. Rain thus became a founding member of Morning Star Ranch, California's first rural counterculture commune. Remaining there over the summer, Rain introduced residents to vegetarian, macrobiotic food; yoga; and meditation. She and her fellow communards also took a "good deal of acid." As her friend Gina recalled in *Home Free Home*, "these were magical times, with us playing archetypes on a Big Grail Quest. We had this sense of wonders to be seen and fantastic games to be won."[27]

In helping to forge an alternative culture, these and hundreds of other hippie foremothers blazed a trail for thousands more "explorers, seekers, thinkers." Young women, harkening from every part of the nation, discovered that a new world awaited them. Some found it by accident or through older siblings, relatives, and friends. Others came across counterculture publications or happened on hippie gatherings. Still others recalled hearing mainstream reportage that, no matter how negative, made the counterculture seem fascinating and appealing. Most, unlike some of the foremothers, were quite young, still in high school or college. Constance Trouble, for example, found hippiedom through an older sister, cousins, and summer camp that was staffed by counterculture youth. Pam Tent, as a high school junior, found the emerging hippie scene in Detroit and began taking psychedelics. "When LSD first happened into the scene, my friends and I latched onto it as an amazingly fun tool for self-exploration." At that point "it was still legal and being sold under the pharmaceutical name of Sandoz." When she graduated from high school, after barely making it through her senior year, she took a summer job with a mortgage company. Still in Detroit, she saw television coverage of the West Coast hippie convergence, a *Time* magazine article on Morning Star Ranch, and *Life* and *Look* features on the Summer of Love, which convinced her "to flee straight life and join the come-as-you-are party in San Francisco."

Similarly, Charlotte Todd, a young bohemian in New Orleans, heard about San Francisco's blossoming counterculture and headed west right after high school graduation. Arriving in 1966, she was welcomed by the Diggers and later moved up to Morning Star Ranch. In contrast, Lelain Lorenzen was quite serious and deliberate. Just after high school, she found a copy of *Mother Earth News* and started corresponding with "people who were advertising . . . for people to come and live with them." She had decided that she "wanted to live close to the bone. I wanted to be a back-to-the-lander. That's why I got involved in communal life, is because I wanted to learn to do things from scratch."[28]

Some had to wait for college, finding little in their home towns to inspire them to a new lifestyle. Roberta Price finished at Vassar in 1968 and then attended graduate school at SUNY Buffalo. During her first year in the Ph.D. program, she received a summer grant to study and photograph hippie back-to-the-land communes. Traveling throughout the southwest, she and her partner were smitten with Libre, a commune in southern Colorado's Huerfano Valley. The following year, she and her companion married, dropped out of school, and moved to Libre. Virginia Logan also had to wait for college to discover the counterculture. She left home for the University of Wisconsin at Madison in the fall of 1964 and fell in love with "kids who had been to arts schools in New York—kids who were interesting, bohemian. And it was, 'oh wow, there's a whole other world, an element of rebellion, that you could dress how you wanted, do what you wanted.'" Shortly thereafter, Virginia met Susan, "who was really different and wild" and undoubtedly connected to the emerging counterculture. Susan gave her some psilocybin, "and it was really scary. I walked outside the dorm and the bushes were on fire, and the trees were talking to each other. When I came down from that I was a little scared to try other things for a while." She also joined campus antiwar protests but shied away from radical student groups. "I never believed in violent opposition to violence, and it was too consuming. I was someone who was playful, spiritual, and wide open to life. And I liked to have a good time. The committed radicals never seemed to be enjoying themselves."[29]

Similarly, Ellen Winner was in medical school when she "met a tall

Beatnik, dressed in black, with a narrow beard and a sense of meaninglessness as deep as my own. I fell in love and my grades hit bottom. Becoming a doctor was now out of the question." Soon after, she entered the counterculture and began a decade-long search for meaning that involved experimentation with drugs and "obscure philosophies." Mara Devine was well on her way to becoming a career diplomat when she left her linguistics program at San Francisco State College to study and teach English in Spain. When she returned to the states, "things were really happening in the Haight/Ashbury where my friends were living. Everybody was taking acid and joining communes. So I followed suit and went out to New Mexico. . . . " Vivian Gotters was fully engrossed in producing a video biography of Johann Sebastian Bach when she began attending lectures at Timothy Leary's League for Spiritual Discovery in New York's West Village. She then dropped out of college, emigrated to San Francisco's Haight Ashbury district, and moved on to Morning Star Ranch. "We didn't even think ahead of how we were going to support ourselves. We were just strongly on this wave of turn on, tune in, drop out, love."[30]

Still others were married or in established careers. Nancy Nina settled in suburban southern California with her husband and two children in the mid-1960s. There she recalled attending a Parent-Teacher Association meeting where an Avon representative gave the keynote address. "And she talked about how important it was to be beautiful for your children, because they would feel ashamed if you weren't beautiful, so you should buy these beauty products." She then turned to antiwar activism and discovered that "this is not my world. This is not my society. I don't pay police to smack open the heads of young women who meditate, and I don't pay presidents and governors that applaud that. This is not my society anymore. I wish it to destroy itself." After taking LSD she severed all ties with suburbia and entered the counterculture. Similarly, Mary Siler Anderson was living in southern California with her college professor husband and two children when she attended a lecture given by Timothy Leary. She also recalled, "there was new music happening, and there was just this sense of change in the air. And I also took drugs. I discovered marijuana and LSD . . . it was a real awakening for me . . . that you don't have to be in this particular rut, doing this particular kind of thing."

Jan Camp, trapped in an unfulfilling, traditional marriage, met the counterculture through her husband's younger cousins. During the day, when her husband was at work, they would drop by with their stash of pot, and "we would have conversations about . . . politics—rules and regulations of the community and how they were shifted to benefit certain people—kind of cultural politics." They also introduced her to music that was "meaningful." From there, it was only a matter of time before she left her husband. Nancy Jean and her husband discovered the counterculture together, beginning with marijuana and graduating to psychedelic drugs, music, be-ins, and sexual experimentation. Nancy recalled, however, that she was countercultural long before the mid-1960s. "It simply reflected my own, pre-existing sensibility: anti-materialistic, spiritual, anti-authoritarian, anti-racist, and pacifist. It was like finding home."[31]

The counterculture's attractions, while lost on most older Americans, were obvious to a generation of young women who came of age during the 1950s and early 1960s. According to Andrew Kopkind, hippie women, like their male peers, saw themselves as creating an alternative to "the old forms, the vinyl and aerosol institutions that carry all the insane and destructive values of privatism, competition, commercialism, profitability, and elitism." Modern industrial society, they maintained, may have improved the material condition of many Americans but at too high a price: conformity; mind-numbing, routinized labor; impersonal, superficial relationships; separation from nature; environmental degradation; emotional and sexual repression; despiritualization of daily life; and a boring, consumption-oriented mass culture. Moreover, they, like youth on the left, viewed the United States as an oppressor—a nation intent on maintaining and extending its power by ruthlessly suppressing domestic and international opposition. An article in the *San Francisco Oracle* stated that hippies concluded that "the system remains and continues to destroy. Our protests have been ineffective because we're psychologically and materially dependent on the system we're protesting. To protest as we have been is to nourish the system that is waging war and degrading people. Effective protest is not proclaiming the faults of the system, but in surviving independent of the system." Hence, they proposed, "the quickest, healthiest most effective way to change our society is to turn on, tune in, drop out."[32]

But "dropping out" had another, gender-specific meaning for young women. It was, above all, an opportunity to escape suburban domesticity, the sexual double standard, and the limits imposed on female creative self-expression and physical autonomy. Thus, women were determined to create a society that embraced a broader countercultural agenda as well as their gender-related longings. Initially though, many simply basked in the novelty and pageantry of the hippie scene. Pam Tent, upon arriving in San Francisco's Haight Ashbury district,

> marveled at the fact that it was midwinter and the trees were still green and the flowers bloomed. The weather was so mild that people walked barefoot. I joined the costumed, painted throng, reeking of patchouli, and strolled up and down the length of Haight Street. Every now and then a young guy would say in passing, 'acid, grass, speed.' If you were interested, you approached him and conducted your business in the nearest doorway. It was that loose.

She went on to explain, "we were a diverse group of intellectual misfits from every corner of society who for various reasons hadn't fit in. We'd come to celebrate life—we were convinced that if we loved enough we could change the world. It was thrilling to find each other and realize our numbers." There, in this small urban enclave, she "found acceptance among these free-living pilgrims and yearned to shed all of my Midwestern inhibitions."

Virginia Logan drove a friend from Wisconsin to Vancouver to help him escape the draft and then headed down the coast to Berkeley. When she arrived in the summer of 1968, the city's hip and student activist communities had recently joined forces to create and defend People's Park. Up and down Telegraph Avenue street musicians, drug pushers, hippie vendors, runaway youth, Hare Krishnas, student activists, Black Panthers, and flower children congregated in what seemed like a never-ending celebration of dissent and nonconformity. Virginia recalled, "my first night in Berkeley, I was in a Eucalyptus grove drinking Thunderbird and smoking dope with Mario Savio's younger brother, and it just felt like the place to be." Renting an apartment right on Telegraph, she was astounded and thrilled by the unfolding drama. "There were Hare Krishnas chanting and the National Guard shooting tear gas at People's Park demonstrators right outside my window. It seemed at that time like anything was possible . . . that the world was completely unraveling, and that something new was taking its place." Although she went back to Madison to complete her degree, she returned to Berkeley the following year.[33]

Like Pam and Virginia, Gina Stillman was in awe of the possibilities. "We were looking for Something. At first I thought I was the only woman desperately seeking an alternative. But it's always been the case that when I feel strongly I'm never wrong. There were thousands of people feeling the same thing. It was the era itself, a time when possibilities opened up to us that had never been revealed before." For her, life prior to the counterculture had been "drab" and disappointing. But once immersed in the new sensibility, "everything was tremendously heightened. I felt a real joy in getting out of my previous existence." Jan Camp also felt completely liberated. After leaving her husband and joining the counterculture, she began cooking, painting, drawing, and making love without a critical audience or preconceived blueprint. For the first time she was able to live "under the radar," free of "the restrictions and norms that other people . . . have to cope with."[34]

Beyond their initial excitement at having found a playful, creative, wonder-filled home, women expressed a profound longing for meaningful relationships and community. Pam Tent recalled that "euphoria suffused this self-made community, where services were exchanged for barter. There was an affinity between strangers that not only prompted tolerance but also led to deep conversations about the meaning of life with people only met in passing." Pamela Hunt relished the opportunity to forge deeper connections with her peers: "You were supposed to think like Ozzie and Harriet. Well, that didn't make sense and it was very boring and, so, with these meetings . . . we were talking about real stuff, real spirit, real community." Kay Hayward, whose San Francisco apartment became a community gathering place, remembered that "it was a wonderful time. It seemed safe, and things seemed marvelous. It just seemed like a golden, blessed time . . . and so full of people. It was just wall to wall people and everyone was experiencing unity, equality." Vivian Gotters, like thousands of other young women, was convinced that this new spirit of fellowship and unity would transform society. "We were so convinced that the world was changing through us—that this was the new age and that all the pain, all the suffering—we could see it so clearly that, you know, just loving and—this was a new time."[35]

Women also desired and found a deeper connection to the natural world, a simpler, less consumption-driven lifestyle, and meaningful work. Matie Bell Lakish, for example, recalled that

> we wanted to reconnect with the land, we wanted to grow our own food, we wanted to have our own babies, we wanted to have our own educational system. And it wasn't just that we wanted our own, it was that we wanted an alternative to what was in existence in society at that time. . . . I think people were really feeling this sense of, this society as removing them from their roots, from their connection with the earth in a lot of ways.

Similarly, Kay Hayward remembered, "We wanted our lives to be better, we wanted to break away from what all of us had known. Not follow particular trends that were fashionable at the time, just simplify, to not value and not go for all those things that were being sought after by the general population at that time." Lelain Lorenzen, as a recent high school graduate when she joined a hippie commune, put it even more simply: "I really wanted to live close to the bone." And this was precisely what she and countless other women achieved. "One way to look at what we're doing is that it's a school. I can recognize the stars now. I can recognize tomato plants. I know how plants look when they are growing. I know how to grow plants. I know what it feels like to drink water from its basic sources. Those seem to me important experiences, experiences which our culture has left out."[36]

Finally, women sought to integrate their quest for spiritual growth and self-realization with other facets of their lives. They longed for a world where work, play, interpersonal relationships, and spirituality were part of a seamless whole. Gina Stillman, for example, recalled in *Home Free Home* that "I wanted to dedicate myself, to be part of a huge, loving, giving, motherly force. I gave up my concern for my personal welfare and concentrated on a concern for the community, for group consciousness rather than on my individual self." Two others voiced similar outlooks in Judson Jerome's *Families of Eden*. Freda, a young woman from Shaker Heights who joined a New Mexico commune, explained that "the reason for my being here is simply wanting to be a better person, to be in tune with myself and realizing that other people help me in that, searching for real values within yourself." Ellen Winner similarly joined the counterculture to "heal my own sense of spiritual isolation and despair" and to break out of "a material world bounded on all sides by the limits of my senses and sealed at the top and bottom with the authority of rational, scientific thought."[37]

Ultimately, hippiedom delivered on many of its promises, creating an opening for women to break with convention and forge dramatically different relationships to their bodies, intimate partners, work, spirituality, children, and nature. Initially, however, the counterculture essentialized female difference in a manner that relegated women to subservient domestic roles and normalized heterosexuality. Despite their intelligence, thirst for adventure, and dedication to a liberatory vision, hippie women entered or helped create a world that appeared to affirm familiar gender constructs and hierarchies. Carolyn Adams, for example, was clearly Ken Kesey's and Jerry Garcia's intellectual equal but filled roles as lover, muse, household manager, and conscientious mother to the children that she had with both men. In a similar manner, Lenore Kandel, a gifted writer and poet, helped run the Digger kitchen while serving as the Haight's reigning love goddess. Her *Love Book* and many of her public pronouncements, while celebrating female sexuality, confined desire to the heterosexual norm and reinforced the notion that women lived solely to love and nurture men. Marylyn Motherbear Scott, an artistic and cultural renegade, seemingly channeled her creative passion into traditional female pursuits. They, and the young women who followed them into the counterculture, often appear — on the surface — painfully unliberated.

The counterculture's setting was quite different, however, from the postwar, suburban, *Father Knows Best* backdrop. Hippie women's domestic labor not only took place outside of the nuclear family structure and the confines of the sexual double standard; it was charged with political meaning and purpose, tethered to a broader agenda for social change. Moreover, the counterculture was deeply committed to so-called feminine traits and values. Indeed, hippiedom was perhaps less hegemonically male than the New Left. Within their extended families and communities, counterculture women formed "sisterhoods" that monopolized very visible and economically vital productive functions. By virtue of occupying and holding their own "feminine" space, hippie women thus felt less burdened by the chauvinism of their male peers. New Left women, in contrast, had to function in an environment that was physically and ideologically dominated by men. Excluded from all avenues of power, activist women not only rose up against male authority earlier, they claimed equality on the basis of sameness rather than difference. Both groups, however, joined their respective movements for similar reasons. They were rebel girls who wanted something more expansive and meaningful than what was offered to their mothers.

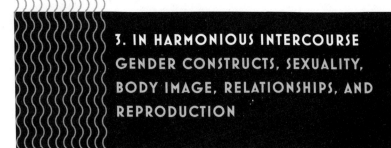

3. IN HARMONIOUS INTERCOURSE GENDER CONSTRUCTS, SEXUALITY, BODY IMAGE, RELATIONSHIPS, AND REPRODUCTION

hen women dropped out of the mainstream, they helped create an alternative culture that was both novel and familiar. The novelty, the outright rejection of conventional middle-class norms by hippie youth, was what captured the attention of older, non-hip Americans. The familiar, the established, the respected, the staid, often got lost in sensational accounts of transgressive behavior. Only a few outside observers, mostly scholars and young New Left feminist critics, noticed that hippie gender constructs and the assumptions that undergirded them appeared profoundly conservative.

In keeping with generations of Americans, hippies believed that women were essentially different from men: more intuitive, nurturing, cooperative, nonaggressive, present-oriented, and ruled by their emotions and bodies. As such, women were naturally suited to be wives, mothers, caregivers, and helpmates. Maggie Gaskin, writing from within the counterculture, remarked, "The women in the hippie community are very, very female. There are a lot of children that are there because they're wanted, and the women are going back and doing very feminine things, like weaving and cooking with a lot of pride, doing it as a woman thing."[1]

Lenore Kandel, the Haight Ashbury's reigning love goddess and author of the *Love Book*, a poetic celebration of hip sensuality, similarly accepted traditional, heteronormative gender constructs and roles. Speaking for a larger cohort, she remarked "a woman is always in relation to a man, really. I don't know any woman who digs being a woman who doesn't want her man a touch stronger. A woman who isn't happy being a woman for one reason or another runs into a lot of problems." A man's job, she stated, is to hunt, protect, and "take care of enemies.

A woman's job is feeding her man, taking care of those things about her. In her way, radiating the feeling of warmth. . . . I don't think it's a man's role to go around changing the diapers. He should be able to when necessary. A women takes care of the washing and putting the kids to bed."[2]

Hippie men were equally forthcoming about gender conventions. A young communard commented, "Chicks, mystical chicks: being witchy and spiritual was the main contribution women were supposed to make to communal life. That and dinner." Peter Coyote, writing about the Diggers' communal households, reflected that "roles were generally divided among traditional male-female lines, with the women looking after the food, houses, and children and the men looking after the trucks and physical plant." In his own relationships, he was just as accepting of the gender status quo. When his lover, Jessie Barton, followed him to San Francisco, he expected her to do the laundry, cook, clean house, and entertain his friends while he immersed himself in the art and literary scene and engaged in "sexual diversions" that were "business as usual" for his male friends and mentors. In hindsight, Coyote reflected, "our division of labor seems archaic, particularly for a visionary community."[3]

Outside observers of the counterculture witnessed much the same thing. Jon Wagner, for example, noted that most hippie communes seemingly adhered to traditional gender roles and had male-dominated decisionmaking structures. Bill Grant, after a tour of northern California and Oregon hippie enclaves, observed that "Women's Lib did not appear to have scored too high in the communes I visited." Some of his traveling companions "gave up, after the third stop, in abject disgust because of the traditional role playing they observed." Ron E. Roberts, equally taken aback by what he witnessed, commented that "often hip communes ignore the contemporary movement for women's rights. Often hip communes, with their prophecies of freedom for the individual, have fallen into the same division of labor as that of the larger society. The women cook, wash, or do other 'womanly' things." Sara Davidson was a bit more charitable, recognizing that hippie "gender roles seemed mutually agreeable and reinforcing: the sex roles are so well defined and satisfying. When men actually do heavy physical labor like chopping trees, baling hay, and digging irrigation ditches, it feels very fulfilling for women to tend the cabin, grind wheat, put up fruit, and sew or knit.

Each depends on the other for basic needs." Indeed, hippie women's own accounts of their division of labor, discussed in the next chapter, mirror Davidson's assessment.[4]

Although hippie gender constructs were somewhat in keeping with traditional ideals, they departed from 1950s middle-class norms in several respects. First, counterculture domesticity was enacted in settings that harkened back to an older, more agrarian era when women's labor was more varied, challenging, and economically visible. As Maggie Gaskin went on to emphasize in *Voices of the Love Generation*, "I feel very sorry for square women because they don't have anything to do. Their husbands are out making so much money . . . so they sit home and have nothing to do because they don't really like being around the children. . . . And they've forgotten how to cook. Everything is frozen. And they've forgotten how to do anything that's all woman, you know. . . . Like taking care of kids, and making a nest, because their nest is all chrome and plastic." Second, women's domestic labor was often performed in the company of other women rather than in privatized, nuclear family settings. As Joyce Robinson, a founding member of the New Buffalo commune in New Mexico, noted in *Scrapbook of a Taos Hippie*, "a great sisterhood grew among the women who lived there, a lifetime bond. Even when I stood for hours in front of a wringer washing machine, it never seemed like drudgery." Third, the counterculture drew upon Eastern, esoteric, Native American, and pagan spiritual beliefs to explain or affirm gender duality. Unlike Christianity or Western philosophical traditions, these belief systems stressed the importance of balancing or harmonizing masculine and feminine forces. At least in principle, women's energy — nurturing, passive, receptive, and intuitive — was viewed as positive and complementary. In this vein, the counterculture, in its reaction against the mainstream, constructed a values system that rejected masculine attributes of competition, aggression, acquisitiveness, and overreliance on reason in favor of so-called feminine characteristics. In time, hippie women recognized that they, by virtue of their "difference," possessed the very qualities lauded by their culture and used this claim of difference to obtain greater power and influence within their families and communities. Finally, the counterculture's construction of the feminine occurred as growing numbers of Americans were challenging traditional moral values, including the sexual double standard. While their roles may have seemed traditional, hippie women's relationship to sex, their bodies, and their partners was most certainly novel and liberating. Indeed, the sexual revolution ultimately provided avenues of escape from the heterosexual norm, allowing women to explore and adopt bisexual, lesbian, and transgender identities and to say "no" to coercive, manipulative demands.[5]

Most hippie women grew up with a sexual double standard that demanded female purity, modesty, and restraint while generally accepting male desire as healthy and normal. "Good" girls waited until marriage to have sex, knowing full well that men never tied the knot with fast or loose women. If they gave in, which many did, the consequences could be devastating: ruined reputations and, in the case of pregnancy, acute shame, embarrassment, and even ostracism. But whether a girl gave in or held out, sex hardly gave free rein to female desire. Well into the 1960s, most Americans believed that the vagina, not the clitoris, was the locus of female pleasure. If a woman was even aware of her own anatomy and brave enough to ask for more than vaginal stimulation, she risked appearing deviant or emasculating.[6]

Other expressions of female desire were similarly taboo. According to religious and scientific authorities, both masturbation and lesbianism were pathological, deviant behaviors, symptomatic of severe social maladjustment. In the context of the cold war, lesbianism was also cast as a political threat. Women who rejected the role of wife, mother, and helpmate undermined the nuclear family—the United States' bulwark against godless communism. Not surprisingly, young women who engaged in either practice not only faced social repercussions but also frequently felt intense guilt and self-disgust. Making matters worse, few girls and women were comfortable with their bodies. They reined in and reshaped their flesh in restrictive undergarments and dutifully observed hundreds of proscriptions against immodesty. Their genitals were not only mysterious, they were disgusting, ugly, and a source of danger. Menstruation was as inconvenient as it was embarrassing. Even pregnancy, childbirth, and lactation, as products of the sex act and thus signs of female desire, weren't topics of polite conversation. As Constance Trouble recalled,

It was pretty awful. You had all this pent up energy and no place to channel it. I also felt ashamed of my feelings and my body: ugly dirty, and most of all very, very confused. On top of everything else, I knew that my mother had gone after my sister's teacher for supposedly corrupting young women's morals. The teacher was a woman. But I didn't know what that meant, because no one, I mean no one, spoke openly to kids about anything outside of the heterosexual norm. It was all about "when a husband and wife really love each other, they come together and make a baby."[7]

Her confusion was no doubt compounded by the ambiguous messages 1950s girls received from popular culture. Sex, as Wini Breines explained, was "commercialized, glorified in movies, advertising, and movie magazines." Thus, girls were caught between "prudish families and narrow, even cruel, sexual norms" and equally strong injunctions to secure dates and popularity by cultivating their sexual appeal. Their worth, they learned, hinged on their ability to attract and fix male attention by parsing out small favors and withholding the ultimate prize.[8]

By the late 1950s some Americans, especially youth, started to rebel against the sexual double standard and the more extreme moral restrictions on private behavior. The *Kinsey Report*, issued in 1953, exposed a huge gap between what adults preached and what they actually practiced. A burgeoning youth culture with a keen nose for hypocrisy increasingly ignored middle-class moralism in favor of racier, more sexualized tastes and behaviors. As noted above, private business, particularly the recording industry, recognized an expanding market and began catering to youth preferences. The Beat subculture was even more scornful of middle-class values and embraced free sexual expression, including homosexuality, as part of its broader rebellion.

In the early 1960s the attacks against sexual conservatism grew even stronger. Helen Gurley Brown's *Sex and the Single Girl*, published in 1962, exploded the myth that women didn't need or enjoy sex, encouraged women to accept their bodies, and skewered the sexual double standard. The "pill," licensed in 1960 by the Food and Drug Administration, reduced the risk of unwanted pregnancy and allowed women to take Gurley Brown's message to heart. As David Allyn observed, "It is almost impossible to overstate the impact of the pill on American culture. It gave women the freedom to have sex when and where they wished and made contraception palatable to the prudest of the prude. It put birth control on the covers of family magazines and symbolically represented scientific support for the sexual revolution. The pill promised a return to the rationalism and optimism of the Age of Enlightenment."[9]

With the decoupling of sex and reproduction came additional challenges to moral convention. The League for Sexual Freedom, founded in 1964 by beatniks Jefferson Poland, Allen Ginsburg, Diane Di Prima, Peter Orlovsky, Julian Beck, Ed Sanders, Paul Krassner, and biology professor Leo Koch, "demanded respect for sexual freedom as a fundamental civil liberty." Eventually attracting a large following among hippies, League chapters attacked laws criminalizing homosexuality, prostitution, public nudity, contraception, abortion, interracial marriage, sex between minors, and any number of sexual acts performed by consenting adults. They also attacked campus regulations aimed at controlling the sexual behavior of college students at about the same time that the hippie subculture started to flower in San Francisco's Haight Ashbury district.[10]

Thus, the counterculture's philosophy of sexual liberation was hardly new or even radical; it emerged within a broader context of liberalization and inherited many of its features from preexisting subcultures and popular or academic critiques of middle-class morality. It was also amorphous and ill defined, a product of youth struggling to find an "authentic" sexuality in the midst of rapidly shifting mores, competing desires, and multiple sexual and social agendas.

As a whole, the counterculture viewed sex as a means of cultural liberation, of freeing itself and society from distorted, obsessive forms of sexual expression. The ills of modern culture, it maintained, were products of repressed desire. Remove the source of repression and a warmongering, competitive, consumption-obsessed social order would give way to one that was more playful, sensual, creative, cooperative, and peaceful. Hippies also decried the lack of intimacy in modern society and viewed sex as an antidote to atomization and alienation. As Leah Fritz put it, "sex—like eating, like walking in fresh air, like all human activity—it should recreate us, help us to find one another, make us real, and tangible as the earth. It should put us together again, body and soul, male and female, in harmonious intercourse."[11]

The reality was somewhat more complex. Most hippie men had been raised to view sexual appetite as an integral feature of masculinity. Sex, as they constructed it, revolved around male desire. For them, sexual liberation meant free, no-strings-attached access to women. In contrast, many women, although woefully confined by the sexual double standard, had been raised to view commitment, emotional intimacy, and sex as a package. While women welcomed the freedom to enjoy sex without the burden of guilt—of being labeled fast, loose, a whore—it was no simple matter to detach themselves from these "strings." Making matters worse, they had the additional burden of contending with manipulative and predatory male behavior. Indeed, many women recalled feeling pressured to have sex in response to charges that they were repressed or hung-up. The sexual liberation movement as a whole also privileged male desire, using it as the standard in attempts to construct a "healthier," more "authentic" sexuality. At least initially, many hippie women had difficulty identifying and asserting their sexual needs and preferences. Thus, women's sexual narratives, while stressing the thrill of breaking free of restrictive norms, are relatively silent on the topic of physical pleasure and enjoyment. Counterculture women, as the following pages indicate, had multiple sexual encounters in a wide variety of settings. But did more mean better? Liberation from the sexual double standard and its accompanying burden of guilt, while no doubt a relief, did not necessarily translate into greater sexual satisfaction.

Moreover, the counterculture, while more tolerant of sexual experimentation than the mainstream, had a decidedly heterosexual bent as evidenced by Lenore Kandel's comment that "a woman is always in relation to a man." Most men and women simply accepted that sex between men and women was the norm. Some hip communities, basing gender constructs on the opposing but complementary "energies" of male and female, even pathologized nonheterosexual relationships. In addition, 1960s-style "free love" entailed the risk of unwanted pregnancy. Up until 1971 some states still banned the sale and distribution of contraception, especially to unmarried women and minors. Even in states with more liberal statutes, poor and rural women often lacked access to family planning services. Planned Parenthood, one of the few agencies that distributed the pill at low or no cost, was largely an urban-based organization. And abortion, in a pre–*Roe v. Wade* era, was either banned altogether or restricted to cases in which the mother's life was in danger. Women who lacked the resources to pay a private physician to perform so-called therapeutic abortions resorted—with often lethal consequences—to underground providers or self-induced termination methods. Sexually transmitted disease was another unwelcome cost of "free" love. During a 10-month period between November 1967 and August 1968, the Haight-Ashbury Free Medical Clinic reported 1,250 cases of "possible venereal disease" and 1,922 diagnoses of "obstetric-gynecologic problems." Gonorrhea, clinicians noted, had "reached epidemic proportions," leaving many girls "sterile from chronic, unrecognized or untreated" infections. They also noted a high incidence of pediatric infectious disease and the often disastrous results of attempted natural home births.[12]

Despite these issues and limits, most hippie women found what they considered to be a more authentic sexuality—a sexuality free of the double standard and more accepting of female bodies and desires. They were part of what Barbara Ehrenreich, Elizabeth Hess, and Gloria Jacobs termed the "hidden sexual revolution that male commentators—even feminist critics have for the most part failed to acknowledge" and that 1980s neoconservatives wanted women to doubt and renounce. Reflecting on the experience of counterculture women, Ehrenreich explained that "newfound sexual freedom" not only liberalized the culture, it "brought the added benefit of a healthy confidence in their bodies—and in their ability to live, at least part of the time without being seriously involved with a man." She went on to note, "they could also, if they chose, experiment with bisexuality or eliminate men from their lives altogether: Casual sex was neither heaven nor hell, but it was an important part of their sexual experience." That women were on balance pleased with their new options is borne out in their strong and enduring support of nonconventional relationships and living arrangements.[13]

Hippie women's sexual explorations ran the gamut: casual, multiple encounters; serial monogamy; open and group marriage; bisexuality; lesbianism; and celibacy. Upon initial exposure to the sexually permissive counterculture, many women, relishing their new-found freedom, opted for casual encounters. Jan Camp, freeing herself from a traditional, nonfulfilling marriage, immediately "started having fun . . . started having sex with whomever came along." She characterized this period as "very liberating, particularly [because] I didn't have to care about being in a relationship to have sex. I would have very deep, intimate relationships with people, and I was also discovering sex, and that it didn't have to be one or the other." Constance Trouble had a similar experience, recalling that "it was exciting and incredibly liberating to freely express that energy without emotional strings, without guilt." Similarly, Near Morningstar, who eventually settled into a sexually open relationship with Morning Star Ranch cofounder Lou Gottlieb, happily recalled, "There is no social pressure to work, to be a housewife, or get married. People smilingly accept relationships that once labeled a woman as a slut." Hippie poet Lenore Kandel echoed this sentiment, stressing that free love liberated women from the notion that their sexuality had to be held in reserve for the right man. Marylyn Motherbear Scott, while opting for monogamy, lauded the counterculture's openness to women's sexual explorations. "And so we learn a lot about power through that time because women started to become aware and confident of their sexual natures, to feel that it was all right."[14]

Most women, after a period of experimentation, settled into heterosexual, couple-type arrangements. But here, too, choices abounded. Many moved from one monogamous relationship to another. Some agreed to "open" marriages while others established long-term, exclusive relationships with a single partner. Pam Hanna (Read), for example, enjoyed a long marriage to her husband, Larry, but it wasn't monogamous. "Even though we were the love generation, some people were just naturally monogamous and remained so. Larry and I weren't. By mutual agreement we had an open marriage before the idea was generally bandied about as bold new experiment. Morningstar people were refreshingly open about the matter. There were more judgmental vibes about food on the set in those days than there were about sex." In fact, when Near Morningstar just arrived at the commune, Larry and Pam shared their bed with her. In *Home Free Home*, Near recalled that "Larry lay in the middle and made passionate love to me. Then he gave Pam a kiss and fell asleep." Later Near hooked up with Lou Gottlieb, but in a nonexclusive manner. As one resident observed, "Their relationship seemed cosmically destined, although Near liked to test its elasticity with handsome newcomers, something which put Lou through the emotional wringer on occasion." Marylyn Motherbear Scott, on the other hand, enjoyed a "sexually liberated" youth but settled into two long-term, monogamous marriages. Free love, she recalled, wasn't "in my nature," nor did it offer the stability that she wanted for her children. Still others, like Roberta Price, started out with an open marriage but later insisted on a closed relationship after affairs on both sides had an adverse emotional impact. But when a young, handsome visitor arrived at her commune, she was incapable of resisting the attraction of "free" love. Monogamy, on the other hand, helped some women draw sexual boundaries. Vivian Gotters reflected that "if you're single, you're open season. That's just the way men relate to the world. . . . So it was very convenient for me if I could say, 'no, no, I belong to a guy, I'm monogamist.' You will get left alone and a lot of energy that I didn't want to lose—I mean I was truly on a spiritual quest."[15]

A smaller number of women chose group sex and marriage. According to Richard Fairfield in *The Modern Utopian: Communes U.S.A.*, at Harrad West, a Berkeley commune, members identified themselves as "a group of half dozen adults and several children who live together in a big old Berkeley house. We function as a family; joyful, angry, helpful, turned on and turned off. Our children are cared for, we care for each other." "Care" extended to sharing sex. As one female member explained in *Communes in the Counterculture*, "we spend two or three nights a week with our pair bond partner, and one night a week with each other member of the opposite sex. Sex every night is not a must, and spontaneity is not ruled out—especially during the day." Questioned about the stability of their marriage, she noted, "Well, we're about as permanent as regular marriages generally are here in California. We've spent an incredible amount of time and energy maintaining the group, and we've had some problems. But I'm sure I'll never return to a monogamous relationship."

During its early years, the Farm, located near Summertown, Tennessee, was also based on group marriage but not on a commune-wide scale. Stephen Gaskin, the commune's spiritual leader, advocated four-marriage, a permanent bond established between two men and two women. This was intended to provide greater accountability in their pursuit of spiritual growth and to keep men's domineering egos in check. In 1972 the Farm phased out four-marriage in favor of the more traditional pair bond but continued to invest marriage and especially marital sex with spiritual significance. "Farmies" practiced Tantric sex, where husbands resisted the rush toward orgasm in order to absorb or open up to their wives' more nurturing, life-affirming energy. In this sexual construct, the woman was the "helmsman, the guide." Her orgasm, or release of female energy, was critical to counteracting the male ego or self-centeredness that stood in the way of men's spiritual progress. Although intended to counterbalance male energy with women's life force, Tantric sex, at least in theory, inverted Western sexual practices that privileged male pleasure. In the bedroom, Farm residents maintained, "ladies" were in control.[16]

Elsewhere, women participated in group sex outside of marriage. Between 1965 and 1967, for example, the League for Sexual Freedom (changed to the Sexual Freedom League) spawned regional chapters in college towns across the nation. In addition to promoting distribution of contraceptive devices to unmarried women and repeal of restrictions and laws that regulated private sexual behavior, league chapters—along with *The Harrad Experiment* and *Stranger in a Strange Land* devotees—hosted parties that led to group sexual encounters. It was more common, however, for young hippies to come together informally, in groups of three or more close friends or fellow communards, to simply "share the love." Indeed, the counterculture as a whole identified organized group sex with white, middle-class suburbanites who, out of boredom, engaged in sex as a form of recreation. Hippies—at least philosophically—viewed sex as "making love," an act that would help foster a more intimate, peaceful, nurturing, life-affirming social order.[17]

Within the counterculture, heterosexuality was the norm. It did, nevertheless, provide small openings for women to explore alternate sexualities or express bisexual and lesbian identities. In cities such as San Francisco, Los Angeles, Boston, and New York, many gay, lesbian, bisexual, and transsexual (GLBT) youth straddled the hippie and gay subcultures. Pam Tent, who arrived in San Francisco in 1967, described a high degree of fluidity and even rapport among heterosexual, gay, bisexual, and transgender hippies. "We were a diverse group of intellectual misfits from every corner of society who for various reasons hadn't fit in. We'd come to celebrate life—we were convinced that if we loved enough we could change the world." Such openness, Pam noted, extended to some of the city's communes, including her own. In Los Angeles, the gay and hippie communities similarly converged in the same neighborhoods and shared many of the same values and outcast status. Both promoted sexual liberation, tolerance, and experimentation, and both were targets of "straight" hostility and suspicion. This affinity bred friendly relations and exchange between the two groups, leading the city's earliest gay newspaper to identify hippies as allies.[18]

Organizations such as the Sexual Freedom League, which by the late 1960s had a mostly counterculture membership, also promoted tolerance. For example, the Berkeley chapter, led by a female president and filled with a mostly hip membership, followed national league policy in welcoming gay and bisexual participants. In 1967 she announced, "if the men want to bring their boyfriends to our parties, or if the women want to bring girlfriends, they should feel free to do so. Don't let up-tight members discourage you." Fluidity and tolerance also prevailed in more rural, back-to-the-land settings. The Triple A (Anonymous Artists of America) commune in southern Colorado's Huerfano Valley was co-founded by lesbian and gay artists Adrienne and Lars and enjoyed close ties to neighboring, mostly straight communities. Similarly, Greenfeel, a Vermont commune, was established by two bisexuals with the intention of creating a "community of lovers" free of mainstream "hangups."[19]

Whether urban or rural, explicitly gay friendly or heterocentric, hippie communes were often tolerant of sexual experimentation and identity bending. Pam Tent, for example, married and had a child with a bisexual (later gay-identified) male partner. Linda, a resident of the Huerfano Valley Libre commune, engaged in a threesome with Lars and Coba, two male members of the Triple A band. As Roberta Price casually noted in her diary, "Lars isn't about to go straight, but this was a triumph of love, of sorts." In such settings women also had more immediate, direct confrontations with the heterosexual norm. Gwen Leeds recounted how her partner, Bill Wheeler, fell in love with another woman and harbored fantasies of having two wives. Gwen valiantly tried to accommodate the arrangement and agreed to a three-way tryst under the influence of psychedelics. "We made love most of the night. I was terrified, incredibly aroused and satisfied at the same time." But in the morning, after the drugs wore off, the relationship shattered, and Gwen eventually moved on to another heterosexual partnership.[20]

Nancy Jean had a similar experience, but in her case it led to a life-transforming realization that she was a lesbian. Although her husband initiated the encounter, and she only complied in the spirit of "free" love, Nancy discovered her deep affinity with women. Shortly after, she left her husband for a female lover and fully immersed herself in an emerging lesbian subculture. Similarly, Mara Devine started out in a heterosexual relationship with a member of the New Mexico Hog Farm commune. After giving birth to a son, she moved back to the Bay Area and joined a Los Altos commune, the Transoceanic Egg. "And when the Egg broke up, that was when I had my first full-blown affair with a woman, and I was really freaked out. I didn't know what it meant, and I decided to run away." After traveling around India and Europe, she returned to the states and joined the Lime Saddle commune near Oroville, California. There, "many of the women were discovering their own sexuality, both as lesbians and bisexuals, and there was a lot of movement toward feminist causes and feminist writing, even amongst some of the men."[21]

Such experiences were not unique. By the early 1970s the counterculture's tentative and qualified acceptance of sexual experimentation provoked demands for greater tolerance and openness. Gay hippie men, fully at home in neither the hip nor the homophile subcultures, began to establish their own communes, gay events, festivals, and institutions — all in keeping with the counterculture's transformative vision. Hippie women of all sexual orientations joined together to forge a feminist identity that emphasized the dignity, if not superiority, of "feminine" values and labor. In some cases they kicked the men out; in others they moved on to form separatist, woman-identified communes.[22]

Hippie women, in conjunction with becoming sexually liberated, developed more comfortable relationships with their bodies. Delia Moon recounted a delightful and emblematic experience that she and a female friend shared while hiking around the Olompali commune grounds. "And we were exploring the beautiful land, and we were at this creek, and there was a waterfall, and we were just mind-boggled. At the top of this waterfall appeared a vision, this wonderful, this naked goddess with a heart-shaped face, and a beautiful bow-shaped mouth, a gorgeous body, and she said, 'welcome sisters to God's land, got a cigarette?'" Nudity and freedom from restrictive clothing went hand in hand with the counterculture's emphasis on returning to nature and removing the barriers to full sensory experience. As early as 1966, residents at Morning Star Ranch took off their clothes. Gina Stillman recalled in *Home Free Home* how it all started with Zilla, "a dancer and an actress, a wonderful, flamboyant creature who blew everyone's mind by walking into the livingroom, taking off her clothes and just continuing the conversation." After the initial shock wore off, and the "summer got hotter and hotter we all started going without clothes. It was only logical. We were down to rags anyway."

In addition to being more comfortable, nudity was also political and transformative. William Thieman reported in "Haight Ashbury" that one woman reflected that the body "is a beautiful thing. I want people to see what I look like, and I want to see what they look like without a bunch of clothes covering them up. Nude, everybody is in the same bag, the same class." Margot Adler, who moved from the New Left into the counterculture, found the freedom to embrace both her sexuality and her body. Joining "a group of men and women that worshiped nature in the nude," she "found the group's attitude toward the body liberating." Indeed, "many of the prejudices I had held for years against my own form melted away."[23]

Women even more readily discarded restrictive clothing. Pam Tent, who left a Detroit suburb for the Haight Ashbury in 1967, recalled that "the first thing we actually shed was our underwear. It went the way of Victorian doilies and the word 'no,' which virtually dropped out of the vocabulary." Helen Swick Perry, an older youth worker and observer of the hippie scene, approvingly noted that young women eagerly cast off "symbols of control—brassieres, garter belts and girdles." She also noted women's "comfortable, flowing garments," lack of makeup, and positive attitudes toward menstruation, sex, childbirth, and homosexual experimentation. Constance Trouble, possibly one of the young women whom Helen observed, recalled, "I know it sounds trivial, but it was a huge deal not to worry about our slips and bra straps showing. We got rid of them. Or shaving. It was suddenly okay to have hairy legs and underarms. And the whole idea of not going out unless you 'put on your face,' that went down the tubes."

The "natural woman" phenomenon, however, oddly generated its own pressures toward conformity. Counterculture women, despite their personal preferences, often felt compelled to conform to the earth mother image. Moreover, cosmetic, "feminine hygiene" product, and clothing manufacturers quickly picked up on that image's market potential, enjoining all women to choose the natural "look." Although Constance Trouble maintained that "nothing that good for women could have come from men," physical liberation was indeed commercialized. Women, especially within the mainstream culture, not only had to look sexy and feminine; they now had to look "naturally" beautiful.[24]

Despite their sexual experimentation, most hippie women valued and formed semipermanent, heterosexual pair bonds. Whether "open"

or monogamous, these ties were extremely fragile; couples formed, separated, and recombined with astonishing frequency. In addition to priz-
ing sexual freedom, the counterculture was philosophically committed
to creating alternative communities that were based on open, intimate,
honest, or what they termed "real" communication among members.
The nuclear family or monogamous couple, they maintained, could not
possibly fulfill every member's emotional, physical, and spiritual needs.
Tribal living, in contrast, offered richer interpersonal rewards and an
antidote to the alienation, atomization, and isolation of modern life.
Communal relationships, based on cooperation, interdependence, and
acceptance of individual difference, would usher in a new social order.
It is not surprising that this emphasis on group intimacy, coupled with
liberal attitudes toward sexuality, often precipitated conflict and tension
in pair relationships. Even the most committed couples found it difficult
to maintain relational boundaries and agree upon limits. Sexual liberal-
ism aside, communal living fostered group intimacy that undermined
the emotional primacy of the pair bond.

Some hippie men added fuel to this emotional stew by using the
rhetoric of sexual liberation and personal freedom to avoid commitment or to push for open relationships. When women demanded more
emotional and physical exclusivity, men often labeled them as "hung-
up" or "repressed." And if another relationship beckoned, or if women
became too insistent, many men simply "split." Indeed, hippie men had
the best of both worlds; they could give free rein to their "natural" desires without the reciprocal, bread-winning obligations that "straight"
society demanded. In other words, the counterculture's critique of the
sexual double standard extended only to women and middle-class moral
strictures, not to the social construction of male sexuality. Peter Coyote,
somewhat remorsefully, recalled that "my casual betrayals of the relationship were exacerbated by the libidinous attitudes of the times. . . .
I couldn't have remained faithful to Sam if she had tied me to the bed,
and my countless infidelities and her imaginative revenges produced
predictable fissures in our relationship."[25]

Women's narratives underscore the chronic instability and tenuous-
ness of hippie partnerships. Nancy Nina recalled how her husband
entered a relationship with another woman at their commune: "I felt
abandoned and cuckolded, and I just felt like a victim." The economic
consequences were also severe. "It was hard sometimes being a mom to

those kids when really nobody else was, and so nitty gritty. The buck stopped with me when diapers needed to be washed. And I was the one who was going to wash them, whereas everyone else would kind of walk away. . . . And we were poor. I remembered when I had two pennies in my pocket and five kids, and a husband that wasn't around, and it was like, 'this is hard, this is scary.'" Gwen Leeds was similarly hurt by her partner's infidelity. When she became pregnant, "the romantic notions of maternal bliss were quickly shattered by my increasing need for emotional support and Bill's reverse need to get away from feeling trapped. New misunderstandings developed between us. We began to feel the desperation of being locked in an irreversible situation." The summer after their baby, Raspberry, was born, Bill fell in love with another woman at Wheeler's Ranch and talked Gwen into a three-way sexual encounter. The next day, "my bond of love with Bill shattered with the realization that he expected me to allow a second wife for his pleasure, but did not have the remotest intention of allowing a second husband for mine. The imbalance toppled our relationship, and I began to search for a way out."[26]

Roberta Price's husband, David, after having an affair with a fellow Libre resident, tried to soften the blow by remarking, "It doesn't mean I don't love you less, you know. . . . We're capable of loving people in different ways at different times, and we shouldn't repress these feelings." Roberta recalled, "I was in a double bind. David's opinion of me would change if I acted angry, possessive, and jealous. I wanted to be the ideal he envisioned, and to act the way he thought people should act. Jung wrote that men are naturally polygamous. There were a lot of people in the Huerfano who shared David's vision. Mostly they were people who wanted to make love to someone else instead of their partner." Anna Marie Daniels was similarly conflicted. Her rakish, but at times very romantic and attentive, husband repeatedly betrayed their commitment. His excuse was two-pronged: as a man, he simply couldn't resist sexual temptation, and Anna Marie was too "uptight" and unaccommodating. Understandably confused, she tried to "lighten up" and overcome her "repressive" upbringing and to make herself more attractive. Already slender, she became anorexic in order to fit what she believed was his ideal. She eventually realized that he was manipulating gender constructs and counterculture rhetoric to his advantage and ended the relationship.[27]

Many women, although left heartbroken or economically vulnerable, expressed relief after their breakups. Many also acknowledged that their relationships were troubled before they joined the counterculture. Nancy Nina, for example, recalled a cross-country trip early in her marriage. "It was a disastrous journey in terms of my own emotional well-being, because I realized that I did not love this man, and I didn't like being with him." Settling in Southern California, and still well before they "dropped out," she remarked "my marriage is pretty much shattered by that time." When Elaine Sundancer's husband left her and their young son, she cut off her hair, took off her wedding ring, and divested herself of her possessions. "My actions were definitely my own. I didn't need to control territory; I possessed myself." She and a group of friends then purchased land and founded the Saddle Ridge Farm commune.[28]

Hearts also broke on both sides. Many women left "straight" husbands to join the counterculture or strayed from their hippie partners. Roberta Price, living with a "perpetual knot" in her stomach over her husband's infidelity, nonetheless engaged in a series of romantic affairs, including one after she insisted on a closed marriage. Despite his assertions that "we're beyond the petty bourgeois possessiveness that plagued our parents," her husband resented Roberta's divided affections and "blew up" at her on more than one occasion. Virginia Logan, although referring to her mutually agreed upon open marriage as "devastatingly horrible," took advantage of its loose structure to assert her own needs. When her husband went abroad to study Sanskrit, she met and had a "karmic" connection with another man. Within hours of meeting, "we both decided to end our marriages and be together." Jan Camp left her straight husband to join the counterculture and after one unfulfilling marriage was determined to be her "own person" and avoid similar entanglements. Over the next several years, she focused on her own creative and artistic development and left a slew of broken hearts in her path. Part of freeing herself and her children involved separating from the "father knows best nuclear family thing," and men, despite their assertions to the contrary, "had difficulty accepting female independence." Similarly, Constance Trouble recalled that "I wasn't willing to settle for anything less than an honest, emotionally and physically satisfying relationship. So, yes, I definitely took advantage of the emphasis on free love to extract myself from confining relationships. It was okay for me to say 'I need space' or 'I can't breathe in this relationship,' and then split."

Sometimes couples simply drifted apart. Angela Aidala reported in "Communes and Changing Family Norms" that one woman recalled that "our problems started before we moved in here. I was kind of in the process of going crazy, feeling like I was providing all the money. He was doing all the fun things. . . . So when we first moved in here, we shared a room, and still lived together, and having other people around kind of allowed me—took some of the pressure off the relationship." She went on to reflect, "and it expanded the parameters of the relationship, and the relationship kept opening till, I guess, the openness of the house and the relationship allowed me to be so independent that I didn't need to be in a relationship any longer."[29]

Residents of the Farm, recognizing that conflict between couples endangered communal peace and harmony, came up with a rather conservative solution. It is interesting that their remedy was based on the realization that both men and women were responsible for infidelity-related disunity. If a couple had sex, they were considered engaged. In the event of a pregnancy, they were expected to marry, and marriage was a lifelong commitment. In addition to stressing male sensitivity and attentiveness to women's physical and emotional needs, they created a female code of conduct that discouraged women from flirting with or seducing attached males. Most members of the counterculture eventually concluded that they, too, needed more stability but not to the extent of reverting to traditional norms. Compared to their straight and New Left peers, former hippies, regardless of gender, continue to be more critical of conventional marriage and the nuclear family and more open to extramarital sex, remaining single, nonmarital cohabitation, and communal living arrangements.[30]

Hippie weddings were just as unconventional as most relationships. Women, dressed in flowing, peasant finery and adorned with floral garlands and wreaths, commonly took their vows outdoors, in the "church of nature." Vows, usually composed by the couple, often drew upon Kahlil Gibran's *The Prophet*, which stressed nonpossessiveness, the individuality of each partner, and the necessity of providing "space in your togetherness." Alternately, they reflected on the themes of community or of opposites coming together and complementing each other. In contrast to conventional marriages, friends often outnumbered blood-

"Alan and Mickey in Meadow," photograph by Irwin Klein.
Copyright 2008, Estate of Irwin Klein.

"Bride and Groom," photograph by Irwin Klein.
Copyright 2008, Estate of Irwin Klein.

"Wedding Feast," photograph by Irwin Klein.
Copyright 2008, Estate of Irwin Klein.

"Wedding Guests Blessing Food," photograph by Irwin Klein.
Copyright 2008, Estate of Irwin Klein.

"Laura and Paul Foster's Wedding at the Hog Farm's Summer Solstice
Celebration, Aspen Meadows, New Mexico," 1968, photograph by Lisa Law.
Copyright 2008, Lisa Law.

relatives as attendees. This underscored the counterculture's commitment to extending intimate relationships beyond the confines of the nuclear family. A minister, often a friend with a mail order license from the Universal Life Church, might officiate, but real sanction came from the witnesses. At communes, weddings provided a break from routine chores and involved the entire tribe. In any event, the ceremony was usually followed by feasting, music, dancing, drinking, and drug use.

Marylyn Motherbear Scott's wedding brought together residents of her commune, the Yin Palace, and folks from the neighboring Whole Earth Truck Store collective. She recalled that "some of the women, Terry in particular, made me my wedding dress out of a white cotton with little lavender flowers on it. It was long and had a high waist—of course I was pregnant, very pregnant." Another friend made the wedding cakes, "seven incredible pound cakes with bright colored frosting, rainbow colors." A minister married them "according to a ceremony that we helped design and . . . said something like 'This is a marriage that has been growing on us all for some time. And it is not a marriage of a two people alone, but a marriage of a community.' It reflected our community atmosphere."

Roberta Price's marriage took place out in the woods and was attended by more than 100 friends who "tramped down the trail . . . carrying salad, bread, cakes, wine, and fruit." Hash, marijuana, and tetrahydrocannabinol (THC)–laced iced tea were also in abundant supply. Her dress was "a turn-of-the-century, intricately embroidered white lawn slip dress," complemented with "a baby's breath tiara and garland a friend wove." Another friend, with a Universal Life Church license, performed the ceremony: "We live in a time when the earth is out of balance, when this country is horribly unbalanced, when it's hard for those who see the most to stay sane. We're gathered today, standing in astrological order, to honor the wedding of David and Roberta, exact astrological opposites, who've found a balance, who complete each other, who are in love." Then the couple exchanged rings "with a row of yin-yang symbols carved into them." Maggie Gaskin's wedding took place in an urban setting but was similarly dominated by friends. Held in a San Francisco warehouse at the height of the counterculture, the ceremony included psychedelic music and a "beautiful light show." Maggie recalled in *Voices of the Love Generation* that "seventy-five of our friends that we loved were there just putting out very holy, holy vibrations on us."[31]

Relationships, whether sanctioned by marriage or by mutual agreement, permanent or temporary, often produced babies. Many hippie women viewed motherhood as the ultimate expression of the "feminine principle." Some even eschewed "artificial" contraceptives in favor of natural birth control or remaining completely open to the "life force." Communal environments often generated additional reproductive incentives or pressures. Women with children were eligible for welfare benefits and hence an important source of income for many communal ventures, a practice critiqued in the following chapter. It was more common for women simply to witness the joy and satisfaction of the mother-child bond and want the same pleasure. Jodi Mitchell, for example, recalled meeting Moonflower and her baby Shanti at Wheeler's ranch. She "secretly envied" the attention that they received and observed that "they were sitting pretty financially" because of their welfare and food stamp benefits. Roberta Price, after witnessing several births at her commune, noted "I got the same dizzy, oceanic feeling I get looking at the stars." She went on to describe it: "The more I've become rooted here, the more I've felt a pull working like gravity." At a group marriage commune in New Mexico, an observer noted more of a collective "pull" toward motherhood. According to Elia Katz in *Armed Love*, "most of the women want to have children. The ones that are pregnant look forward to bringing new children into the Family, though they might not know who the biological father is. The children are cared for by all the women in the Family." At the Farm, in rural Tennessee, the incentives were even greater. Giving birth conferred status and brought women into a sisterhood of mothers. Ina May Gaskin, the Farm's head midwife, recalled, "Well, I mean, once you become a mother, okay, and you've done it under your own power, then you get power from that . . . then you believe you can do anything." Marylyn Motherbear Scott put it in more spiritual terms: "We embody the Goddess who creates life . . . there is a moment of conception . . . a moment of union and magic of the highest order, and that is a mystery to be revealed to any one who wants to go there. You know at that moment, even in sex, that it can create life."[32] Women viewed pregnancy as a natural process and delighted in the changes to their bodies; within their essentialist gender constructs, they had become "women." Pam Tent recalled, "Throughout my teens, I'd always identified with the pubescent girl with the silver airplane on the cover of the Blind Faith album. Now my body was finally taking on the curvaceous shape I felt I lacked, and I was thrilled. It never occurred to me that pregnancy wasn't sexy because I'd never felt more like a woman." When Gwen Leeds discovered she was pregnant, "I said to myself, 'There's a tiny being living inside me right now!' I felt honored and in awe of my body. My days began to revolve around the developing child within me. I planned to give birth at home. Since there were no doctors around who encouraged home deliveries, I felt I needed to be in the best shape possible when my time came." The voluntary poverty and overcrowding of many hippie households and communes often presented problems, however. Gwen, for example, moved out of her home—the bustling communal hub at Wheeler's—to the relative peace and quiet of the garden during the latter part of her pregnancy. "Bill moved our mattress to the garden and hung a tarpaulin over it. We added a small extension to the garden, built shelves, set up a table and a wood stove and put our clothes in a wooden box. Our bed was surrounded by growing things. We ate our own vegetables and went naked all day long." For Pam Read, the problem was hunger. During her second pregnancy, milk and other sources of protein were in short supply. One day, with nothing to eat but cooked chicken feed, she "burst into tears. There was just nothing in it that my body wanted." Some friends, witnessing her distress, bought her a half gallon of milk and a dozen eggs. "I was so grateful. Later Jonie asked me how I was—'didn't I feel better.' Infinitely. 'How many of those eggs did you eat,' she wondered? All of them, I mumbled, embarrassed." In fact maternal malnutrition, often leading to prenatal and perinatal complications, was not an isolated problem. Voluntary poverty and rustic communal settings often compromised the health of women and children.[33]

Hippie women, viewing birth as a natural process and an opportunity for communal or familial bonding, preferred home birth to delivering in an institutional, medical setting. Hippie babies, as discussed in Chapter 6, were thus born surrounded by family and friends in gardens, forests, tipis, rustic cabins, domes, buses, and communal gathering places. Self-taught midwives often assisted, but many women coached themselves through the process. On communes, births—like marriages—were cause for rejoicing. As Iris Keltz noted, "Birthing was a celebration.

Taking control of our lives was important to us. Herbal remedies and midwives were rediscovered as healthy and viable alternatives to 'buying into' the medical establishment. 'Old Way, Good Way' was one of our mantras." Keltz stated that Pam Hanna (Read), a midwife who lived at Morning Star, estimated that she delivered forty-three babies there. Her own daughter, Minka, was delivered by another commune midwife "in a beautiful home birth in the mid-'70s."[34]

Women's narratives are full of descriptive home birth stories, pointing to the individual and collective significance of bringing a new member into the "tribe." Gina Stillman and Gwen Leeds were part of a baby boom at Wheeler's Ranch. Gina was assisted by a Reichian masseur, her partner Ramon, and close friends Lou, Near, and their son, Vishnu; Bill, Gwen, and their daughter, Raspberry; and Gina's brother. As Ramon observed, "Having a baby seemed to turn Gina into a Gypsy dancer. It was a slow labor, but she kept on top of it by 'oming' during each contraction." After Sol Ray's birth, "the whole community rejoiced with us. Everyone showered us with love and many kindnesses, bringing us cooked meals and many presents for the baby." Gwen's birth had also gone smoothly. As she recalled, "Everybody was crying and screaming, and Bill was saying it was the most beautiful thing he had ever seen. He placed her on my stomach, and I turned to gaze in her eyes as she turned to gaze into mine. She was looking to see what mother she had gotten as I was looking to see what child I'd been given."[35]

At a New Mexico commune, Rose Gorden recalled her birth experience, as reported by Iris Keltz. "Paul delivered Nova, our daughter in the shelter—our resident midwife watched over him. A doctor who was visiting checked me out and gave my baby her first shots. . . . Some weeks after the birth, I went to Safeway and weighed her in one of their produce scales, somewhere between the lettuce and zucchini." Pam Hanna (Read), who later assisted many births, had her second child in a campsite with only her husband in attendance. "Psyche Joy Ananda was born under a starry sky. We think it was after midnight on June 28 (we were clockless). She had bright coppery red hair and hazel eyes, and she nursed immediately. She was sweet and lovely from the very first. Larry made her a beautiful redwood burl cradle and for awhile all was well." Ruby Tuesday, in contrast, had her baby, LSD guru Ralph Metzner's son, in a loft in New York City. Tuesday, a young performance artist who had lived at Millbrook the previous year creating psychedelically enhanced art, recalled "I think it was probably . . . the first or one of the first births ever done on LSD." Nancy, a member of the Hog Farm commune, had her baby, Blue, on the road, in a bus, with fifty members in attendance. Wavy Gravy recalled, "A doctor friend of ours agreed to assist by telephone from Los Angeles and we had a fast car on hand just in case. . . . Gradually we began to blend our breaths with Nancy's. All together now. Uunnggg! Slowly the head began to emerge. Uunnggg!!! Little by little. The children were fascinated. Nancy's four-year-old boy David was right at wombside asking questions."[36]

While most births went smoothly, there were, as suggested earlier in this chapter, tragedies and near misses. Some women, as a consequence, dedicated themselves to perfecting the home birth process. Pam Hanna (Read) moved from California to New Mexico in 1968, shortly after giving birth to her daughter, Psyche. Once there, at the Morning Star East commune, "word had gotten out that I'd had both my babies outside a hospital, so maybe I knew something about it." A young girl in labor came to her camp asking for help. "Her water had broken and she was only eight months along. I didn't have any lobelia (which can stop labor), so there was nothing I could do except keep her quiet and elevate her legs. She started bleeding toward sundown and was bundled up and taken to the hospital in Espanola where she delivered two dead female babies (named Una and Ulna) that night." Iris Keltz noted that Pam, Tish Demming, and other New Mexico hippie midwives began using doctors "to be an emergency backup if the pregnancy and birthing warranted it." She also observed that "now there is an official birthing center in Taos that can trace its roots to those days." Nancy Nina gave birth at her commune in the middle of winter to a premature, breech baby. She and her child survived, but they had to go to the local hospital, where the staff treated her like a "dirty hippie." This negative experience prompted her to go to nursing school and into a career as a neonatal nurse. Ina May Gaskin similarly gave birth to a premature baby while she and her fellow communards were on the road looking for land on which to settle. The baby died, and Ina May went on to become a trained midwife and establish a state-of-the-art clinic at the Farm. She and other Farm women, although promoting an essentialist, pronatalist ideology, helped inspire and inform the contemporary natural/home birth movement.[37]

Hippie "womanhood," while essentialist and heteronormative, broke with middle-class convention in several crucial respects. It was enacted outside the isolated confines of the suburban nuclear family and within a broader ideological framework that placed a positive valuation on "feminine" attributes. It also, as the next chapter explains, unfolded in settings that enhanced the visibility, value, and creative potential of women's labor. Most important, women attached political significance to their work, viewing it as an integral part of their effort to transform self and society. Their seemingly traditional roles thus departed sharply from those of their middle-class, suburban mothers. Even the process of giving birth and assuming the mantle of motherhood were charged with new meaning, new possibilities. Children, however, also brought new responsibilities. All hippie women had to make a living, but those with children had fewer choices and less flexibility, especially since male partners were often unreliable breadwinners. Indeed, many hippie men willingly fathered children but "split" as soon as their freedom was compromised. Thus, many counterculture women, as discussed in the following chapter, filled both domestic and provider roles.

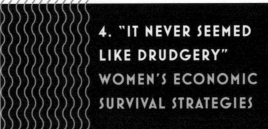

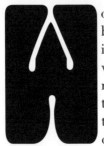

omen of the counterculture, like their male peers, believed that the technology and consumer-driven industrial capitalist economy had despoiled the environment; severed the connection between man and nature; contributed to the centralization of power and the proliferation of impersonal, bureaucratic institutions; and, most important, reduced workers to mere cogs in the machinery of production. Their parents, they maintained, had sacrificed creativity, autonomy, passion, and the very capacity for self-realization for a false sense of security and virtue. As Peter Coyote put it, the counterculture wanted to create "a society liberated from the carnivorous aspects of capitalism, a culture offering more enlightened possibilities for its members than the roles of employee or victim."

Even worse, in the counterculture's estimation, the older generation had submitted to mind-numbing labor in order to obtain status or transitory fulfillment from consumption. Truth, beauty, love, meaning, and transcendence, they maintained, are found not in things but in communion with self, nature, and the human family. Indeed, "mindless" consumption not only obscured the truly meaningful; it fostered greed, competition, war, and environmental degradation.[1]

Women, however, had additional, gender-related incentives to "drop out" of the "system." If they took "straight" jobs, they could expect far fewer rewards than their male peers. Indeed, while many of their middle-class mothers had entered the paid labor force, it was more to boost family spending power than for status or personal fulfillment. Low pay and lack of challenge, as Wini Breines and Stephanie Coontz observed, encouraged most postwar working women—regardless of class—to define themselves as wives and mothers. Home and family, at least in their present forms, however, were even less appealing to young hippie women. Without any role models or clearly mapped alternatives, counterculture women thus adopted a series of strategies to minimize their participation in the "straight" labor force and reconfigure domesticity: voluntary simplicity, scavenging, crafts production and other small business ventures, temporary straight jobs, theft, welfare and other government entitlements, communal living arrangements, and rural self-sufficiency. In many cases women employed several strategies simultaneously or moved from one to the other as their needs or circumstances changed.[2]

What remained constant, however, was the counterculture's division of labor. Regardless of their living situations or level of participation in the paid labor force, hippie women took primary responsibility for domestic tasks such as cooking, cleaning, laundry, gardening, and child care. Those who opted for voluntary simplicity or rural self-sufficiency devoted even more time to domestic tasks. Without electricity, prepackaged and processed foods, washing machines, running water, vacuum cleaners, and a host of other laborsaving amenities, routine chores easily filled each day. While hippie men often devalued and took advantage of women's domestic labor, there was no denying its importance in maintaining counterculture households and communities. Moreover, it was usually performed in the company of other women and demanded a level of skill, creativity, and adaptability that was alien to suburban domestic environments. Thus, many women found great satisfaction—and eventually power—in their seemingly traditional roles.

Another constant was men's insistence that they needed to escape the breadwinner responsibilities or "hassles" of their fathers. If women placed too many demands on them, compromising their freedom and autonomy, many men "split" for greener pastures. Although the middle-class contract that governed their parents' relationships (that men bring home the bacon and women cook and serve it) was challenged by a rising divorce rate and increasing female labor force participation, it was still the legal and culturally sanctioned standard. Many counterculture men, however, equated the ideal of mutual, reciprocal obligation as a hindrance to pure, uncorrupted, on-the-road freedom. As a consequence, many hippie women, particularly those with children to support, were forced to take "shit jobs" out of economic necessity. Unlike relatively unencumbered men, they could not afford to be as selective.[3]

Voluntary simplicity, or intentionally reducing consumption, was almost universally adopted by women across all segments of the counterculture. Helen McKenna, addressing an urban hippie audience, cautioned, "There are withdrawal pains involved when a habit gets kicked. Middle class affluence is a habit with many comforting goodies to give up." She then outlined a series of steps toward a less costly, more ecologically sound lifestyle: buy used clothing or sew your own clothes; keep your old car in good repair or, better yet, walk, bike, or hitchhike; eat at home, not in restaurants; avoid purchasing goods that you don't need; and most important, "reassess your job."

Women who moved back to the land were even more determined to scale back. As recounted by Mary Siler Anderson in *Whatever Happened to the Hippies*, Nonie Gienger recalled that "we were living very consciously, trying to make everything count. . . . I never got anything for myself. Literally, I didn't buy a thing. We would patch together clothing, very beautiful patchwork clothing out of things we got out of the free-box. Or my family would send us cloth and I would sew things by hand." While clearly sacrificing comfort and convenience, most women expressed satisfaction with their choices. Helen regarded her plan as a recipe for "Revolution." Nonie observed, "We weren't living a life of abundance. We were living like people in Third World or Asian nations. But I liked it. It made me feel very strong, very resourceful and rugged."

Judson Jerome provided examples of others who felt liberated. One woman realized that her "old life" was so cluttered and busy that she never had the chance to enjoy and savor anything. "It was like a meal where there's so much food, and you suddenly realize that you haven't really chewed and tasted and enjoyed a single bite." Another commented, "We just don't want to be trapped by a system that makes you try to meet a standard of living that's too high; makes you eat food that's too rich; live in a house that's overheated in the winter and air-conditioned in the summer. I like to wear sweaters—this house stays around sixty with the cook-stove going. In the summer, it gets up to one hundred, but then you just take your clothes off. It doesn't cost anything."[4]

Hippie women and the counterculture more generally believed that the United States, although prosperous enough to afford citizens the freedom to pursue truth, beauty, love, and knowledge, opted instead for an "economic model of unlimited growth" that channeled human creativity, talent, and energy into generating an ever expanding array of products—products that consumers neither needed nor truly wanted. Scavenging thus became a noble pursuit, a way to obtain life's necessities without submitting to the system of wasteful production and mindless consumption. It also meshed with the counterculture's environmental ethic that called for reducing the waste products of human activity.[5]

Women scavenged in dumpsters for food and in streets, alleys, abandoned buildings, and even dump sites for construction materials, furniture, clothing, tools, and useful household items. Constance Trouble recalled finding most of her clothes outside thrift stores. "At night, after closing time, people who wanted to dump their stuff would just leave it in the back of Goodwill or Salvation Army stores." Her commune, located near a college campus, "practically furnished the whole house with stuff that students had left out on the street when they vacated their housing at the end of the school year." She and other hippies viewed their recycling efforts as a mode of resistance, a political act that rewarded them, in Trouble's words, "with a sense of moral virtue."

Digger women were the ultimate scavengers, feeding their own communes and stocking their free food distribution projects with dumpster and produce market discards. Peter Coyote recalled how "Nina Blasenheim, Judy Goldhaft, Phyllis Wilner, Myeba, Siena Riffia, Rosalee, and Vicky Pollack, attended by a rotating 'staff' of allies, perfected the art and sustained the effort necessary to glean surpluses from the various grocers at the Farmers' Market." Apparently, the mostly Italian men who ran the markets were more tolerant of women scavengers than of men. Another commune that ran a free food program also relied on women to secure the goods. According to John MacDonald, "some knew well enough how to glean from the grocers, and their good manners and attitudes resulted in sympathetic cooperation. Once the local grocers had identified them as worthy people, they were permitted access to the throw away produce and other perishable items."[6]

Despite their efforts to scale back and live off the waste of society, most women needed a source of income. Seeking to avoid participation in the capitalist system, some started or joined worker-owned enterprises and consumer cooperatives. Others, looking more favorably upon entrepreneurial activity that was small in scale, creative, highly personal, not excessively profit driven, and environmentally friendly, started their own businesses. Most hippies, in fact, were not anticapitalist. They simply objected to its more "carnivorous aspects." At some point, however, most women were forced to settle—at least temporarily—for "shit" jobs in a pre–affirmative action–comparable worth labor market. There, they struggled mightily to find work that was compatible with their values.

In both worker- or consumer-run and entrepreneurial ventures, women often focused on food preparation and procurement, an area of expertise that grew out of the counterculture's traditional division of labor. Beginning in their households, hippie women experimented with new diets and foods that they considered to be healthy, natural, environmentally sustainable, and conducive to spiritual growth. Laura and Barb, members of a Seattle commune, wrote: "We eat only natural foods. You really feel high when your body is free from the poisons found in meat and processed foods from the grocery stores. We make our own whole grain breads and yogurt, and we sprout seeds for their nutritional value." Elaine, from a Midwest commune, offered a similar perspective in *Celery Wine:*

> We want to eat food that has the things our bodies need to grow, food that doesn't have poisons in it. We want to eat natural food that hasn't had all the goodness processed out of it, food in its proper season. And we like to eat food that's been grown and picked and cooked with love, by people who enjoyed what they were doing, food with good vibes in it. We want to stand in good relation to the soil—to feed it well, so we will be fed by it.

Indeed, as early as 1967, women attached political significance to their food-related work, viewing it as a critical element of cultural transformation. Else Gidlow, who wrote a food and gardening column for the *San Francisco Oracle*, asked, "Who feels called to the war against processed nonfood for processed nonpeople, and to the creative work of production for health and sanity without which there is no dance or song, music or joy? I do!"[7]

It wasn't long before their enthusiasm and skill translated into business ventures. In *Storefront Revolution*, Craig Cox recounts how Debbie, Susan, and Jeannie Shroyer learned, through communal living, "that they could feed themselves nicely by growing some of their own food and buying in bulk quantities grains, beans, honey, molasses, dried fruits, and nuts." When they moved back to the city, they decided to open a food co-op "to sell the kinds of food they'd eaten at the commune." North Country, the first food co-op established in the Twin

Cities, launched a local food revolution that grew to include several co-operatively run natural food stores. Across the country, other women followed their lead, helping to establish tens of thousands of co-ops or food conspiracies that were egalitarian in structure and committed to worker participation. As interest in whole foods grew, mostly male, for-profit entrepreneurs stepped in to claim a share of the market. They, in contrast to egalitarian-minded hippie women, had the business expertise and connections to secure investment capital and loans. Only nominally loyal to counterculture values, they successfully marketed hippie tastes and preferences to a wider base of consumers.[8]

Women, however, continued to influence U.S. diets through other avenues. Some, for example, branched out into prepared foods and restaurant businesses. Mara Devine joined a commune that ran a soy burger business, and when that experiment failed, launched her own company. Making soy burgers, she commented, is "right livelihood. It's important to me. I think about how—when you look at all the people in the world and how many of them actually make a living doing what they like to do—how many are there?" Alice Waters, who started the "California cuisine" food revolution when she opened Chez Panisse in 1971, definitely fit in Mara's select camp of satisfied entrepreneurs. Financed in part by her psychedelic and pot-dealing friends, Alice's vision of serving fresh, seasonal, faultlessly prepared, and wholesome food in casual, elegant, warm surroundings added an element of refinement to the counterculture's palate. Alice Brock, owner of Alice's Restaurant, not only fed her hippie patrons but also provided a community gathering place for western Massachusetts' counterculture. Similarly, Moosewood Restaurant in Ithaca, New York, established as a collective in 1972 by Molly Kazen and twenty of her friends, offered wholesome food in a convivial, hip-friendly environment.[9]

Women also contributed to food columns in the underground press and published dozens of cookbooks. Most authors combined recipes with commentary on the health, humanitarian, and environmental benefits of vegetarianism and eating fresh, locally grown produce. Some even framed women's domestic labor as inherently creative and political. In the underground press, food columns were one of the few venues open to women writers. For example, Jeanie Darlington's "Food and Fun" in Washington, D.C.'s *Quicksilver Times* and Ita Jones's syndicated "Grub Bag" enjoyed long runs and a loyal readership. Ita Jones, in fact, produced one of the first counterculture cookbooks, *The Grub Bag: An Underground Cookbook*, published by Random House in 1971. It was followed in 1972 by Lucy Horton's *Country Commune Cooking*, Anna Thomas's *The Vegetarian Epicure*, and Crescent Dragonwagon's *The Commune Cookbook*. Kathleen Taylor not only cooked lavish vegetarian meals for various communal households; she hosted a PBS television program, "Cooking Naturally," and wrote *Nutrition Survival Kit: A Natural Foods Recipe and Reference Guide*. The first chapter, "Politics in the Pantry," alerted consumers to the environmental and health consequences of depending on the "profit oriented food industry." In 1977 Molly Kazen compiled the *Moosewood Cookbook*, which, according to the *New York Times*, became one of the top-selling cookbooks in history. Its phenomenal popularity indicated that counterculture food preferences had gone mainstream.[10]

It was *Laurel's Kitchen*, however, that best captured hippie women's relationship to food. Echoing Frances Moore Lappe's *Diet For a Small Planet*, which was issued in 1971, *Laurel's Kitchen* outlined the ecological and humanitarian implications of a meat-based diet. Home-cooked vegetarian meals, the authors proposed, were not only more healthful; they could help stave off global famine and environmental collapse. Women, as "keepers of the keys," givers of the "gift of life," possessors of the "nurturant impulse," and those who had "the eye for the good of all," were in a position to influence the fate of the planet by turning their hands to the "very real problems that are crying out for creative attention and hard work to solve. By forgoing the temptation to feather your own nest, you free yourself to tackle them. No paycheck comes at the end of the month, and no promotion: the incentive here is much less obvious, and much more worthy of you as a human being." The authors also took on critiques of the counterculture's division of labor: "We can talk back firmly to those who would belittle the significance of our work; better yet, we can demonstrate by quiet personal example that no other job or career involvement can be quite so effective in bringing about the world we all want to see." Like the *Moosewood Cookbook*, *Laurel's Kitchen* enjoyed widespread popularity (eleven editions in five years) and helped bring natural foods and vegetarianism out of the counterculture and into the mainstream.[11]

Aside from food-related businesses and publishing, women engaged in a wide variety of entrepreneurial activity. Craft production, as one anthropologist noted, "is the most honored economic enterprise among hippies," embodying "the notion of one actively engaged in the full process of production; someone free from arbitrary structuring of his activity; someone in harmony with his environment and his material." Women usually produced crafts in their homes and sold them at "head" shops, flea markets, craft fairs, arts cooperatives, and along tourist and hippie thoroughfares such as Berkeley's Telegraph Avenue. Some even lived nomadically, producing goods on the road and traveling from one craft fair to another.[12]

Bead work, although labor intensive, had low overhead costs and was thus an attractive option for many women. Mary and five friends who lived together in a San Francisco commune formed the Great Ooga Booga Bead Company and sold their wares along Telegraph Avenue. Later they moved to rural Humboldt County, "figuring we could carry on our bead business at craft fairs." In a similar fashion, Vivian Gotters lived in an old Victorian in the Haight with a group of art students and made her share of the rent money by crafting and selling beaded neck-laces to a local psychedelic shop.[13]

Other women worked in fiber, wood, and wax. Lelain Lorenzen joined women at the Garden of Joy commune in launching a cottage industry devoted to making and selling quilts. Sherri Cavan provides examples of women elsewhere who knitted, crocheted, and produced macramé. A vendor at a San Francisco street market produced crocheted wool caps and macramé belts right in front of her customers. Others turned out goods for hip merchants. About fifty women, for example, worked on consignment for a single San Francisco head shop, doing "sewing, knitting, crocheting, and candle making." Still others worked in wood. Karen Lee Robins, who moved back to the land after traveling out west in search of community and enlightenment, "joined the craft fair scene," selling her sculpted furniture and cooking utensils. Cavan also mentions a Berkeley woman who similarly made walnut tables that she sold on consignment to hippie merchants.[14]

At times, the life of an artisan could be difficult. Melissa Hill lived in a truck with her partner and eked out a precarious living making candles and selling them at craft fairs. When sales were poor, she augmented her income by "selling blood and hawking flowers." According to Cavan, the maker of walnut tables was ripped off by the vendors who agreed to sell her wares. When she returned to collect her share of the sales, they claimed to have no knowledge of her tables. "I could get no satisfaction from them. [Male] friends told me it was because I was a woman artisan and didn't have the right means to intimidate them." Still, craft production had its rewards: autonomy, creativity, flexibility, and the pleasure of creating objects of beauty. Rain Jacopetti, a fiber artist, documented the stunningly gorgeous and diverse products of hippie artisans in her 1971 publication, *Native Funk and Flash: An Emerging Folk Art.*[15]

A smaller group of women managed to amass the capital to start their own businesses. Susan Lydon, in *A Few Folksy Fashions*, describes the work of Jeanne Colon, who made colorful, richly decorated clothing in ethnic and peasant styles for San Francisco's rock luminaries. Her underlying philosophy was to "free the mind" by "free[ing] the body. . . . Clothing is like breathing; it should be a natural, easy thing to have happen." Later she became a successful herbalist, publishing a series of books on herbal body care and healing. Trina Robbins, one of the few women comic artists who contributed to the underground press, supplemented her income by making clothing and running a boutique on Manhattan's lower east side; she had to because male cartoonists and editorial staff did not take her work seriously. Similarly, Peggy Caserta, Janis Joplin's lover and clothier, owned one of San Francisco's first hip boutiques. Ami Magill also traded in counterculture fashion. Shortly after moving to the Haight Ashbury in 1965, she opened Headquarters.

> My sister did this extraordinary facade of all these beautiful monkeys chasing their tails. We found this old costume shop going out of business and bought hundreds and hundreds of these vintage beaded jackets for a dollar apiece and sold them for three, which showed you what level of retail brilliance we were on. At one point, the entire Haight was running around in those jackets! When Paul McCartney came through, that's what he saw, so that's were Sgt. Pepper came from.

The occult and healing arts, which women quickly cornered with their "natural" intuitive abilities, provided another lucrative small business option. Women, setting up shop as psychics, tarot card readers, astrologers, massage therapists, and herbalists, paved the way for a much larger group of female New Age entrepreneurs in the 1980s and 1990s. Flower vending was another popular venture, possibly because of the low overhead. Kathleen Taylor, for example, opened Berkeley's first flower stand on Vine Street. Organizers of the People's Park Memorial Day march used her wholesale license to purchase flowers that participants later stuffed into the gun barrels of national guard troops stationed around the park perimeter.[16]

Finally, female entrepreneurship sometimes extended to marijuana cultivation and small-scale drug dealing. Constance Trouble recalled that "many, many women friends—starting back in high school—sold acid, mescaline, speed and dope. But they mainly got the stuff from boyfriends who dealt with the bigger suppliers. Still, you could make a lot of money quickly if you were willing to take the risk." Cultivation was potentially even more lucrative. Carolyn Adams, who moved her family to the more rural, child-friendly environment of Marin County, played a pioneer role in developing more potent strains of marijuana. After people began stealing her plants, she wrote *Primo Plant,* a guide to home pot cultivation. "A lot of people who became serious growers started with my book—that's what I meant it to be. By that time, I had a whole circle of friends who were doing it, and I'd go observe the plants in their gardens, this whole group of women growers who started up in Mendocino."

Mary, who moved up to Humboldt County, remembered that "we'd been growing it [marijuana] to smoke almost from the very first. Smoking marijuana was as common to our lifestyle as love beads and brown rice, only more important." She went on to describe how this soon led to cultivation for sale: "The lure of being able to finish your house or replace your broken-down vehicle with one that ran was just too great." Moreover, "you could use part of the money to buy beautiful homemade things and so support local artisans." Marijuana money also financed local schools, volunteer fire brigades, environmental organizations, clinics, and food co-ops, but it eventually led to violence, soaring land values, and a massive law enforcement crackdown in the 1980s.[17]

Women who failed to find an entrepreneurial or cooperative niche often had to settle for "straight" or "shit" jobs. Their relative youth and inexperience, combined with a gender-stratified labor market, limited their options to child care, waitressing, modeling, go-go dancing, retail sales, clerical jobs, and various adult entertainment options such as strippers, escorts, and massage "therapists." Women viewed these jobs as temporary, using them to make rent or travel money or to tide them over until a better opportunity came their way. Constance Trouble, for example, took a series of minimum wage jobs until she found a commune that provided support through various cottage industries. "At one point the only job I could find was in a massage parlor. Initially I thought 'cool, I get to make money healing tired, broken bodies.' But I soon discovered that it was essentially a front for prostitution. I quit as soon as I found a retail job, and it was almost as demeaning. But at least it paid the rent."[18]

In order to supplement their incomes or avoid "shit" jobs, many women resorted to alternatives that the mainstream regarded as truly deviant. Some stole or "liberated" goods from private businesses. Theft, according to the counterculture's code of ethics, was justified if you were in need and if you stole from large, impersonal, profit-driven establishments that "ripped off" their workers and charged inflated prices for their goods. Crescent Dragonwagon, for example, commented that "I never rip off things around the corner and I won't at any country store where people treat you like a human being."

A similar rationale applied to government assistance. The state, like private corporations, was viewed as an agent of repression, aggression, greed, and corruption. In contrast, the counterculture was constructing a new, humane social order that deserved support. Roberta Price's husband, for example, told her to think of food stamps "as a kind of NEA grant to fund this experiment in living." He added, "it's a small investment for the government. And it's worth it to them to get the trouble makers out of the cities and subsidize us on communes/reservations in the middle of nowhere."[19]

Despite their elaborate rationale for accepting public assistance, hippies were, in very real terms, depending on the system that they deplored. Quite understandably, hard-working adults viewed them as irresponsible freeloaders who used tax dollars to subsidize hedonistic, antiestablishment lifestyles. It was like biting the hand that fed you. Bill Wheeler, the hippie founder of a northern California commune, candidly explained local resistance to his experiment. From his straight neighbors' perspective, "the hippies are living on welfare, living off the fat of the land. Why are they having such a good time while us people have to slave in factories eighteen hours a day?" Indeed, counterculture dependence on government entitlements fueled much of the mainstream's antagonism toward hippies and contributed to a growing backlash against federal antipoverty programs—a backlash that ulti-mately injured the truly needy.[20]

While many households and communes, like the Farm, opted for self-sufficiency and independence from the "establishment," most, at some point, relied on government entitlements such as food stamps, food com-modities, and welfare benefits. Indeed, hundreds of hippie households and rural and urban communes wouldn't have survived without such benefits. For example, Terry Klein, who moved among various commu-nal households, recalled that "we used to get food stamps. That's how we got by, pretty much. I don't remember ever working. I don't remem-ber ever having money. And I don't remember ever worrying about it either." According to Mary Siler Anderson, Sue Perkins's welfare ben-efits not only financed her move back to the land; they allowed her to purchase property: "I had to pay $72 a month out of my welfare check for the land. Most people were on welfare. I got food stamps, but there were so many children staying at my house all the time that we used to go down to Mendocino and get commodities too." Jodi Mitchell, a young runaway who ended up at the Wheeler's Ranch commune, recalled the generosity of Moonflower and her baby, Shanti. "I secretly envied Moon-flower's Earth Mother status and all of the attention it seemed to attract towards her on the land. It also attracted food stamps and welfare their way, so compared to most they were sitting pretty financially. They were extremely generous toward me and shared everything."[21]

An interesting result was that welfare payments led to women's in-creasing assertions of power within counterculture families and com-munities. Bennett Berger states in *The Survival of a Counterculture* that many, already contributing a disproportionate share of labor, by the early 1970s realized that "men provided neither regular income nor sta-tus nor security nor reliable emotional support." Firmly in control of their welfare checks, a growing number of women made bids for indepen-dence. In some cases they expelled their former partners or "brothers," concluding "that they didn't even need men for sex." In other cases, they used their economic clout to demand a more egalitarian division of labor or greater respect for their "feminine" contributions. In this latter case, some men complied with the new demands while others "split," leading to male depopulation of many communal households.[22]

Communal living was both an economic survival strategy and a countercultural ideal. It reduced expenses, allowing hippies to focus on the "real" work of creative, sensual, and spiritual regeneration. It was also a rebellion against the "atomistic tendencies of modern society, a full-scale attack on the received notions of how people relate to one another, and an attempt to recover 'the world we have lost.'" The alternative to urban and suburban isolation and loneliness, they maintained, was a new tribalism—communities of like-minded individuals whose social interactions were governed by reciprocity, interdependence, cooperation, generosity, and trust.[23]

From the mid-1960s to the mid-1970s thousands of hip communes took root across the United States. Their physical location, size, spiritual or philosophical orientation, and membership requirements varied. Some were urban, some rural. Some housed hundreds of communards, others only a few. Some were organized around shared religious or philosophical values or a particular leader, and others were open to individuals of all persuasions and had no formal structure or hierarchy. Some required members to contribute all of their assets and income to a shared resource pool, while others operated on voluntary contributions or by dividing living expenses among members. Despite these differences, most hippie communes—at least until the mid-1970s—shared common features: women took primary responsibility for cooking, cleaning, child care, laundry, tending the ill, comforting the distraught, and soothing bruised egos. Moreover, in many cases women contributed more than their fair share of economic resources in the form of welfare checks, food stamps, and income from outside jobs and crafts production.[24]

Commune men often grasped the significance of women's contributions but had difficulty expressing their appreciation. Bob Carey, a member of the Family of Mystic Arts, commented that "it's really unbelievable what those chicks have learned to do over a fire that's nothing more than a hole in the ground. . . . If the chicks don't have any energy and don't want to do anything, like be chicks, you know, wash dishes, cook, then you're in trouble because there's nothing worse than not getting your food, having all the dishes stacked up." Similarly, Peter Coyote acknowledged that women performed most of the day-to-day chores that sustained Digger communes and free food programs but confessed that "all of our 'appreciation' of the women and their work did not extend to valuing that work as dearly as our own." As already mentioned, Coyote later realized that such a division of labor was archaic.[25]

Outside observers noted that women performed a disproportionate share of communal labor and often characterized women's work as oppressive, exploitative drudgery. Richard Atcheson, for example, visited a New Mexico commune and observed, "It's Mary Louise and the other women who do all of the work, look after all the practical matters, keep things together." He also noted, "If anybody on that particular mesa had penetrated to the duality of sexual identity . . . we had seen no sign of it. We had seen, on the contrary, a perfect hip mirror to middle class life, an unconscious parody of the traditional sex roles as played out every day and night in all the suburbs of America." Feminist observers were even more critical. Vivian Estellachild, visiting a hip commune, noted that the men did "odd jobs," sat around, or "played All-American on an $8000 caterpillar and wrecked all the cars" while the women were caring for children, contributing their welfare checks, "baking bread, making supper, and doing an endless pile of dishes left from the interminable snacks." During a visit to another commune, she observed "at least half of the women were unhappy" — a state she attributed to their limited roles.[26]

Most commune women, however, viewed their work in different terms, infusing it with value, richness, and complexity lost on most hippie men and outside observers. Moreover, the rigors of communal living, especially in rural areas, often precluded a strict division of labor. Women — particularly those who were single — had to master a wide range of survival skills. In their own eyes they were pioneers pushing beyond the confines of nuclear families, creating and sustaining meaningful relationships, acquiring new skills, and testing their physical and creative limits. Although many eventually insisted on a more egalitarian division or labor, few characterized their work as drudgery. Joyce Robinson, a founding member of the New Buffalo commune in New Mexico, spoke for the majority: "I didn't know I could work so hard. I enjoyed those traditional roles more than I thought I would, but there was also the freedom not to cook everyday." To her this was the foundation for a feeling of sisterhood.[27]

Open land communes, including Gorda, Tolstoy Farm, Drop City, Morning Star Ranch, and Wheeler's Ranch, afforded the best opportunity

"Sandy in Her Kitchen," photograph by Irwin Klein.
Copyright 2008, Estate of Irwin Klein.

"*Woman Picking Fruit, El Rito,*" *photograph by Irwin Klein.*
Copyright 2008, Estate of Irwin Klein.

"The Weaver," photograph by Irwin Klein.
Copyright 2008, Estate of Irwin Klein.

"Woman Chopping Wood," photograph by Irwin Klein.
Copyright 2008, Estate of Irwin Klein.

"Hog Farm Members in Free Kitchen, Woodstock," 1968,
photograph by Lisa Law. Copyright 2008, Lisa Law.

"Portrait of L. P.'s Sweetheart," photograph by Irwin Klein.
Copyright 2008, Estate of Irwin Klein.

for women to test their capacity for self-reliance. There were no rules, no membership requirements; everybody was welcome, and residents contributed as much or as little as they wished. It was pure, unadulterated, "do-your-own-thing" anarchy. Arriving alone or with partners and friends, women faced the immediate challenge of securing shelter and food. They pitched tents, erected structures from scavenged materials, hauled water, cooked over open fires, gathered wild foods, planted gardens, tended livestock, bathed in creeks and ponds, made their own clothes, bartered and shared with other residents, and otherwise made do under very primitive conditions.

In 1967 a young pregnant woman moved to Wheeler's Ranch and made a shelter in the garden under a tarp. She spent the entire summer gardening and canning her own organic baby food and then gave birth while consulting the Chicago *Policeman's Handbook*. Over the next three years she helped other women give birth, hauled water and firewood for cooking and washing diapers, and learned about healing with herbs, yoga, and massage. She wasn't alone in her desire for self-sufficiency. Trudy, an eighteen-year-old from a wealthy Chicago family that made its fortune from barbed wire, arrived at Wheeler's in 1969. She then proceeded to build her own house. Gwen Leeds, a fellow resident, "often saw her carrying lumber. Another day I saw her on the community run to get a few things she needed to finish her house." Later, when Gwen went to see the finished product, she "found a solid platform with canvas sides, many windows, a bed loft and a canvas roof. There was a small pile of chopped wood under the cast iron stove. Although sparsely furnished, the house was immaculate and Trudy was beaming."[28]

Alicia Bay Laurel, another Wheeler's communard, inspired thousands of young women to test and refine their survival skills. Only a year older than Trudy, she took over the garden, constructed her own shelter, and generated income by selling her crafts. According to Bill Wheeler, she earned the distinction of being "the only person on the Ridge who was neither 'without income' nor on welfare." As her fellow residents soon discovered, she was also working on a book: a self-illustrated guide that "demonstrated with childlike fluidity how to build a shelter, shit in the ground, chop wood, have a baby, etc." *Living on the Earth* was published in 1970 by a small independent press in Berkeley. The first edition of 10,000 copies sold out in two weeks, prompting Random House to purchase the rights. The next edition, published by Random House in

1971, sold more than 350,000 copies and made the *New York Times* best-seller list. Pioneering, like natural foods, was apparently catching on with the mainstream.

Adhering to the open-door ethic of sharing, Alicia used her royalties to treat Wheeler's folk to a series of celebrations over a period of several months. The marathon fetes culminated with an Easter extravaganza where "Alicia arrived dressed as a bright pink Easter egg and her friend Sunny in a baby blue bunny costume. Gifts were distributed of home-made marzipan Easter eggs seasoned with Clear Light acid. Hundreds of dyed chicken eggs had been hidden in the bushes and grass. Baskets in hand, the children spread out to find them." The hunt was followed by yet another elaborate feast. At Wheeler's and elsewhere it wasn't all work and no play.[29]

Most women, neither open-door barbed wire heiresses nor successful authors, still found communal work much more varied and interesting than critics implied, even in more structured environments. Elaine Sun-dancer, who cofounded Saddle Ridge Farm with several friends, recalled sharing child care with another woman. "We would informally divide the work: 'Okay, I'll take them in the morning and you in the afternoon.'" This left time for her to read, write, and learn new skills like cooking for large numbers of people on a wood stove, experimenting with new recipes and ingredients, canning, brewing, gardening, composting, and animal husbandry. Lelain Lorenzen similarly relished the opportunity to "learn to do things by scratch." A year after graduating from high school she joined the Garden of Joy Blues commune and learned how to grow her own food, milk goats, raise rabbits, dye wool, make quilts, and bale hay. She especially enjoyed "gathering wild foods. Sometimes we would go gather a lot of walnuts, and we would gather sorrel, you know sheep sorrel, kind of sour. We'd make a soup out of that."[30]

Other women preferred to specialize. Noelle Barton, for example, was head cook at the Olompali Ranch commune in northern California. There she routinely cooked for between sixty and eighty people and took pride in preparing healthy meals. "I threw out people's cigarettes. I threw out people's coffee. I threw out people's white sugar. I threw out their white bread. I threw out their meat. I tried to make them eat health foods." She went on to note, "Some people are more organic now than I am because of me." Pamela Hunt and several other women who joined the Farm specialized in midwifery. She started delivering babies on the commune's cross-country bus caravan in search of land and continued after they settled in rural Tennessee. Midwives, she recalled, were respected and supported by other commune members. "I had women that were helping me with my kids and with the housework and with the laundry so that I could go and deliver babies." She also recalled that midwives "were the first ones with the phones on the Farm. We were the first ones with transportation and people were real good to us." Pamela also practiced allopathic medicine. Indeed, healing was widely regarded by the counterculture as women's work. Ann MacNaughton, from Libre, recalled how women possessed "female knowledge," including "herbal information, dietary information, childcare, child birth, physical information like that . . . we had to figure it out, how to solve it when someone had pneumonia."[31]

Most women—even those who later became critical of the counterculture's division of labor and men's devaluation of their work—reflected fondly on their experiences. Roberta Price, who lived at Libre, recalled, "I can mix cement, blow dynamite, bank a fire, use a chain saw, split wood, milk goats, make yogurt and parmesan cheese, bake donuts, ride bareback, hunt mushrooms, start fires, frame roofs, cure bacon, punch cows." In the process of learning these new skills, she "memorized the shapes of three thousand clouds, calibrated a hundred sunset reds, catalogued one hundred eleven rainbows, and watched five babies slide out into life." In the end, she noted, "my life is fuller, happier, more real" because of her communal experience.[32]

Still, communal living, especially in rustic settings such as Wheeler's and Morning Star, imposed serious hardships on residents. The counterculture's rejection of modern technology had a disproportionate impact on women. Routine chores, without laborsaving devices, electricity, or running water, multiplied the demands on their time. Women with children were even more caught up in a series of domestic chores. Communal literature, in fact, is replete with accounts of men hanging around strumming guitars, smoking pot, and discussing philosophy or the next "important" project. When women participated in creative ventures—as did Alicia Bay Laurel—they were more often than not single and childless.

Rustic and crowded conditions also led to the spread of communicable disease. Aside from sexually transmitted infections, communes were plagued with outbreaks of hepatitis; dysentery; food poisoning;

respiratory, eye, ear, and throat infections; scabies; fleas; ringworm; and lice. Many communes and communards were, as clinicians noted, hygienically challenged, subsisting on scavenged food prepared under unsanitary conditions and relying on open, easily contaminated water sources for drinking and bathing. When illness struck, many resorted to herbal or home remedies instead of the medical "establishment." For more serious conditions, delay often had dire health consequences. Finally, maternal and infant malnutrition should not go unexamined. Because of their ideals and youthful ignorance, some members of the counterculture neglected the basic health needs of women and children. I am haunted by the memory of a young acquaintance who gave birth, completely unassisted, on a southern California beach. She and her child survived, but the overly zealous dietary proscriptions, youth, and voluntary poverty of his parents turned him into a lethargic, emaciated toddler. Today, I would have notified child protective services, but at the time I lacked the mature judgment to take such action. Even more tightly knit, structured communes, such as the Farm, struggled early on to meet the nutritional needs of members. Young, city-bred communards, while firmly committed to an agrarian, self-sufficient lifestyle, often lacked the skills and knowledge to successfully raise crops and livestock.[33]

Many women, including some who lived in rural communes, strove for complete self-sufficiency. This was by far the most challenging of women's economic survival strategies and the greatest test of their physical, emotional, and creative capacities. Alicia Bay Laurel's Wheeler's experience was an idyll, a romp in the woods, compared to the daily challenges and hardships faced by self-sufficiency purists. Moreover, her delightful guide to living on the earth was about as useful to purist pioneers as the *Girl Scout Handbook*. Ayala Talpai, who moved to the land with her husband and five children, recalled:

> by the time we moved to this ranch, I was pretty much of a Superwoman. If it was time for supper, I'd pick up a basket and go out to the garden, that's how it started. . . . I just milked twice a day. So I was making cheese and butter and cottage cheese and yogurt and buttermilk and whipped cream and ice cream and everything. . . . But that was a major dent in my time, you know. I was cooking on a wood stove. So I was doing everything on this wood stove, and I was

knitting my husband's socks out of yarn that I'd spun and dyed my-self, and he'd go off to work with his sandwiches of homemade bread and mayonnaise and homegrown lettuce and homemade cheese and a hand-knitted hat on his head and homemade shirts, and oh my God.[34]

Nonie Gienger's life was similarly rigorous. She and her husband moved back to the land in 1971 and lived in a tent while they constructed their first home, a 7 x 10 cabin. She gave birth to her first child, a son, while still in the tent, hauled water for washing dishes and diapers, gath-ered firewood, cooked on a wood stove, and sewed clothing and baby blankets by hand. The first winter, they lived on deer meat, rice and beans, and a gallon of milk per week. Later she planted a garden and took trips to the coast to "gather seaweed and nettles, plantain and dan-delion, berries and wild apples, too." They did purchase some staples such as rice, beans, oil, and grain, "But we were even grinding our own flour to make bread. I was a pioneer housewife and we were living off very little money. But it felt good because I knew where everything came from." She also handled family medical crises. Just before the birth of her second child, they contracted dysentery from a contaminated water supply. "It showed up first in my son. . . . One day I found him outside crying and his intestine was hanging out. I didn't know what happened. I was horrified." She consulted the herbal reference book, *Back to Eden,* and used white oak bark and golden seal as remedies.[35]

Marylyn Motherbear Scott also started from scratch. "When we went up there, there was nothing on the land except a cattle trough. So we were building homes, building water tanks, building roads, just build-ing, building, building. And having babies still. Looking back on it, honestly, I don't know how we did it all. But I had a lot of energy and could do multiple things at the same time, and I did." She went on:

I had my babies at home. I nursed my babies. I slept in the same bed. I schooled them at home. We'd get up and do the gardening, built houses, and cooked from scratch. Everything. I made my own bread. I made my own cheese. I made my own tofu. I gardened and had vegetables. I was even the first person I know who grew blue corn and a lot of new food stuffs like that. I raised every kind of seed, every kind of bean, and every kind of vegetable.[36]

Marylee Bytheriver, along with her husband and baby, started out with more basic comforts. They moved onto a 360-acre sheep ranch, complete with a barn and a house, which her parents had purchased. Still, her life was arduous. She hauled "twenty years worth of manure" out of the barn and dug it into the soil from which she produced "all our own fruits and vegetables." In addition to gardening and canning, they raised and butchered their own animals. The hostility of the local population and lack of intellectual stimulation, however, eventually took their toll. "After three years, I bought some land in Ettersburg and started living by myself there." Her two children stayed with her husband because "he was just better at raising them than I was, so that's what he did and I pursued my other interests." Her new life included building her own house, putting in an organic garden, installing her own water and electric systems, writing astrology books, working as a paralegal, travel to China and Tibet, returning to college, and a second marriage. Like many women, she found complete self-sufficiency too limiting but never abandoned her commitment to living lightly on the earth.[37]

In time, those who remained on the land established networks and associations that provided essential services, intellectual stimulation, and emotional support. Mary Siler Anderson described how the approximately 800 back-to-the-landers in southern Humboldt County came together. Once they had addressed the basics of building shelter, planting gardens, preserving food, and finding ways to dispose of waste and generate energy,

> we began to organize ways to provide basic services for ourselves. Food being basic, we began with buying clubs that evolved into food co-ops. We started our own schools to provide what we felt would be a better education for our children. We didn't like the medical care in Garberville, so we formed our own health center. And we became aware that our environment had been damaged and needed our help. Out of that came a recycling center.

Women, like their pioneer counterparts 100 years earlier, were central to community building efforts.[38]

Maggie Carey, for example, established the first free school in Mary's community. When it failed because parents "were busy building their homesteads and didn't have time for the school," she and other women placed their children in the local public school district and gradually took it over. Maggie won election to the district's board of trustees, serving for a twelve-year period. Mary, on the other hand, helped start the community's first newspaper, child care center, and recycling center and organized town meetings and a Chamber of Values "to consciously practice ways of being together that encourage the full participation of everyone there and foster a sense of a cohesive community." In the same community, Nonie Gienger and her husband devoted years to legislative lobbying and networking with environmental organizations and Indian tribal representatives in an effort to obtain wilderness classification for the surrounding Sinkyone forest. Another neighbor, Mara Devine, devoted her time to sustaining the local battered women's shelter and rape crisis network.[39]

Whether women choose voluntary simplicity, scavenging, temporary odd jobs, public assistance, communal living, or rural self-sufficiency, their goal remained constant: to fashion livelihoods that were individually and socially transformative. Daily labor work, they believed, should harmonize with and reinforce counterculture values of cooperation, autonomy, creativity, intimacy, spirituality, and environmental sustainability. At times, their desire for right livelihood took on tones of desperation. A letter arriving at a commune from a young woman in Muscoda, Wisconsin, summed it up: "Dear Brothers and Sisters, I'm female, nineteen, and a college dropout. Right now I'm trying to keep from being swallowed by a monster—plastic, greedy American society. All of my friends are working to get through school, to start a job or get married and settle down. But the thought of following this pattern completely turns me off. . . . Help me!" Fortunately—from her perspective—help came in a variety of forms. In addition to economic alternatives, the counterculture offered a number of other escape routes: mind-expanding drugs, a dizzying array of spiritual paths and self-transforming therapies, and travel.[40]

5. "I WAS OPENING UP LIKE A TENDER FLOWER"
WOMEN'S PSYCHEDELIC, SPIRITUAL, AND TRAVEL ADVENTURES

arijuana, hashish, LSD, peyote, mescaline, and psilocybin were the counterculture's drugs of choice. Although taken recreationally, these substances, unlike "harder" drugs, were widely regarded by users as catalysts of a new world order. According to their advocates, psychedelic drugs fostered a sense of unity with all of creation, cleansed the mind of received truths, unleashed repressed creative and sensual energy, and facilitated spiritual growth and telepathic communication among cosacramentalists. As Carolyn Adams noted in *Can't Find My Way Home*, "my whole approach to drugs had been for them to enhance your perception or feeling of the joy of life."[1]

Women willingly ingested large quantities of these substances over extended periods of time, with apparent satisfaction and even zeal. Their experience was largely ignored within the counterculture, distorted by the mainstream media and law enforcement agencies, and later, censored by women themselves, however. As a consequence, there is no single body of literature—primary or secondary—that explores what women hoped to achieve through drug experimentation.

Countercultural literature is virtually silent on the subject of women's drug experiences. The underground press, dominated by male editors and staff writers, highlighted the accounts of drug "experts" and younger male users. Timothy Leary, Richard Alpert (Ram Dass), Ken Kesey, and Augustus Owsley Stanley, as pioneer experimenters, manufacturers, and advocates, occupied the top of the psychedelic hierarchy. Next were younger males for whom drug use was often a means of testing and asserting masculine authority and dominance. The ability to handle high, frequent doses; avert bad trips; interpret psychedelic visions; and maintain a normal persona while tripping in straight surroundings conferred status within countercultural peer groups. There was also the allure of going against the mainstream. Being busted, serving time, or evading arrest without implicating others were additional measures of manliness.[2]

Within this context of male celebrity and posturing, women were cast as secondary players: psychedelic disciples to more-experienced, enlightened males or distressed damsels who needed to be rescued from bad situations during bad trips. Outside of the counterculture, the media, social critics, and law enforcement officials had much to say about women drug users but little to say about women's actual experiences or reasons for "turning on." The mainstream or "straight" media, clearly uncomfortable with the concept of female agency, initially placed women in the role of victim. For example, in a late 1960s episode of *Hawaii Five-O*, a young college student, turned on to LSD by a sleazy, gurulike professor, killed herself by attempting to fly off of a cliff. *The People Next Door*, a CBS Playhouse Drama that aired during the same period, portrayed another unwitting young woman who was lured into drug use by a seemingly innocent boy next door. She ended up in a psychiatric ward. An episode of *Ironside* ended more happily when the good guys rescued a girl who had been similarly lured into the seamy hippie drug scene.[3]

By late 1968, when some television programmers began reaching out to an audience more sympathetic to the counterculture, they offered viewers another, albeit still stereotypical, image of drug-using women: the spaced-out hippie chick. For example, Goldie O'Keefe, a character on the *Smothers Brothers*, poked fun at the perceived dangers of marijuana and LSD but trivialized, sexualized, and domesticated female experimentation. In one episode, where Goldie is showing the audience how to make whole wheat bread, she instructs: "The more you knead it the higher it rises. The higher it rises, the lighter you feel. Ohhh—I feel good already! Ladies, ladies, ladies, get it on this way. My bread is getting high. And I'm beginning to rise."[4]

Contemporary observers of the counterculture did little to challenge or nuance these images. Tom Wolfe, in *Electric Kool-Aid Acid Test*, not only placed women in supporting roles to more daring and edgy males; he portrayed them as casualties of psychedelic excess. "Stark Naked," for example, goes stark raving mad while high on drugs and is picked up by Texas authorities and institutionalized midway through the

Prankster's cross-country journey. In an equally tragic vignette, Wolfe describes another drugged-out woman who is gang-raped (Wolfe doesn't call it rape) by a horde of Hell's Angels "until she had been fenestrated in various places at least fifty times."[5] Joan Didion's *Slouching toward Bethlehem,* which emphasized the shallowness and banality of the counterculture, reinforced the already prevalent stereotypes of female victim and spaced-out hippie chick and introduced a new image: the negligent, drug-obsessed mother.[6]

Added to this was the downright consternation and disapproval of the law enforcement community. Female drug users, from its perspective, were either hapless victims or selfish, shallow thrill seekers. Jan, a young hippie interviewed by a couple of criminologists, was described by them as "pretty," "clean," and gainfully employed but in an unfortunate relationship with a boyfriend "who preferred to be supported by Jan, or, if she was no longer willing, other women." When asked, "What's a nice, pretty girl like you doing in a place like this?" Jan angrily responded, "What I do with my own body is my affair. I like to smoke marijuana and have been on several LSD trips. It's my business." After Jan rebuffed their attempt to cast her as a victim, the interviewers concluded that she was simply another delinquent "busily engaged in glorifying youth, sex and irresponsibility."[7]

There are, of course, elements of truth in some of these accounts. During the Summer of Love, for example, the Haight-Ashbury Free Medical Clinic staff reported in the June 1968 issue of *Clinical Pediatrics* that "many young people 'freaked' on acid—that is, they experienced the feeling they had lost control of themselves. Many fear they may be permanently 'mad.'" Still, between November 1967 and August 1968, only 2 percent of total clinic visits involved "acute drug reaction," a category that included bad trips, overdoses, and withdrawal from harder drugs such as STP, methamphetamine, and heroin. Marijuana use, as the clinicians noted in the same issue, caused "few acute or chronic abuse problems or untoward reactions." A more serious problem, in their estimation, was that youth wasn't limiting its experimentation to psychedelics and marijuana. Some young hippies, like many of their rock and roll icons, had moved on to harder, more addictive substances such as speed, heroin, and cocaine. This was particularly the case by 1967. Hippiedom, as its denizens observed, started to attract a "criminal element" that introduced ever increasing quantities of hard drugs.

Dawn Reynolds, who arrived in the Haight Ashbury during the summer, remarked in *Can't Find My Way Home* that "it was like one minute we were smoking pot, and then we blinked, and the next minute we were doing heroin." This shift did indeed produce many female victims, spaced-out hippie chicks, and negligent, drug-obsessed mothers. But they were only one group of actors in a much more complex, interesting story. Thousands of other women viewed drugs—particularly psychedelics and marijuana—as a ticket out of suburbia's straitjacket.[8]

Getting at their stories, however, was somewhat of a challenge. Because of negative stereotypes and judgments, and the privileging of male experience within the counterculture, many of these more serious experimenters eventually denied or downplayed their 1960s drug use. By the early 1980s additional pressures reinforced their silence. Many had become parents or participants in the "straight" labor force. Moreover, political leaders waged national Just Say No and War on Drugs campaigns and framed their own prior drug use as mere experimentation or youthful indiscretion. The tendency toward self-censorship even extended to counterculture-friendly gatherings and conferences. A participant at a 1980s Naropa Institute conference recalled how a younger member of the audience asked the panel about the use of psychedelics during the Beat and hippie eras. A panelist responded, "Well, drugs were a part of it, but only a small one. Those days were mostly about achieving altered states through meditation." Diane Di Prima, who bridged the two eras, gutsily stood up and objected: "Now wait a minute. I think that everyone should know that drugs *were* an important part of our experience. To deny that because it's the Reagan age of 'just say no' is crazy. We were changing our consciousness back then and a lot of what we were doing through psychedelics was very positive."[9]

Diane Di Prima, and other counterculture women who have been willing to disclose their drug experiences, not only talk up the life-altering effects of psychedelics but also reveal a pattern of heavy and sustained drug use by women. Teresa Murphy, for example, admitted taking LSD sixty times over a two-year period and didn't consider that to be "frequent use."[10] Data from youth surveys bolster such personal testimony. A study of 250 hippies conducted in the Haight Ashbury district revealed that the average number of psychedelic experiences per participant "was conservatively estimated to be between 75 and 100." Gender and other measures used in the study had no bearing on the pattern or frequency of drug use. A more detailed assessment of eighty youth (thirty-four women and forty-six men), drawn from this larger sample, revealed that all but one used marijuana on a daily basis.[11] Another survey, conducted among Berkeley hippie youth, led to similar conclusions. More than 97 percent of women had used marijuana and hashish, 91 percent had used LSD, and more than 80 percent had used mescaline and peyote. Again, gender was not a significant determinant of frequency in regard to the use of marijuana or psychedelic drugs.[12]

Women used marijuana and hashish to relax, enhance social and sexual interactions, and alleviate the boredom or dullness of everyday life. Many reported that, when stoned, the most mundane encounters, chores, and surroundings seemed "new," weighted with deeper significance or meaning, and infinitely more interesting.[13] In contrast to the recreational and often daily use of marijuana, women used psychedelics to achieve life-altering, spiritual, and psychological insights. And in account after account, these drugs delivered on their promise. In most cases, however, most women admit that psychedelics simply confirmed or brought into sharper focus existing insights, desires, and in some cases fears.[14]

Women's initial experiments with psychedelics, for example, drew attention to their dissatisfaction with straight society or radical youth organizations and confirmed that they belonged within the counterculture. As reported by Keith Melville in *Communes in the Counterculture*, a middle-class housewife explained that marijuana and LSD presented her with new options:

> I started smoking and took acid a few times, and I began to look at things differently. Like when I started smoking, I stopped dusting. It just didn't make any sense spending all that time dusting all those things. Then I took acid, and when I put that little pill in my head all of a sudden I understood a lot of things for the first time. I knew what was important, the love and the sharing, and these other things just weren't important at all.

After failing to convince her husband to adopt a new lifestyle, she "split" and moved to a commune in Grants Pass, Oregon.[15]

Similarly, Mary Siler Anderson was a married mother of two children seemingly living out the ideal middle-class dream when she "discovered marijuana and LSD . . . it was a real awakening for me . . . that you didn't have to be in this particular rut, doing this particular kind of thing." She went on to describe how she "had this sort of feeling coming out of the '50s that, really, life was about destroying the imagination." She ended up leaving her husband, joining a couple of urban communes, and eventually moving back to the land.[16]

Others described a no less dramatic shift from political activism to the counterculture's emphasis on self-transformation. Kate Coleman started out as "an idealistic left-wing activist at Berkeley in the early sixties" who "thought there was something deranged about drugs." But by the late 1960s the combination of LSD and travel abroad had shifted her perspective. "I was completely softened. All my hard edges had been worn down. I hadn't taken much truck with this spiritual shit, and I was always cynical, always the tough guy. . . . No matter how far I'd gotten, I'd been a conservative little old lady underneath everything I did, but now I was opening up like a tender flower." She went on to describe her experience as an "ego death," a breakdown of defenses that filled her with joy, "lifted" her cynicism, and opened her to "all the wackiness and heartbreaking humanity of what was happening around me."[17]

Virginia Logan was simultaneously involved with Berkeley's activist community and searching for a meaningful spiritual path when she took LSD. The trip was psychologically devastating, destroying all sense of meaning and order in her universe and landing her in a hospital emergency room. Nevertheless, it clarified where she thought she belonged.

> I had been doing a lot of protesting and marching, and during that bad acid trip I had the realization that the evil I'd seen was a projection of the evil inside me. And what I needed to do, rather than fight the evil outside—because that's how we characterized the government, the administration, and the war machine—was confront the evil inside. So that acid experience, although really horrible, shifted my life direction, and that was when I fully committed myself to the inner journey.[18]

Once embedded in the counterculture, most women embarked on a quest for a more "authentic" or "real" spiritual experience. Here, too, psychedelics played a significant supporting role. Countercultural women, raised in varied mainstream religious traditions, eagerly embraced Native American, Eastern, and occult alternatives. Psychedelic experiences often confirmed the "righteousness" of exploration, reinforced connections among varied belief systems, pointed to a particular spiritual path, or encouraged women to create eclectic spiritual blends that met their individual needs.

Indeed, spiritual themes predominate in women's drug use accounts, pointing to the counterculture's idealistic pursuit of individual and collective enlightenment. Virginia Logan's story, for example, moved from her conviction that she belonged within the counterculture to her full-fledged commitment to finding a spiritual path. Prior to her bad trip, she had studied various spiritual traditions and regularly practiced meditation. Her LSD experience, which demolished her ego boundaries and her sense of a solid, predictable, ordered universe, convinced her that Buddhism held the greatest promise of individual and cultural transformation.[19]

Anne Waldman, a Bennington College student ready to expand her horizons beyond the "restrictive intellectual mentality of the East Coast," traveled west to attend the Berkeley Poetry Conference. Once there, she dropped acid and "visualized, witnessed, and encountered every person I'd ever known . . . in a sort of rainbow gathering or convocation." She also encountered "other living, breathing" beings "that locked me into a net of interconnectedness . . . an endless web of relationships between Karma, between people and animals and everything else that moves and breathes in our pulsing, expanding universe." This vision drew her to Tibetan Buddhist practice and contained the essence of the "Dharmic axiom: Nothing is solid. You are impermanent. Life is precious. You can't hold on. You will die. You are connected up with everything that breathes—the trees and the birds and the fish and so on, not to mention the inanimate beauties. Thought forms evolve thought forms, endless concentric wheels of aspiration."[20]

Although psychedelics had an interesting synergy with Buddhism, they also encouraged eclecticism. One young college student, raised Catholic but turned atheist, started using pot, hash, and LSD during the same period that she was studying the anthropological literature on altered states of consciousness. She recalled that her own drug experiences

> were good for my head. I was able to break out of conventional ways of thinking. I was able to intuitively understand things that were too non-logical for me to hold in my mind without drugs—for instance,

the nature of matter. I had read that physics proved that matter is not so solid but I couldn't grasp the idea. LSD gave me the experience. It opened my mind to possibilities and let me understand the metaphysical nature of myth as a vehicle for truth.

She went on to describe, "No longer was something 'true' or 'false' based on whether it was 'proved.' There were other questions that were important to ask. These ideas led me to Jung, who led me to Joseph Campbell, who continues to be one of the main philosophical influences in my life." After her drug epiphanies, she explored shamanism and eventually became a "practicing pagan and yoga enthusiast." [21]

Maggie Gaskin, raised by a fundamentalist Christian father and an Episcopalian stepmother, discovered that acid was a catalyst for a more "real" spiritual experience that included serious study of the Tarot, Kabala, yoga, and Eastern religious traditions as well as marriage to one of San Francisco's psychedelic gurus, Stephen Gaskin.[22] Rain Jacopetti, a young artist, wife, and mother who moved in the summer of 1966 to what would later become the Morning Star commune, embarked on a series of psychedelic journeys that eventually led her to yoga, meditation, macrobiotics, and Subud and then on to Native American, earth-based, and goddess-centered spirituality.[23]

A few women credited psychedelics with helping them find new meaning in their own religious traditions. Ruth, for example, was raised a Catholic but as an adolescent started to "rebel against the 'Mother Church,' which I thought was the most tyrannical thing there was." At sixteen she entered her church while on acid and "I felt as if something new were coming to me, like I was having a religious experience. From then on I was able to ignore the politics and just connect with the spirit that had given hope and comfort to so many people."[24]

Women also described an almost spiritual longing for community or tribal membership that was illuminated or clarified during their psychedelic drug experiences. Diane, the middle-class housewife who stopped doing housework when she turned on to marijuana and acid, wanted to break out of the confines of her nuclear family in order to experience "the love and the sharing" associated with communal living. She left her husband partly because he "still wanted things of his own, and didn't want to open the house to others."[25] Gina Stillman, another early resident of the Morning Star commune, recalled a group acid trip where she realized that "I wanted to dedicate myself, to be part of a huge, loving, giving, motherly force. I gave up my concern for my personal welfare and concentrated on a concern for the community, for the group consciousness rather than on my individual self."[26] Nancy Nina, a suburban housewife who became a committed antiwar activist, took LSD and similarly decided that she needed to live communally with like-minded individuals—people who refused to support the existing "police state" and wanted to create "something that loves the earth and all the species and can embrace diversity and doesn't use violence to solve its problems."[27] Yet another woman described how an LSD trip focused her desire to belong to a "tribe" or extended family and triggered her search for a community that shared her ideals.[28]

Beyond their role in focusing spiritual and communal longings, psychedelics informed women's more general search for personal growth. Indeed, these drugs were widely perceived as deconditioning agents that could free the mind of repressive cultural baggage that obscured a truer, more sensual, creative, "together" self. For a generation of women raised to "save" themselves until marriage, confine and restrain their flesh within foundation garments, and never "let themselves go," marijuana and psychedelics helped ease sexual and sensual inhibitions. Jan Camp, brought up within a highly religious Italian Catholic family, refrained from sex until she was eighteen and married. The marriage, from a sexual, creative, and emotional standpoint, was stifling. Her husband, who regarded her as an appendage or possession, was emotionally distant and verbally noncommunicative. She recalled two disappointments on her wedding day. The first was that she had to carry her own suitcases, the second was sex. "The papers were signed and chivalry was off. It's 'you belong to me, you carry the suitcases.'"

After discovering the counterculture, Jan mustered the courage to leave the relationship and "started opening up." At a body-painting party, where the artist was covering people in paint and pressing them against canvas, she recalled that the younger men were attracted to her. One of them approached her, asking if her hard, erect nipples meant that she was aroused. "And I said, 'I don't know; let's go take a shower and find out.' So we went into a shower stall, and I climbed up on him, my arms around his waist. And we had sex. And I was tripping, and I had the most fantastic orgasm. And I just sort of got off, climbed down, and said, 'thank you.' And he was, like, 'Wait!' And it was just like theater, and I just loved the idea of life being theater."[29]

Sandra Butler credited LSD with freeing her from a sexually repressive, conservative upbringing and allowing her to redefine her sexuality as healthy and natural. "If you're around nature, or pretty things, or just happy, you feel good, and you feel sexual. . . . And you've got to go on your feelings. And that's why I was so mixed up. People are so far away from the natural flow of their feelings."[30] During a bad trip on mescaline, Keely Stahl, an eighteen-year-old college student, came to a similar conclusion about the benefits of "letting go." Initially she experienced physical ecstasy: "It was as though my body had become pure sensation, vibrant and glowing, no longer comprised of bones, fibers, and cells." But the sensation of "losing control" provoked anxiety, panic, and excruciating physical pain. Disturbed by her experience, she quit school, went into Reichian therapy, and discovered "that the disconnect between my mind and my body had been the cause of the horrific episode." She went on to conclude that her fear of "letting my bodily sensations get away" ruined an opportunity to be at one with the cosmos in "a sort of mutual orgasm without sex and self-manipulation." Keely, as a consequence of this experience, dedicated herself to helping others heal or bridge the mind-body divide.[31]

Women also believed that psychedelics could liberate them from psychological baggage that impeded personal growth. Jan Camp, an artist whose lively imagination and creative gifts were largely ignored by her family, was used to having her thoughts, feelings, and ideas discounted. During her first LSD experience, "I realized the power of my mind. I could see my mind working, and could tell that it not only had the capacity to understand, but to make things happen." When a fellow tripper discounted her insight as "stupid," she saw him as all of the people in her life who had trivialized her ideas. She understood that "I could think whatever I wanted, regardless of other people's judgments." Later, during the same trip, she hallucinated that she was an artist with a vast audience of appreciative fans who were asking for her blessing. Both visions contributed to her growing confidence in her artistic and creative abilities.[32]

Marylyn Motherbear Scott had a similar, life-altering experience with mescaline. Prior to the trip, which was her first, Marylyn was long plagued by feelings of anxiety and dread that accompanied impending events or transitions. After taking mescaline, she realized "that the waiting and the anticipation of something happening was difficult for me" because when she was seven her father had been killed in World War II. She went on to describe how "I came into awareness that in a second life can be gone—in an instant, in a half of a breath it could be over, done. The fact that now I understood how precarious our lives were—in a visceral way—moved me into another expression of that which was to be really present at living. That altered my whole reality, and affected the work that I do today."[33]

Although some women had "bad trips," they expressed few regrets in regard to their drug experiences. The consensus, represented by Marylyn Motherbear Scott, was that psychedelics allowed the counterculture "to move forward into a more enlightened state" that rejected violence, intolerance, overconsumption, and despoliation of the planet. "We were given the job to work on that, to bridge this time of awakening that was so necessary for our survival. We didn't have eons of Buddhism in our lineage, so we had to get it fast, get it in a second, because Western culture needed it."[34]

Gina Stillman put it in more personal terms:

We were looking for Something. At first I thought I was alone, that I was the only woman desperately seeking an alternative, for something different. But it's always been the case that when I feel something strongly I'm never wrong. There were thousands of people feeling the same thing. . . . Then psychedelics came along in 1964 and there was a change in consciousness. New possibilities opened up—worlds we had never dreamed of, almost like a new spectrum of colors. It was as if I had been living in a prison and never realized it. Our appreciation for the beauty of life increased—for things we had always taken for granted. A leaf, a blade of grass, everything was tremendously heightened. I felt a real joy in getting out of my previous existence.[35]

Although many women used marijuana and psychedelics for fun, recreation, and adventure, most regarded these substances as catalysts of spiritual discovery and awakening. Indeed, most, like Dawn Reynolds, ultimately concluded that "it was about learning how to blow the mind without drugs. Immersed in Zen, Vedantism, macrobiotic vegetarianism, reflexology, shiatsu, vitamin therapy, and yoga, she started finding some of the very things she had looked for in acid." Like their drug experiences, women's spiritual journeys were largely ignored by the mostly male insiders and mainstream observers who chronicled the counterculture's beliefs and practices. The resulting gap or silence masked the central role that women's spiritual paths played in the genesis of New Age alternatives—alternatives that for better or for worse profoundly altered the religious landscape of the United States in the late twentieth century.[36]

During the 1960s most counterculture women believed that spiritual truth was located within the self, waiting to be discovered or awakened by opening up to the individual's natural intuitive capacity to recognize the divine. Hence, the widespread use of psychedelics to free the mind of received truth. The search for the divine, inextricably connected to self-realization, was an on-going, continually unfolding process, a lifestyle that involved both the rejection of traditional religious authority and the separation or compartmentalization of work, leisure, consumption, and worship. To counterculture women, middle-class submission to institutional expertise and authority, impersonal and unfulfilling work regimes, consumerism, and the management and control of desire and emotion were obstacles to spiritual growth and self-realization.

Their rejection of institutional authority and their reliance on inner direction led them to embrace a dazzling array of alternatives. Some of these alternatives, such as Tibetan and Zen Buddhism, Sufism, Native American spiritual traditions, variants of Hinduism and Sikhism, paganism, Wicca, and Christian and Jewish revival movements, constituted spiritual paths or disciplines. Others, such as the tarot, kabbalah, sweats, peyote rituals, vision quests, alchemy, yoga, meditation, encounter groups, magic, crystals, astrology, fortune telling, and Jungian psychology, were tools for recovering the authentic self or for aligning the self with divine, cosmic forces.[37]

Consistent with the counterculture's construction of gender, many of these alternatives accepted as a given the duality of male and female natures. Controlling, channeling, or integrating masculine and feminine energy was often a crucial aspect of spiritual growth. Some even venerated female deities and archetypes or recognized the dual nature of the divine. Moreover, women's supposed intuitiveness, connection to nature's cycles and rhythms, attunement to emotions and feelings, and rootedness in the here and now gave them a distinct edge in spiritual practices and disciplines that called for "letting go of the ego," "getting in touch with feelings," being "here now," and nonrational ways of knowing.

For many women, this was an improvement over the strictly patriarchal traditions of their childhoods and a doorway to greater influence. By the late 1960s and early 1970s some counterculture women began to argue that it wasn't enough to harmonize or balance male and female energies; there was simply too much yang (male energy) and not enough yin (female energy). If the counterculture was serious about creating a more cooperative, peaceful, emotionally expressive, life-nurturing world, then it had better place women, who possessed these qualities in abundance, in charge of spiritual growth and self-realization. In the transition from the Piscean to the Aquarian age, a woman named Pelican argued,

> We as women are in a crucial position . . . because we are first of all less tied to the Piscean forms which were developed by men for the benefit of men. The Piscean Age has been dominated by the glorification of masculine energies and the negation of feminine energies. Women have a natural intuition and sensitivity to cosmic vibrations. It is our task now to emphasize with our lives the positive feminine powers as we develop the new ways of the new age.

This realization, which would lead to women's dominance in the New Age spiritual movements of the 1970s and 1980s, unfolded gradually, beginning with their break from established traditions and experimentation with alternative religious practices.[38]

Hippie women came from Catholic, Protestant, Jewish, and atheist or agnostic backgrounds, but after joining the counterculture they were less likely than their mainstream peers and hippie males to claim a traditional religious identity or preference. For some, the counterculture provided the opportunity to satisfy spiritual longings that had begun in childhood. For others, joining the counterculture, taking psychedelics, and being exposed to religious alternatives were decisive factors in their break with convention. Most, however, took time to explore, moving from one alternative to another before settling on a particular path. And for many, the particular path would be eclectic, fashioned from different traditions to create the perfect, individually tailored fit.

Some women, however, elected a particular path because it offered structure and security during a period of crisis or vulnerability. Bennett Berger, in his study of communes, observed "the sexual ethics and out-law spirit rendered men free to 'split' whenever they felt like it," leaving women, sometimes pregnant or with children, to fend for themselves. Other women simply "burned out" on drugs or were overwhelmed by the emotional and physical costs of "free" love. For these casualties of counterculture excess, many of the more structured religious sects offered food, shelter, protection from sexual exploitation, and clear moral and behavioral guidelines. The International Society of Krishna Consciousness, for example, banned drugs, alcohol, tobacco, and sex outside of marriage. Similarly, most of the Jesus Movement communes prohibited the use of intoxicants and premarital sex. As Timothy Miller observed, these and other more structured alternatives appealed to "hippie dropouts," particularly those who had come up against the lim-its of freedom.[39]

Most women, however, opted for less, rather than more structure. Jan Camp was raised in Westfield, Massachusetts, by devoutly Catholic, Italian American parents who "made a pact to raise children for God." From a very young age Jan "wanted to be a cloistered nun. This was not encouraged in any way, however, and it fell by the wayside." For women in her community, marriage and having children were alternate routes to fulfillment, and, at eighteen, Jan married a "shy, quiet boy" whom she met on a blind date. The marriage, however, was emotionally unsat-isfying and stifling. He didn't want her to work outside the home, and controlled her social life. When he ended one of her close friendships, Jan had a nervous breakdown and "couldn't stand to be around him after that." When they went to a priest for help with their marriage, "he told us to have sex. But I couldn't breathe when we had sex." Her second negative encounter with the church occurred around the same period. "I went to confession after missing mass on a Holy Thursday. The priest said that he had to determine the weight of my sin by asking me some questions. 'Was I married?' yes; 'did my husband miss mass?' yes; 'do you have any children?' no, but I want them; 'do you think God is going to send you children if you miss mass?' I didn't answer the last question. I simply got up and walked out of church never to return." Jan, who had suffered several miscarriages and desperately wanted children, regarded this counsel—like the last—as insensitive and insulting.

But she remained "thirsty for spiritual life, so I studied many religions by going to different churches and talking with people about their faith." After leaving her husband and entering "the counterculture wholeheartedly, I felt permission to visit all types of religious belief and take from each a style of expressing/manifesting things like compassion, prayer, service, tithing, raising one's voice in praise, creating a place for God in my heart, etc." Still attracted to the cloistered life of prayer, she satisfied that longing

> by using a synthesis of Western, Eastern, and psychic thought practices in everything I do no matter where I am and who is around. One of the things Tom [her current partner] and I realized when we got together was that we wanted to have a shared spiritual practice. We tried a few things and have settled on morning silence and sharing thoughts, sometimes with Tom doing automatic writing and sometimes choosing a Zen meditation card or reading from a spiritual philosophy book.[40]

Virginia Logan, raised in Iowa and Wisconsin by Methodist parents, recalled "always, since I was a child, I was looking for a spiritual home. Although I loved Methodist hymns, and liked Jesus because he was kind to children and compassionate toward the poor, the whole Christian world view didn't make sense to me." She wanted to be Jewish at age nine "because I really liked the ritual, how it all had meaning and was integrated into life." Later, she wanted to be Catholic and, despite her mother's disapproval, "would lie in bed at night saying the rosary."

Like Jan, her ability to explore different spiritual traditions expanded when she joined the counterculture. Her first husband, an East Asian studies scholar, introduced her to Buddhism and Hinduism, but "Buddhism made the most sense and I began practicing meditation and looking for a teacher." She also became a strict vegetarian. In the meantime, she and her husband drifted apart. Their open marriage was "devastatingly horrible," and the insights she received in her women's consciousness-raising group added to her dissatisfaction. But what she really wanted was a spiritually meaningful partnership. "Joe studied Buddhism as an impartial scholar, and I had become a practitioner."

When he left for Nepal to collect and microfilm Buddhist texts, Virginia remained behind and fell in love with a man who shared her spiritual longings. Indeed, the first night they spent together, she had a "satori experience. It was as if everything fell together. Everything was completely meaningful, so evident that it's humorous that I hadn't seen it before. I experienced the world as totally perfect in all of its imperfection—that everything was exactly how it should be—that everything was related to everything else." She related this experience as "the most important moment of my life."

After she introduced her new partner, a former student radical, to Buddhism, they both embraced that path and added Tai Chi to the mix. Virginia then discovered that she was pregnant and made the wrenching decision—despite her new husband's opposition—to have an abortion. He left and became a Buddhist monk. "So here's a great irony. I left Joe because he didn't have a spiritual calling—the relationship had no spiritual content—and I married a man who left me to become a Buddhist monk."

Never abandoning meditation and basic Buddhist precepts, Virginia then embarked on another spiritual path. In a series of workshops, she discovered her psychic abilities and began to give readings. This soon translated into a spiritually and financially rewarding vocation. Later, with the advent of computer software capable of generating astrological charts, she added astrology to her practice. Eventually her spiritual journey took her in yet another direction: devotion to the "Divine Mother." After a series of meetings with Mother Mira, Virginia became aware that the "divine feminine wishes to—needs to—manifest on this planet at this time. So I turned my attention to that, embodying that in my own life." She went on to relate that "the mother part is really important. The archetype of the father has been with us too long. What we need now, as a species, as a planet, is the love of the mother—the nonjudgmental, forgiving, unconditional, and totally accepting love. This aspect of our consciousness, her embodiment within us, is what is going to change the world."[41]

Two other women cited personal crises as having precipitated their spiritual quests. In her Web site, Shakti Gawain, "a pioneer in the field of personal growth and consciousness" and the author of several books on creative visualization, intuition, and inner transformation, reveals that she was raised by atheist academics who "created in Shakti an attitude of both openness and skepticism that [led] to a great need for testing everything herself." A devastating breakup, however, provoked a "deep existential crisis" and a "search for the true purpose of life." As reported in *For the Love of God*, this led her to experiment with "mind expanding drugs" and to go on a journey around the world. At the end of her travels, she landed in India with "almost no possessions, but it was an extremely liberating experience for me." There, she "had a mystical experience with the God Shiva," and when she returned to the United States "knew that I wanted to pursue consciousness whatever that was—and my personal growth."[42]

Ellen Winner recalled that "by the age of nineteen I felt trapped in a material world bounded on all sides by the limits of my senses and sealed at the top and bottom with the authority of rational, scientific thought. I decided to become a doctor like my mother; I thought that by healing others, I might heal my own sense of spiritual isolation and despair." Exposure to the Beat subculture and then immersion in the counterculture led instead to "a life long search—through obscure philosophers and drugs, through madness and self-deception, through religions of all sorts—trying to find my way back toward that moment of fourteen-year-old clarity [when] I understood that the body was not important—I was consciousness, and consciousness is eternal; that was all that mattered." She eventually discovered shamanism, studied with shamanistic healers in Nepal, and became a healer in her own right.[43]

For women who were not spiritually inclined, the counterculture offered a host of therapies and techniques to find, liberate, or transform the self. In her study of a northern California hippie community, Jentri Anders found an intense interest and investment of marijuana cultivation profits in a wide range of group and individual therapies, dream analysis, and communication skills workshops. Indeed, for many women, the promise of self-discovery and transformation was the most exciting and liberating aspect of the counterculture experience. Beneath the surface, however, most of these alternatives shared two major philosophical tenets: rejection of received truth or knowledge and the self as the final authority—tenets that would later carry over into 1980s New Age spiritual movements.[44]

It is interesting to note that some women shied away from both the spiritual and self-help smorgasbords. Anna Marie Daniels, a self-defined skeptic, witnessed a downside to such exploration. "I could understand the spiritual longings of my peers, having experienced them myself, but there was too much damage: loved ones who, under the sway of a particular guru or 'enlightened' figure, relinquished their self-confidence, self-determination, responsibility for their children and the planet, and their financial resources." The practice of borrowing from other culture's religious traditions was also troubling to some. Indeed, this concern was shared by many Native American activists and anthropologists who deplored the desecration of sacred sites, the commercial trade in spiritual artifacts and objects, and the appropriation and selective modification of complex cultural and religious traditions. Above all, they voiced concern that this type of borrowing occurred in isolation of any deep understanding of indigenous cultures and the struggles and privations of "real" Indian people. As Philip Deloria noted, "Indian people were basically irrelevant. Indianness—even when imagined as something essential—could be captured and marketed as a text, largely divorced from Indian oversight and questions of authorship."[45]

Others, like Constance Trouble, expressed misgivings about the counterculture's focus on self-realization and transformation. "Early on we saw self and social transformation as a kind of joint project you do together. But self-improvement got separated from the social part at some point, and it became all about 'me.'" Trouble, however, is a bit too nostalgic. Even during its celebrated "golden age" (before hard drugs, Altamont, and the Manson family), the counterculture, especially in regard to its spirituality, had a highly individualistic and even entrepreneurial bent. Indeed, these very features explain why, by the late 1970s and 1980s, its therapeutic and spiritual alternatives caught on with the American mainstream. By the 1980s self-cultivation was completely stripped of its connection to social change. In *Habits of the Heart*, Robert Bellah and his coauthors observed that "finding oneself" by rejecting external sources of authority had become a major middle-class lifestyle objective—an objective that was at odds with basic human longings for love, intimacy, and community, not to mention civic engagement and activism.

> There are truths we do not see when we adopt the language of radical individualism. We find ourselves not independently of other people and institutions but through them. We never get to the bottom of ourselves on our own. We discover who we are face to face and side by side with others in work, love, and learning. . . . Finally, we are not

simply ends in ourselves, either as individuals or as a society. We are parts of a larger whole that we can neither forget nor imagine without paying a high price.

The tension between self-realization and the obligations and responsibilities of community is as old as the United States, and neither the counterculture nor its New Age offspring succeeded in reconciling them.[46]

Wanderlust was the final expression of women's quest for spiritual and personal transformation. During the 1960s young Americans traveled abroad in unprecedented numbers, joining their European, Canadian, and Australian peers in a vast, unsupervised, democratized version of the Grand Tour. European cities such as London, Amsterdam, Paris, and Copenhagen initially were the major centers of youth tourism. From there, travelers gradually moved to other areas, including the Near and Middle East, South and Southeast Asia, East and North Africa. By the late 1960s a favorite route was the "hippie trail," a route that began in Europe and extended overland into "Turkey, Iran, Afghanistan, Pakistan, and India to Nepal."[47]

With little more than backpacks and a few hundred (or fewer) U.S. dollars, young men and women took advantage of inexpensive train, plane, and bus fares; favorable exchange rates; and a welcoming network of youth hostels and hippie encampments to escape the confines of their own culture. Constance Trouble recalled,

> Kids at my high school began working and saving for their great escape in their junior year. We waited tables and babysat during the school year and took jobs picking and processing fruit during the summer. Some of the guys took off for Alaska and made a small fortune in the canneries. And some of my friends didn't have to work at all. Their graduation present was a round-trip ticket to Europe, as long as they promised to come home in the fall and start college.[48]

The exodus, as sociologist Erik Cohen noted, was fueled by the lure of inexpensive drugs, the desire for "real" experience, and disgust with "the Vietnam war or with the modern political system in general." The airlines, he observed, "realized that they could capitalize on the very alienation of this youth, by providing them with cheap opportunities to escape." Even the guidebook industry, that had traditionally catered to "sedate, middle class tourists," began issuing publications that appealed to "counter-cultural consumer demands." Word of mouth, however, was the most potent force behind youth tourism. As wave after wave of hippie travel enthusiasts returned, they not only spurred additional flight, they directed their peers to "already well-trodden itineraries."[49]

Hippies initially found food, lodging, and diversions in quarters that had originally catered to "the lower class local population." But by the late 1960s and early 1970s, counterculture travelers had established their own settlements "near Kathmandu in Nepal, in Goa in India, on Ibiza in the Beleares, on the French Riviera, outside Eilat on the southern-most tip of Israel, on some of the Greek islands, in Morocco, on the island of Lamu in northern Kenya, and probably in other localities." In some cases these new communities enjoyed convivial, cordial relations with local populations. In others, they were regarded as a nuisance, scaring off more affluent tourists and exposing local youth to drugs and corrupt Western values. As Cohen noted, "in a rather paradoxical manner, the very youths who in their way rebelled against their own culture and rejected it, came to be considered as the most fearsome representatives of its 'negative aspects.'" Indeed, young hippies of the 1960s and 1970s brought tourism and its attendant impacts on local economies and cultures to previously "uncontaminated" quarters of the globe.[50]

Globe trotting, especially on a low budget, was also risky. Disease (especially dysentery), hostile locals, corrupt officials, thieves, reckless drivers, fleas, bedbugs, and generally poor sanitary conditions plagued even the most seasoned travelers. Trading the comforts of home for a more "authentic" experience, however, became a badge of honor. As Agnieszka Sobocinska noted, "travelers boasted of the tortures they had suffered at the hands of the Indian railways, Nepalese drivers, or Singaporean customs officers. . . . Whinging about inconvenience of every kind was a way of proving that a traveler had experienced the 'real' Asia and had a genuine experience."[51]

Despite the lure of exotic locales, even greater numbers of hippie youth took off across the United States, using their thumbs, legs, bicycles, broken-down vehicles, and interstate buses to find love, community, and spiritual enlightenment. As Roberta Price noted, "all over the country, Children of the Sixties are getting into revamped school buses, VW vans, Chevy trucks with campers, step-vans, beat-up old Saabs, Peugeots, and slope-back Volvo 544s, heading west, north, up country, into the woods, the mountains, the desert, to the islands. Away!"[52]

An astonishing development was that young women—in increasing numbers and despite their parent's reservations and the counterculture's focus on male mobility and freedom—joined the domestic and international exodus. Wandering, drifting, hitting the open road, escaping the constraints of home, and casting aside comfort for the sake of adventure were celebrated in countercultural film, literature, and music as vehicles for discovering a truer male identity. Nevertheless, hippie women found small kernels of encouragement for their own wanderlust. They read themselves into male-authored travelogues, scripts, and lyrics and seized upon rare anthems to female freedom, such as the Beatles' "She's Leaving Home," It's a Beautiful Day's "White Bird," and The Band's "Tears of Rage." Women similarly found little or no validation from straight culture—a culture that accepted travel and adventure as a male rite of passage but regarded women wanderers as deviant or driven by personal or economic misfortune. By the 1960s some middle-class parents tolerated and even encouraged travel as long as it was an adjunct to formal education and a prelude to settling down, but most could not understand or accept their daughters' unfettered, seemingly purposeless sojourns. It not only overturned gender conventions; it represented a rejection of middle-class culture. There were, after all, prodigal sons, but no prodigal daughters. But leave they did, crisscrossing America and the world in search of broader horizons. Marilyn Stablein left for Europe after her freshman year in college, having saved enough for a round-trip ticket to Paris by cleaning houses on the weekends. In September, when her flight was scheduled to return, she tore up the ticket, deciding that she had more to learn there than here. She and a new boyfriend then traveled the hippie trail through "Tangiers, Algeciras, Tripoli, Torbruk, Luxor, Cairo, Alexandria, Istanbul, Tehran, Karachi, Delhi, Kathmandu." She ended up staying seven years, mostly in India, Nepal, and Tibet. "There are times when I ask myself, what am I doing here? My answer: to uncover its secrets; to listen to the whisperings, the sacred oral traditions; to read the texts in the languages they are written in; to learn by heart the names and the faces of deities so I can capture their images on paper and strive to imbue each image with the greatness of its namesake, its spiritual essence."

Drugs were also part of her journey, sold in government shops and routinely offered to deities and consumed in large quantities by the locals. As she happily noted, "drugs are plentiful; drugs are inexpensive.

Conveniently drugs are legal." On a trip to Dharmasala she met up with Richard Alpert, who was there to interview the Dalai Lama about the spiritual benefits of LSD. He supplied her with several hits that she took on a backpack trip through the mountains of Kashmir. This was followed up with a mescaline experience at a monastery in Nepal. But mostly her journey involved immersion in other cultures, reflecting her desire to "learn everything the hard way with no preconceived knowledge or experience. Life and art are inseparable. Life is preparation for the creative act. I am young and eager, entranced by the magic of art, ritual and music." At one point she asked herself, "Do women travel differently? I'm not interested in destinations as much as the journey along the way. To go, to move, to travel is to exist, to be alive."[53]

Cherie Lemke left home for Paris after graduating from college. For her, U.S. culture was beyond repair. Even the counterculture, just starting to emerge, held little promise of effecting change. The escalating war in Vietnam and white resistance to racial equality were, in her mind, symptoms of a deep, incurable cultural malaise. In Paris she found a youth subculture that blended leftist politics with the joie de vivre and spiritual leanings of the counterculture. She could read the tarot, throw the I-Ching, meditate, whip up lavish meals, decorate her home with flowers, experiment with drugs, demonstrate, and engage in serious political and philosophical discussion with no apparent contradiction or divided loyalties. She learned to paint, took lovers, played in a jazz band, and earned a meager living as a part-time translator and artist's model. After suffering through an open relationship, she devoted herself to Siddha Yoga and made several trips to India to study with her guru. After twenty-five years she returned to the United States, a stranger to U.S. culture and her family.[54]

Some left only to discover that home was more attractive. At seventeen, Anna Marie Daniels and her boyfriend rode bicycles from northern California to British Columbia in search of a safe haven from the draft and a community that shared their values. "This was in the days before we had fancy touring equipment, so we carried everything in backpacks. I remember running into another couple who were camping out of their VW bus. To me, after several days of biking in the rain and sleeping in a leaky tent, that was the height of luxury." They made the same trip the following spring and summer and, failing to find the right community, headed off to Europe.

For more than a year they toured Europe, Ethiopia, Egypt, Tanzania, Mauritius, and Seychelles, and finally ended up in Australia. "We stopped and worked whenever we ran out of money. I worked in Paris as an artist's model, as an au pair in Switzerland, at a concession stand at a campground in Spain, and in a department store in Australia. And we slept out in the open, in campgrounds, hostels, and cheap, seedy hotels. In some places you took your stuff into the shower with you so it wouldn't get stolen." The worst segment of the journey was on a boat from Spain to Ibiza. "We could only afford third-class tickets, so they put us in the hold down by the engine room where diesel fumes mingled with odors from chicken, onions, and vomit in one-hundred plus degree temperatures. And they wouldn't let us on deck for fresh air." Her partner had a taste for risky adventure and a roving eye, "and we must have broken up twenty-eight times during our trip." Alone in Australia, she had a single goal: earning enough to buy a ticket home. "Everywhere we went, women were treated like second-class citizens, either denied basic rights, or treated like sex objects. I realized that as bad as things were in the states, I—as a woman—had more opportunities here than anywhere else."[55]

Like Anna Marie, Ladybear first explored the United States, starting out in an old car and, when that broke down, using her thumb. Still craving adventure, she traveled to Europe and set out on the hippie trail through Turkey, Afghanistan, and Iran. She stopped in India and studied with a guru before returning home. Similarly Mara Devine moved from San Francisco to a commune in New Mexico, back to the Bay Area and several other communal households, and then on to India to study yoga. "I took my son, he was still in diapers, and we lived in this ashram . . . under this crazy guru named Swami Gitananda who was a real charlatan." She and her son then traveled around India and Europe before returning home and joining yet another commune."[56]

When they returned, hippie women brought back more than memories. Their appreciation of Asian and Middle Eastern textiles, furnishings, art, crafts, and clothing fueled new hippie fashion and home decorating trends—trends that caught on with mainstream consumers and retailers by the mid-1970s. Women similarly translated their knowledge of non-Western healing practices, yoga, and meditation into successful New Age business ventures. These, too, eventually appealed to a broader, middle-class clientele base. Finally, their exposure to new foods transformed the U.S. diet. Alice Waters's travels, particularly to France, left an indelible stamp on her approach to cooking and serving food. Counterculture cookbooks, such as *Moosewood* and the *Vegetarian Epicure*, carried recipes for Macedonian, Indonesian, and Balkan salads, felafel, gado-gado, samosas, spanakopita, dolmades, ratatouille, dal, bryani, and dozens of other international dishes. Soon, Americans more generally acquired a taste for the "exotic."

Other women, for economic or safety reasons, confined their roving to the United States. Terry Klein began hitchhiking between Portland, Oregon, and San Francisco while a senior in high school and remained on the road for several years to come. "We would just stumble on these scenes. . . . I was very loose. I guess hitchhiking was a huge part of it for me, because it was so footloose and fancy free, so 'here today and gone tomorrow.' I went for years where I didn't have a permanent residence and I never thought of myself as homeless." Sylvia Anderson similarly spent the Summer of Love in San Francisco, moved to Wheeler's Ranch and lived in a tent for a year, and then moved on to other communes before settling down for a longer period at the Farm in rural Tennessee. Jodi Mitchell, perhaps the most daring of all, "hitchhiked back and forth across the U.S. . . . numerous times, including once smack dab in the middle of a howling blizzard, crossing northern-most Interstate 80 of course!" A young runaway from West Virginia, Jodi was searching for an alternative family that would appreciate her curiosity, creativity, and need for freedom. She undoubtedly felt alone out on Interstate 80 between rides, but thousands of teenage girls across the United States had embarked on similar journeys. Their stories are the subject of the next chapter.[57]

6. LITTLE SISTERS
GIRLS OF THE COUNTERCULTURE

outh in the United States, from our nation's beginnings to the present, have run away in search of adventure and opportunity as well as to escape poverty, abuse, slavery, and involuntary servitude. During periods of upheaval — war, rapid industrial and urban expansion, and economic depression — runaway numbers have surged. In the 1930s, for example, boys and girls left home in unprecedented numbers, prompting the federal government to establish camps, shelters, vocational training, and work programs for transient youth. For the most part, however, these runaway episodes had a minimal impact on middle- and upper-middle-class Americans. When their boys ran off, it was generally as Huck Finn–like adventurers in search of thrills and excitement. A common and not unfounded stereotype was of the amusingly precocious son who ran off to join the circus or attend a forbidden amusement. Far fewer girls ran away, and those who did were cast in similar terms or as mentally unbalanced and misguided.[1]

This changed with the emergence of the counterculture. Quite suddenly the number of runaways skyrocketed. According to a report of the California state legislature, the FBI reported that in 1968 alone more than 100,000 runaways had been apprehended by authorities. This was only a fraction of the number that remained at large. According to Jeffrey Blum and Judith Smith's study, *Nothing Left to Lose,* "sensible" estimates put the national total at around a million. In large cities such as Boston and Chicago, the number of warrants for missing children doubled between 1965 and 1971. In the suburbs the increase was even more dramatic. By 1967, 11 percent of Americans under the age of eighteen were labeled as "delinquent," a majority for running away from home. Ken Libertoff stated that "what made this such an extraordinary occurrence was the fact that many, perhaps even a majority, of these youths were from comfortable middle- and upper-class families. Unlike most of their predecessors who, over the years, had frequently come from poor families, these runaways were both leaving and rejecting considerable material comforts, educational advantages, and future professional prospects."[2]

Even more troubling to middle-class parents, their daughters were a large part of the emerging "problem." By 1966 missing person reports filed on behalf of girls outnumbered those for boys. And once youth shelters were established later in the decade, intake workers reported that more girls than boys used their services. Although these figures do not necessarily indicate that female runaways outnumbered boys, they do point to a significant upturn in numbers—numbers that provoked a differential level of alarm and intervention. Perceived as more vulnerable by parents, law enforcement, and juvenile authorities, girls were arrested and incarcerated in greater numbers and institutionalized for longer terms than their male peers.[3]

Mainstream perceptions of female vulnerability were heightened by suspicion of the counterculture. Girls were no longer running away from unbearable home situations or chasing harmless amusements; they were flocking to hippiedom. In the minds of older adults, this meant exposure to sex, drugs, disease, filth, and antisocial, hedonistic values. Worse yet, the only slightly older hippies willingly harbored runaways and rarely cooperated with authorities during periodic sweeps of communes and "pads." Parents, juvenile authorities, and the media, uncomfortable with the notion that girls would willingly leave their clean, comfortable middle-class families for such an environment, portrayed female runaways as deviants in need of rehabilitation. Indeed, in 1970 the American Psychiatric Association classified running away as a mental disorder.[4]

If caught, girls were often incarcerated in juvenile detention facilities for "their own protection" and subjected to rigorous redomestication programs. For example, in April of 1971, 30 percent of the girls at Connecticut's Long Lane facility were confined for running away. An additional 58 percent were locked up for other, so-called status offenses such as sexual misconduct, truancy, missing overnight, and incorrigibility—predictors of more extreme rejections of adult authority such as flight. In contrast, only 2 percent of the boys at the state's male facility were in for running away. Another 10 percent were serving time for truancy and incorrigibility (none for sexual misconduct), but the majority (more than 75 percent) were in for real crimes such as theft, assault, and breaking and entering. Moreover, the girls, despite their "far less serious delinquencies," served longer terms of confinement with a staff devoted to turning out "good homemakers." As the former superintendent explained, Long Lane's treatment program consisted of "prevocational training with special emphasis on homemaking since the girls will eventually be homemakers, religious training, extra curricular activities through Girl Scouts, Tri-Hi-Y, Garden Club, Acrobatics Club, etc." There, and elsewhere, helping girls accept the middle-class domestic ideal was the apparent goal.[5]

But others had a different perspective on the "problem." Runaway shelters, founded and staffed by members of the counterculture as a response to the "deluge" and as an alternative to incarceration, served thousands of youth per year in the late 1960s and early 1970s. Their counselors, while agreeing that runaways were vulnerable, credited youth with greater agency. From their perspective, the runaway "problem" was part and parcel of a more general and healthy erosion of authority: "As young people see authority undermined and questioned on every front . . . it is natural that they will see the authority which affects them the most, that of the family, to grow more palpable, perhaps oppressive, and possibly intolerable." They went on to note that youth, witnessing their slightly older siblings ignore parental authority and set out across the United States in search of alternatives, found it difficult to wait until they were eighteen to do the same. Shelter workers, in keeping with their own dissatisfaction with mainstream culture, suggested that youth were fleeing from meaningless work, the alienation of suburban life, the sexual double standard, the substitution of material goods for "real" sources of happiness, and a destructive, amoral political structure. Girls, like their older female siblings, had additional reasons to rebel: the sexual double standard, confinement within the domestic sphere, and the lack of any rewarding, challenging career prospects. Why, they wondered, should on-the-road freedom be reserved for men? If conforming to traditional gender norms was difficult for the first wave of female hippies, it was even more problematic for girls; they had older role models who had already made a break for freedom.[6]

Girls' testimony supports this latter analysis and offers additional insight into their motives and experience. Constance Trouble recalled how her mother unwittingly sent her to a summer camp that was staffed by "drug using, sexually randy eighteen and nineteen year-old hippies. The older girl campers couldn't wait to be deflowered, and male staff and campers willingly obliged. It was one big sensual free-for-all, punctuated with serious discussions and antiwar songs around the campfire." When she returned home after the summer, she resented her mother's efforts to set limits. "Plus, my older sister, who was only sixteen, was amorously involved with a full-fledged, psychedelicized, free-love hippie. Spending time with them was like taking a class called Freedom Is Us 101." She began cutting school, hanging out with other hippie kids, sneaking out at night, and dating a man in his late teens. "My mother had me picked up by the police and incarcerated in juvenile hall for incorrigibility. On release during Thanksgiving, I ran away, was caught, and then sent away to a private girls' boarding school."[7]

Some parents, caught up in the media hype and fearful that their daughters were falling into the hippie lifestyle, took preemptive action and cracked down on seemingly trivial issues such as dress and hair. Diane ran away from Malden, a working-class community near Boston, because her parents were concerned about her appearance, insisting that "she cut off her long brown hair" and not "wear blue-jeans to school." They also "kept her inside the house for days at a time. After being grounded for weeks, she took off, dressed in blue-jeans, a coat, and a sweater, and now all she wanted to do was 'put as much distance' between herself and her parents as possible; what she wanted was to regain the sense of freedom she had before her parents had become so restrictive."

Ellie, a girl from western Massachusetts, had conflicts with her mother over dress and friends. Just prior to her flight, her mother called her a "disgrace to the family" for wearing jeans to a family gathering and "caught her lying about the friends she was seeing." Ellie made her way to Boston and found temporary housing at a runaway shelter, where counselors observed that "she was involved in making new friends, finding some place to stay, selling underground newspapers, and planning where to stay next." Julie, a runaway from Georgia, not only clashed with her mother over friends and clothing but over values as well. She described her mother as "really prejudiced . . . she doesn't like colored people and she doesn't like freaks. She doesn't like me in general because I'm different from everyone else in the family. . . . I wear my hair differently, I wore wire-rim glasses, I wore blue-jeans all the time. She expected me to change . . . not to have any colored friends . . . [or know] any people with long hair."[8]

Parental values and judgments also prompted sixteen-year-old Ellen to leave home and join a nearby commune called Oz. Her father, apparently reluctant to force her back home, attempted a dialogue:

ELLEN: "We were all going through the rebellion stage. . . . Our parents were down on us for the way we dressed. We knew what we didn't want—living like our parents who were brought up to hate. The hating begins with cliques in high school and carries over to the Apple Valley Country Club."

FATHER: "I just don't want you to spend the rest of your life contemplating your navel. We're living in an exciting time, a New Renaissance, when technology is pushing out frontiers for man. Look at the space shot."

ELLEN: "It doesn't impress me that we send men around the moon. It's internal discovery that's important."

FATHER: "I don't care what experiences you have. As long as they don't destroy you and you do something productive."

ELLEN: "What's productive? As long as I'm perceiving the world in all its beauty and dimension, I don't have to paint pictures."[9]

Once girls left home, they faced the daunting task of finding shelter and a means of support. Most gravitated toward college towns such as Berkeley, Santa Barbara, Boulder, Ann Arbor, Cambridge, or Boston; centers of hip culture such as the Haight Ashbury or Greenwich Village; or rural communes where they could connect and blend in with their slightly older peers. Unlike adult women, who could secure jobs, welfare, or food stamps, runaways had to rely on the generosity of others, panhandling, and free services provided by hippie institutions.[10]

As the numbers of runaways burgeoned, members of the counterculture stepped in to provide a host of free services: food, clothing, shelter, medical care, counseling, and legal assistance. By 1967 these providers began consolidating runaway services under a single roof. Starting with Huckleberry House in San Francisco, others soon followed: Looking Glass in Chicago, Bridge Over Troubled Waters and Sanctuary in Boston, Amicus House in Pittsburgh, and Runaway House in Washington, D.C. Rejecting the notion that runaways were delinquents or deviants, these providers believed that girls had the capacity to make their own decisions and supported their bid for autonomy and freedom. Although they encouraged contact and reconciliation with parents, they refused to force the issue. This approach was both philosophical and practical, based on respect for youth autonomy and the knowledge that many children would simply return to the streets if they felt pressured to contact their families. Parents and law enforcement officials were incensed, but many girls who would have otherwise been out on the streets found a nonthreatening, safe haven.[11]

Outside of these shelters, girls were much more vulnerable to sexual exploitation, poverty, and disease. Moreover, because they lacked a complete education and job skills, their odds of remaining on the streets even after reaching legal age were higher than for the older youth population.[12] Women's narratives describe these vulnerabilities, but also include accounts of resourcefulness, adaptability, accomplishment, and self-reliance.

Constance Trouble, whose rebellion landed her in a girl's boarding school, recalled, "I was immediately looking for a way out." On a field trip she split off from the other girls and approached a sympathetic-looking young couple who helped her "escape" to a nearby hippie beach enclave. She went on,

> At fourteen, I'm pretty sure I was the youngest person there, but at least a dozen others—girls and boys—were underage. We younger folk formed a little tribe, panhandling and hanging out at the beach by day, and sharing meals, music, romance, and marijuana by night. The only downside I remember was having my period and not being able to afford tampons, and being short on money for food. A couple of nights we made soup out of diluted catsup and ate it with little packets of saltines that someone had stolen from a restaurant.

In terms of sexual exploitation, "I never encountered any. For me, it was consensual and with a younger guy. In all, I was gone about three weeks, and my parents must have been frantic—it was right around the time the Manson thing was happening." She was finally caught by an undercover police officer, sent home, and incarcerated for three months in a juvenile facility until her father agreed to assume custody. "We reached an agreement: if I went to school and got good grades, I could pretty much have complete freedom. But looking back, I think I was pretty lucky."[13]

Jodi Mitchell, raised in West Virginia, met up with the counterculture in New York City during a summer stay with her grandmother. "I went back to W. VA a changed person, a master plan brewing in the back of my mind." Shortly after returning home, she ran away and ended up living on the streets of Berkeley, "surviving on a wing and a prayer and little more." There, she got by on "survival sex, dumpster diving, panhandling, petty theft, and just plain living by my wits." A local church offered regular free meals, and the People's Park free box provided clothes. She washed up in campus bathrooms and slept at crash pads in exchange for sex or—if she didn't feel like "paying"—in abandoned buildings, on roof tops, and in bushes on the streets.

One day, two young men from Wheeler's Ranch, "rescued" her off the streets and brought her home with them. For her, "Wheeler's was a place to heal and to grow, a retreat, to be nurtured in nature." A new friend, Sun, gave her a "tent, sleeping bag, kerosene and a lantern, matches, cook-pots, and food—just about everything I would need to set up housekeeping." Over the course of her stay, which spanned her late teens, others were equally generous. Older women shared food stamp and welfare-generated resources, information about edible and medicinal plants, and advice on spirituality, health, and nutrition.

Men, she noted, "never forced sex upon me or expected payback, they acted like brothers. Aware of my vulnerability and prior exploitation on the streets, they were extremely protective and caring." Wheeler's, as an open door commune, attracted some very strange characters, however. Bowie Bill, "a thuggish Daniel Boone type," was one of them. Although kind and protective toward Jodi, Bowie kept a "very tight rein on" Diane, the fourteen-year-old runaway who lived with him. Younger than Jodi, and much younger than Bowie Bill, Diane may have run out of other options. On Jodi's last day at Wheeler's, "I stopped by to say goodbye to her and she confessed she was a 14 year old runaway using an alias, her hair was died black, and her picture had been on the evening news as her parents had been desperately searching the Haight Ashbury district for her."[14]

Girls were indeed easy prey. If their older female peers had trouble setting limits, it was even more difficult for these economically dependent, emotionally immature youngsters. Some male members of the counterculture viewed sex with minors as perfectly normal. Underground comix and rock lyrics, such as R. Crumb's "Fritz the Cat" and Frank Zappa's "Brown Shoes Don't Make It," spoofed it, and poster and album cover art sexualized young female bodies. And the counterculture's belief that children were inherently wise and capable of making their own decisions helped assuage male opportunists' lingering doubts about the ability of minors to make their own choices. On the other hand, some young girls insisted that they *were* ready for sexual relationships and resented the sexual double standard that labeled them as helpless victims or promiscuous deviants. For all runaways, though, the issue of free choice was often complicated by their dependence upon older peers—those who could offer shelter, protection, food, and other essential resources. In the context of such dependence, the notion of having a "choice" was highly questionable.

Shannon Perry, like Diane at Wheeler's Ranch, clearly had few options. Only thirteen, Shannon moved among several communes during the nine months that she was on the run. With the exception of one rural, family-oriented commune in southern Oregon, she felt extremely confused and anxious: "My mind's saying one thing. My mind's saying 'sex is wide open, anything goes, it's all okay,' but emotionally it wasn't. Not being safe, and not having boundaries. And having some real situations where I felt taken advantage of by some of the men." One the other hand, Shannon maintained, "I developed a lot of strength, and a lot of independence."[15]

Other young runaways seized the initiative when it came to relationships with older men. Girl Dreyer, who had fallen in love with a budding psychedelic rock musician, ran away with her friend, Martha Wax, in order to join her lover. Singer David Crosby, at that time with the Byrds, hid them in Santa Monica's Tropicana Motel, and from there Girl and Martha traveled up to Big Sur and on to San Francisco. Arriving in the city, they connected with Girl's boyfriend, David Freiberg, who had just been released from jail. To keep Girl out of juvenile detention, the couple married, and shortly after Freiberg and four other musicians formed the soon-to-be-famous band, Quicksilver Messenger Service. Girl, however, still had a thirst for on-the-road freedom. "From time to time, being a wife and mother just no longer appealed to the young ex-runaway and off she would go."

Martha Wax, Girl's friend, became a partner of Rock Scully, who managed the Grateful Dead and inspired Paul Kantner of the Jefferson Airplane to write the song, "Martha," about her. Two other runaways also married Quicksilver men, and the band's collective household in Mill Valley "became something of a haven for runaway girls," who no doubt sought fame and glory as rock star groupies or consorts. Indeed, police made a practice of raiding the house to round up the latest batch of underage girls.[16]

Youth advocates, attempting to negotiate the fine line between coercion and free choice, decided that the best solution was to provide a safe haven in a nonjudgmental, nonthreatening environment. Girls such as Diane and Shannon, who escaped parental authority only to face exploitation at the hands of predatory males, would have another alternative. Others, such as Constance, Jodi, Girl, and Martha, could—if their luck or courage ran out—also find refuge. By the early 1970s state and federal legislators adopted their approach, decriminalizing status offences such as running away and appropriating funds for community-based programs that provided youth services outside of the traditional child welfare and juvenile justice systems. This development had a disproportionate impact on runaway girls. Parents reported them more frequently, and the police, perceiving them as more vulnerable, apprehended them at a higher rate than boys. And once caught, girls were more likely than boys to be committed to locked facilities because there were fewer placements for them in structured, community-based programs.

In the meantime, whether caught or not, most runaways remained connected to the counterculture. Phyllis Wilner, whom Peter Coyote regarded as the "first among equals in the Diggers," was never apprehended. She fled her parent's home in New York at fourteen and, as Coyote tells us, lived nomadically for several years, "spending time with the Hell's Angels, homesteading in the New Mexico wilderness, making numerous cross-country jaunts to New York City and then back, baking at the Free Bakery in Oakland, and gardening and looking after babies at Black Bear Ranch in the Trinity-Siskiyou Wilderness." Later she obtained her general equivalency diploma (GED), attended nursing school, and worked in a Himalayan refugee camp before returning to San Francisco and taking a job in the psychiatric ward at San Francisco General Hospital. In 1974 she moved back to the country near Arcata, California. Constance Trouble, although caught and placed in her father's custody, simply became "a hippie with good grades." As soon as she graduated from high school, she left home and joined a commune where she remained for the next eight years.[17]

While many girls ran to hippiedom, others were born into it. Girl children of counterculture parents often arrived in the world "naturally," delivered by fathers, family friends, and midwives in noninstitutional settings such as tents, buses, rustic cabins, gardens, forests, beaches, urban pads, and central gathering places on rural communes. Their names frequently reflected parents' spiritual, land-based, and tribal values: Moon, Rain, Rainbo, Sunshine, River, Sierra, Wind, Shakti, Raspberry, and Morning Star. As infants, girls remained close to their mothers, who usually ascribed to the notion that babies should be breast fed and given plenty of physical contact. For the sake of convenience and "bonding," parents and children frequently shared the same bed.[18]

In the sexually liberated environment of the counterculture, parents' relationships were tenuous at best. Men and women paired and re-paired with astonishing frequency, but children usually remained with their mothers. For many girls, their close relationship to their mothers would thus extend well beyond infancy. In communal settings, however, girls usually had several surrogate parents. Gilbert Zicklin says that at one commune, for example, "five-year old Heather went to one of several adults to be read to, to get food, to find clothes and to be put to sleep." Though her mother was attentive and the primary caregiver, "the child easily approached other women when her mother was busy or not interested in interacting with her." According to several studies, such arrangements produced children who were, as John Rothchild and Susan Wolf put it, "more self-confident, adept at creating and sustaining relationships, and less self-centered than their 'straight' peers." And while some communal families were less attentive to children's emotional and physical needs or banned kids completely, most treated them with respect and provided ample affection and guidance.[19]

The counterculture's definition of guidance, however, differed significantly from that of the mainstream. Like their peers who started runaway shelters, hippie parents placed a premium on child and youth autonomy. Regarding themselves as products of repressive, authoritarian child-rearing practices, they were determined to raise creative, tolerant, physically and emotionally expressive, egalitarian children. They rejected notions that children "belonged" to parents and had to

"Mother and Baby through Adobe Doorway," photograph by
Irwin Klein. Copyright 2008, Estate of Irwin Klein.

"Girls with Sheep," photograph by Irwin Klein.
Copyright 2008, Estate of Irwin Klein.

"Guppie and Expectant Mother in Kitchen," photograph by Irwin Klein. Copyright 2008, Estate of Irwin Klein.

be shaped into productive, responsible citizens. In their view, children were untainted by the fear, prejudice, and greed of the broader society and hence possessed a natural wisdom and keener sense of self. As such, children should be free to learn, explore, and grow in accordance with their self-defined interests, needs, and desires. Adults could gently guide and protect but only in a manner that enhanced this exploratory process.[20]

For girls this translated into very few limits and boundaries. As Chelsea Cain remarked, "Our parents offered us a rare freedom to create our lives as we chose. It was part of a larger commitment to freedom that came to define the hippie counterculture. . . . Those of us who felt safe in this freedom reveled in it, those of us who did not feel safe pined for structure, curfews, limits."

Suzanne Cody, apparently raised without limits *and* a sense of safety, was determined to offer something different to her own daughter. In her contribution to *Wild Child: Girlhoods in the Counterculture,* she swore to her infant "I will give you limits and guidelines and discipline when you willfully and unreasonably defy me." Moon Zappa, who felt similarly unmoored during her girlhood, also contributed to *Wild Child:* "At my house there were no rules, so there was nothing to rebel against. I hated it. It always left me with an awful floating feeling . . . of too much space, of too many choices. I felt very often (and still do) like I was doing a moon walk and my cord came loose from the ship. Ick. I craved rituals and rules like my friends had. I prayed for curfews and strictly enforced dinner times. Uniforms and organized events and people with goals amazed me."[21]

Parents not only eschewed setting limits but also actively rejected societal values and norms. This could be embarrassing and confusing for children, as described by Gilbert Zicklin in *Countercultural Communes.* Lara, not even in her teens, "knew," for instance, "that other children didn't curse the way she did or do 'freaky' things like invite a guest at the farm to fuck her in the barn. On trips to town, Lara would observe the way parents treated their children and comment about how straight they were." She also recognized that her extended communal family existed outside of larger, societal limits. On one trip to town "she saw a sheriff's car and excitedly burst out, 'Pigs, Rachel, pigs! We could get busted.'" Rachel, one of her surrogate mothers, "reassured her that the 'pigs' had no reason to bust her, but Lara seemed uneasy when the police were around." Similarly, Francesca Fortunato recalled,

> I remember (knowing that pot was illegal) the constant fear that the "man" would come and bust my parents, haul them off to jail and leave us (brother and self) even less cared for than we were already. I was terrified when, at school, I made friends with a police officer's daughter. I found excuses to spend all our playtime at her place, the playground or the mall. No way was I letting such a potentially dangerous person in our house.[22]

Other girls simply longed for normalcy. Rain Grimes recalled in *Wild Child* that "I was so free to become who I wanted to be that I just wanted to be like everyone else." Similarly, Adriana Barton was so "desperate to be normal, I rarely invited kids over. They would see the outboard motor stored in plain view in our dining room. They would see my hyperactive 6-year old brother leaping around the house, naked as a monkey, slowing down only to retract his foreskin to gross us out. My friends would inevitably turn up their noses at the snack foods they were offered." Whiz Perry, echoing this sentiment, stated that "what I really craved was the seemingly normal lives the other kids had—real moms and dads, normal clothes, lockets and friendship bracelets, posters of movie stars and TV sets. Most of all, I wanted to be a Girl Scout just like the other girls in my class."[23]

Parents, while valuing girls' freedom, also valued their own—especially when it came to mobility. This, too, could provoke longing for a "normal" childhood. Before the age of seven, Carin Clevidence lived "in a Canadian commune, an apartment in Greenwich Village, a tree house, a teepee and a white Dodge van named Hippo." In the meantime, Carin's uncle was recreating Mayan agricultural practices on an experimental farm in Belize. When Carin was seven and her sister, Shelly, was five, her mother decided to lend a hand. Once in Belize, they lived in a house on stilts with "an old-fashioned palm roof" that "had two rooms furnished almost entirely with hammocks." The girls bathed in the river, ate rice and beans for "breakfast, lunch and dinner," attended the local school, and socialized with the local residents. When her uncle temporarily suspended his experiment and returned to Minnesota with his family, Carin's mother took a job working in the sugarcane fields—"the only woman who did"—to support her family. After she contracted hepatitis, she returned to the United States with Carin and Shelly. A year later, she told her daughters that they were going back to Belize, and Carin refused to go.[24]

Rain Grimes, born on a kitchen table in a cabin in rural Pennsylvania, also remembers a life of travel. A year and a half after her birth, her parents packed up and moved to the state of Washington. "We lived my parents' hippie dream in various New Age communities in Washington's Skagit Valley and, later, in Sedona, Arizona. When I was six, we traveled across the country again, this time to Ithaca, New York, in a red Dodge van." Finally they settled in Beantown, Wisconsin, where they remained for "thirteen long years." Rain's relief at finally settling down was offset by her exotic, outsider status as a member of one of the few hippie families in the area.[25]

Lisa Michaels was doubly on the move. After her parents divorced, Lisa moved between them. Her mother and stepfather, after taking Lisa on a cross-country trek in a refitted mail truck, finally settled down in a rural community in northern California to pursue *their* dream of self-sufficiency. But like Rain, Lisa felt like somewhat of an outsider in the mostly straight community. Periodic stays with her preoccupied, restless father, a former member of the Weather Underground, contributed to her feelings of being uprooted and on the sideline of her parents' countercultural-radical experiments. Joelle Fraser similarly recalled having several "fathers" in dizzying succession, which "almost always meant a hasty move to a new house in town, which often required a new school." She reflected how it soon became "natural . . . to withdraw a bit, to keep my distance" and that she "was accepted or rejected and often a combination of the two. Trust became something hard to hold on to, harder to hold than air, than water." At the same time she regularly visited her biological father, a man with a serious drinking problem, who lived in Hawaii.[26]

The counterculture's attitudes toward sexuality posed additional perils and opportunities for girls. Most hippies ascribed to the notion that the industrial capitalist system was built on the sublimation of sexual desire. If erotic impulses continued to be suppressed and channeled into maintaining the status quo, the future was bleak: more human exploitation, consumption, materialism, greed, atomization, and environmental degradation. But if desire was liberated—especially from the constraints of monogamy and prohibitions of pre- and extramarital sex — utopia was at hand. Play, sensual pleasure, and cooperative and egalitarian relationships would rise to the top of the human values hierarchy.[27]

Thus, free, open, unconstrained sexual expression was construed as a revolutionary act, one that was an integral part of creating a new world order. Children, parents believed, were as yet untouched by the sexual inhibitions of straight society and should remain free of the hang-ups that plagued the older generation. They should be free to explore and discover their own, authentic, "natural" sexuality. Girls, then, were caught up in a radically shifting construction of both childhood and sexuality — constructions that were still vague and abstract and that lacked concrete rules and guidelines. Many adults, especially those who were attempting to exorcize their own inhibitions, were ill equipped to set limits for their children.

Many girls, as a consequence, were exposed to adult language and sexual behavior. Moreover, they were relatively free to engage in sexual play with childhood friends and allowed to decide when they were ready for more serious encounters. In this sexually "liberated" environment, girls were less constrained by the sexual double standard and encouraged to feel positive about their bodies and sexual desire. At the same time, some parents had difficulty balancing their respect for youth autonomy with factors that might prevent their daughters from making their own choices: age, confusing sex with the need for affection, wanting to fit in, seeking adult and peer approval, and not wanting to be perceived as repressed or "hung-up." In a few cases, allowing young girls to "decide for themselves" or failing to provide adequate supervision led to child sexual exploitation or molestation. Fortunately, most parents drew the line at child-adult sex.[28]

Nevertheless, girls — with varying degrees of success — had to decide for themselves how, when, and where to express their sexuality. Elizabeth She recalled in *Wild Child* that "my parents, happy practitioners of free love, didn't teach me safety, or boundaries. I was primed to be the sexiest, the wildest, the least hung up. . . . Untainted by rules and regulations. Unconstrained. Free. These days I have so many hang-ups, I'm surprised I can walk down the street without tripping." Others recalled feeling embarrassment and pressure. For Francesca Fortunato, "the sexual 'freedom' really was embarrassing and difficult to deal with. I, too, remember living room floor orgies and whipped cream cans littering every corner in the morning." As Jody West stated in David Allyn's *Make Love Not War,*

> [I] really appreciated that my parents were so open about sex, but, at the same time, I felt more pressure to lose my virginity from my father and stepmother than from anyone else. When I had my first date with a boy—I'd never even been kissed—I brought him over for a soda or something. My father found out he was coming over and put condoms on every bed in the house. I was so embarrassed I wanted to cry.

Earlier, when she was eleven, her parents had asked whether she wanted "to watch them have sex. I said no, of course, but that only reinforced my image as the family prude."[29]

Whiz Perry's early sex education made her a "smarter teen" but caused some embarrassment as well. Having watched her midwife mother deliver babies, she understood the connection between sex and pregnancy. "Anytime I was tempted to have unprotected sex in the heat of the moment, I just remembered that view from the birthing room and I was suddenly okay with waiting." She went on to observe: "But this openness about sex and reproduction was another two-sided gift from my mom. . . . In the fifth grade I tried to correct some of my classmates' misconceptions about sex. I explained in graphic detail where babies really came from—and how they get made—to a group of kids on the playground. Some simpering girl went home, told her mom, who in turn called the school outraged." The next day she was reprimanded by the principal and sent home with a letter of warning for her mother.[30]

Drugs posed an additional problem. Counterculture parents, as frequent users of marijuana and stronger psychedelics, struggled with the issue of setting appropriate limits for their children and adopted a wide variety of positions and strategies. On the more liberal end of the spectrum, some were open about their own drug use and shared substances with curious or insistent children. For example, if girls expressed interest in trying marijuana, parents or older adults often passed them a joint. This, as one sociologist observed, was part of a larger pattern of valuing children's judgment and autonomy and including them in family and group social rituals. LSD, peyote, and mescaline, however, were generally shared with greater discretion and supervision.

On the opposite end of the spectrum, a smaller number of parents were discreet about their own use and strongly discouraged their "naturally high" children from using any drugs at all. Most parents, however, fell somewhere in between, neither hiding their own drug use nor actively encouraging and supplying their children. As Ben Schwabe recalled in "The Hippie Mom and Others Respond," "there were many hippie parents, like mine, for example, who were able to raise freedom-loving children without exposing us to more danger than your average (let's say square for old time sake) kid. My parents didn't impose any freedoms on us; we had to find our own pot to smoke. As a result I ended up trying pot later than many of my square classmates."[31]

Whether they joined in or not, girls were often exposed to the consequences of parents' drug use: fear of legal authorities, parental neglect and distraction, and violence associated with drug dealing. Whiz Perry "got to see firsthand that drugs don't make you a freer person. They chain you to addiction, numbing your motor skills and rendering you incapable of motivation and responsibility." Her peers, she reported, felt the same way: "The Farm kids knew all too well that drugs did not encourage mom to feed you regularly, or to remember to sign your homework, or even get you to a doctor." Some children also felt embarrassed about how drug use reflected on their families and communities. "When somebody at the Farm got busted for growing pot, we were humiliated, and downplayed the event [at school], saying it wasn't the same place we lived."

Everywhere, growing, manufacturing, and using drugs were risky. Gabriel Golden recalled that "in my case, my mother's desire to divorce my father and 'find herself' resulted not only in a total lack of discipline and boundaries, it also resulted in her murder when I was ten years old, the result of a drug deal gone bad." Although spared such dire consequences, Francesca Fortunato expressed disgust at her father's seeming lack of self-control. "I remember one of Dad's friends (and a fellow member of his amateur rock band, 'Diablo') writing a song about his [her father's] enthusiasm for all manner of drugs (called 'Junk Man's Dream'). What a sweet tribute to a friend." These and similar stories suggest that many counterculture girls were probably less likely to experiment with drugs than their straight peers.[32]

Despite their sometimes grim and gritty assessments of the particulars, girls appreciated their parents' efforts to try something new. As Lisa Michaels was quoted in "The Kids Are All Right," in retrospect they often felt "a real sense of gratitude for the freedom and respect they were given" and were eventually able to place their own experience within a broader cultural and historical context. Straight kids, they observed, felt crippled and victimized by too many restrictions, domestic violence, an authoritarian mode of discipline, and parents' alcohol abuse problems and often envied their hippie peers. Age and education also brought the realization that their experience wasn't wholly unique. As Micah Perks observed in "The Kids Are All Right," "I realized my childhood was in some ways a quintessential American childhood. . . . What came together in the '60s wasn't some weird, anomalous moment in our history. It's something that's happened over and over in America: a desire for utopia. From the colonial period to the religious communities of the 19th century to the '60s, this is a movement that rises up again and again."

Most "wild as a baby goat" countercultural children survived their unstable upbringings and became responsible and productive adults. All fourteen of the women who recorded their stories in *Wild Child: Girlhoods in the Counterculture* are creative and interesting adults who work as actors, writers, photographers, filmmakers, playwrights, and mothers. Their stories underscore the observations of a straight peer, Alan Sailer, in "The Hippie Mom and Others Respond": "I knew quite a few 'hippie children' in high school. They were for the most part, infinitely funnier, smarter, better read, more spontaneous and less hung up than the rest of us. And they were far happier too." In the end, their parents' struggle to escape their own restrictive upbringings and test a new ideal yielded results no less imperfect than those realized by successive generations of well-meaning U.S. parents.[33]

Finally, narratives indicate that children's experience varied according to whether they were born into the counterculture or introduced to it later. Jan Camp had two young children at the time she abandoned the straight world and became a hippie. Her five-year-old daughter had much more difficulty adapting to the lack of structure than her younger son, and eventually she went to live with her father, remarking that "I need to go live with my dad where there's two parents when I come home from school and carpets on the floor." Her daughter's discomfort with the hip lifestyle reached its height in fourth grade, when—in their mostly straight community—peer pressure to be "normal really kicked in." In contrast, Jan had relocated to a hippie-dominated community by the time her son had reached the same age, and he—already immersed in the counterculture—was much less self-conscious.

Finally, most counterculture women were more likely to delay child-bearing than their nonhippie peers, waiting until their late twenties and early thirties to start families. This meant that a majority of children born to hippie parents arrived after the attractions of free love, drugs, and physical mobility had subsided. Anna Marie Daniels, for example, had her first and only child at age thirty-eight, long after she had settled into a stable second marriage and career. By that time, she and many other counterculture mothers had modified their child-rearing philoso-phy. While still emphasizing intellectual autonomy, creativity and in-dependence, emotional and physical affection, acceptance of the body, and openness about sexuality, she sheltered her daughter from adult sexual behavior, drug use and language (no television!), provided a safe and structured physical environment, and regarded marital harmony and stability as absolutely essential to successful parenting. Like girls raised a decade earlier, her daughter ate organic food, attended a "free" elementary school, frolicked in the nude, played with handcrafted toys, was at home in the adult world, and felt free to express her emotions and question adult authority. The difference was that these activities now occurred in a more structured, stable setting, with firmer limits and boundaries. Indeed, this modified style of hippie parenting had, by the 1980s, become mainstream, almost completely alleviating the stress and embarrassment associated with being "freaky" or "weird." As the next chapter discusses, parenting wasn't the only aspect of hippie culture to enter the mainstream. Indeed, counterculture women were integral to the New Age lifestyle movements of the 1980s and 1990s—movements that permeated middle-class culture and transformed relationships to self, spirituality, health, work, and the environment.[34]

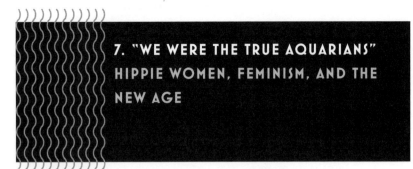

omen of the counterculture embraced feminism slightly later than their New Left peers, in the early to mid-1970s as opposed to the late 1960s. Moreover, most hippie women adopted a feminism that affirmed and celebrated "natural" or "essential" female characteristics, in contrast to the radical feminist position that gender, as a social construct, was at the root of women's oppression. By the late 1970s counterculture women, much like nineteenth-century social housekeepers, were using the notion of female difference to carve out spheres of influence in emerging movements: New Age spirituality, holistic health, ecofeminism, antinuclear and peace activism, and food politics. Indeed, women's claim of a deeper connection to nature, the body, and emotions and of greater intuitive and nurturing abilities gave them a decided edge in many of these new movements—an edge that they parlayed into leadership positions and successful entrepreneurial ventures. Thus, hippie women's influence, as agents of cultural transformation, increased and extended well beyond the 1960s and 1970s.

Although the counterculture's role in shaping lifestyle choices of the 1970s and 1980s is increasingly well documented, much of the literature focuses on the role of male "cultural entrepreneurs," such as the *Whole Earth Catalog*'s editor Stewart Brand, in brokering hippiedom's tastes, preferences, and practices to a broader public. Women, as this chapter argues, were even more central to this process. They not only dominated many New Age movements; they were the primary consumers of holistic, "natural," and self-help products and services. Before becoming cultural intermediaries, however, hippie women first became feminists. Indeed, their feminist awakening—and the type of feminism

they chose—explains both their influence within and the unique characteristics of various New Age movements.[1]

Feminism, many contemporary observers noted, came late to the
counterculture. Throughout the 1960s, hippie women were focused
on highly personal, individual quests for self-realization and spiritual
enlightenment that were exciting and stimulating. At the same time,
they were pushing the boundaries of cultural and social convention in
ways that seemed plenty edgy and novel. Women were not simply cooking, cleaning, and minding children; they were bursting out of nuclear
families, establishing and joining new tribes, experimenting with sexual
freedom and open marriage, devising methods for educating "free" children, and learning a myriad of new skills: organic gardening, composting, canning, animal husbandry, midwifery, holistic healing, and crafts
production. In short, they were filled with a sense of purpose, on a mission to recreate themselves and cultivate a new social order.[2]

Conflicts arose when many women decided that men were not only
less committed to this utopian vision but also devalued women's work.
As reported by Richard Atcheson, Ian, a male member of a Palo Alto
commune, summarized the lack of male commitment in this way: "The
girls were first and foremost into having a commune. I think they worked
too hard at it. After a while they got mad when the guys wouldn't work
as hard, would, you know, forget to do stuff, miss their jobs, or leave
a mess. They were into fair sharing but the guys were undependable
and the girls couldn't stand it." Peter Coyote, as noted in an earlier
chapter, acknowledged that women's labor was essential to sustaining
the Diggers' communal households and food distribution networks, but
confessed that "all of our 'appreciation' of the women and their work did
not extend to valuing that work as dearly as our own."

Indeed, by the early 1970s many women concluded that men weren't
doing much of anything except indulging in male posturing, ego-
tripping, endless theoretical discussions, philandering, tinkering with
trucks and tractors, getting high, and pursuing what Jentri Anders referred to as "existential, on-the-road freedom."[3]

As their dissatisfaction grew, most women turned to a feminism in
keeping with the counterculture's gender norms and values system. Although hippies challenged some of the mainstream's most sacred mores, they unquestioningly accepted the notion that women, because of

their reproductive function, were ruled by instinct, emotion, sentiment, intuition, and the senses rather than reason. They also accepted the corollary assumption that women, as "givers of life," were receptive, nurturing, cooperative, averse to conflict, and inescapably bound to the body and nature. It is interesting that this construction of the feminine corresponded with the counterculture's ideal of the new person and new society. The Aquarian age, according to hippie disciples, would usher in a new social order based on what Allen Ginsberg termed the "affection-ate feminine" in which kindness, tenderness, cooperation, reciprocity, interdependence, open expression of affection and sexual desire, egali-tarianism, tolerance, nonaggression, and playfulness would form the basis of human interaction.

In their nonrepressive culture, Eros would reign supreme. The West-ern notion that instinct, intuition, emotion, and sensuality are "eternally hostile and detrimental to reason" would be replaced with an exuberant, life-affirming irrationality that would overcome Western civilization's death wish. Along with Herbert Marcuse, hippies believed that Western culture, in order to save itself, needed to embrace the "female principle of sexual pleasure which it has historically characterized as fatal in the work-world of civilization." Indeed, the counterculture maintained that the so-called rational was what had led the United States into the abyss of war, overconsumption, greed, competition, environmental degrada-tion, and the death of the imagination.[4]

Given this convergence of counterculture values and gender con-structs—that women naturally possessed the very qualities that the counterculture lauded—it should come as no surprise that most hippie women seized on difference to claim authority and power within their movement. In contrast, women of the New Left were struggling to gain credibility and influence within the very public, male-identified arena of political activism—a sphere in which rational debate over theory, tactics, and strategy constituted work of value. As long as women were perceived as inherently irrational, emotional, sentimental, and intuitive, their male peers could justify treating "sisters in struggle" as second-class citizens. Thus it made sense for many women of the New Left to adopt a feminism that denied or at least attempted to denaturalize dif-ference, one that branded "feminine" characteristics as fictions or social constructs.

To large segments of U.S. society the denial of difference was highly alarming, even incomprehensible. It threatened not only individual identity but also deeply entrenched personal and institutional relationships. Many hippie women, in light of their emerging difference-based claim to power, shared some of the mainstream's reservations. Radical feminists had, after all, characterized their labor on behalf of social change as mere drudgery, sexual exploitation, and domestic slavery. In contrast, hippie women viewed their work as an expression of the "affectionate feminine," the very values that would create a more nurturing, compassionate, generous, peaceful world. Marylyn Motherbear Scott put it this way:

> I had turned away from political feminism. I had thirty years of marriage. I was not, by nature a political feminist. And when these women wanted me to go to these meetings, I wasn't interested. I'm totally grateful for the feminist movement . . . but then it was devoid of the spiritual, and it was like women were becoming men, taking on male roles. Yeah, it was female, but they had to masculinize in order to compete.

She went on to reflect that her feminist consciousness took root on the land:

> It was being on the land where the Mother Goddess began to speak most intimately to me, by being in nature, by knowing the passage of the seasons, by experiencing it full on. It wasn't book learning, it was experiential.[5]

By the mid-1970s counterculture publications began to affirm the "experiential" basis of hippie women's emerging feminist consciousness. For example, *The Green Revolution,* a publication geared toward back-to-the-landers, devoted its January 1976 issue to women. The author of the lead editorial, like the authors of *Laurel's Kitchen* cookbook, stressed that women could change the world by applying their "natural" qualities in the home. "Why," the author asked, "do Women Liberationists clamor for equality with men, as though they'd thereby be raised a notch?" She went on to argue: "But isn't woman's best chance of changing the world dependent on her having the freedom to exercise her superior nurturing, loving qualities? And could there be any better place for those qualities to blossom than a truly-functioning home?" By "home" she was referring not to the traditional nuclear, suburban family but to "a home on the land inhabited by an extended three or four generation family (with or without blood ties)." The same issue featured a poem entitled "Mother's Day," celebrating the warmth, beauty, and joy that homemakers lovingly bestow upon their families.[6]

Affirmation of a difference-based feminist vision also came from a wider community of counterculture women. In Mateel, a hippie community in southern Humboldt County, Jentri Anders observed that the feminist awakening involved women's "learning to accept and love themselves as women" and to realize that other women afforded greater support and affirmation than their freedom-seeking men folk. "Forced by motherhood to recognize their dependency, they could relate to each other from more tribal self images." She went on to note, "The bonds created by women helping each other give birth and mother, organizing play groups, schools, and child care arrangements to share the responsibility and provide early social training for children, are among the strongest unifying forces in Mateel."[7] Karen Lee Robins also pointed to the importance of female bonding as a counterculture version of radical feminist consciousness-raising. "As a new mother I found myself entering a whole new very emotional, yet very earthy realm of life. I loved the kids but was very confused and frustrated over the role. Meantime, though, my circle of women friends was defining itself. Precious bonding experiences were occurring and eventually, Mother earth herself was wrapping me in her arms and ancient and nostalgic feelings were surfacing from deep within."[8]

Through "learning to accept and love themselves as women" and their "precious bonding experiences," hippie women began to elaborate on their feminist vision. In the process, many concluded that their "sisters" provided greater support and affirmation than men and that women were the true keepers of Aquarian values. They began to emphasize not just individual empowerment but also, according to Mimi Albert in "Women of Wisdom," "the importance of reawakening and reclaiming feminine wisdom for all humanity." Pelican, for example, in her article "Birth of a New Age," asserted that "it is our task now to emphasize with our lives the positive feminine powers as we develop the new ways of the new age." She went on to state that the collapse of the old male-dominated order "is frightening [but] is making way for spiritual rebirth of the feminine energies on earth." Patricia Mische, writing for *New Age* magazine, made much the same point: "The values that have been labeled 'feminine'—love, compassion, cooperation, patience—are badly needed in giving birth and nurturing a new era of greater peace and justice in human history."[9]

This difference-based feminist vision, as detailed in other parts of this chapter, encouraged hippie women to move outside of their homes and communes and into New Age movements. But in the shorter term, it led many women to demand authority and respect in their personal relationships and extended communal families. Women at the Diggers' Black Bear Ranch, for example, launched a feminist coup around 1974 and kicked the "cowboys" out. Bennett Berger observed several communes where women similarly took over, pushing out men who wouldn't conform to the new, women-centered order. In some cases, the sexually liberated climate of the counterculture led women to adopt bisexual, lesbian, and transgender identities. This generated additional impetus for a woman-identified feminist model. For example, at the Lime Saddle commune near Oroville, Mara Devine recalled that "many of the women were discovering their own sexuality both as lesbians and bisexuals, and there was a lot of movement toward feminist causes and feminist writing, even amongst some of the men." Eventually, however, the men "just all left en masse," feeling too threatened by the new power dynamic and the fact that "a lot of the women were coming out as lesbians."[10]

Indeed, according to Bennett Berger, a growing number of hippie women "began to realize that they didn't even need the men for sexual gratification" and joined together with lesbian and bisexual defectors from the radical feminist camp to celebrate and affirm women's difference through separatist institutions, gatherings, concerts, workshops, and communes. For example, Nancy Jean, who was a married mother when she first joined the counterculture, discovered her lesbian identity during a group sex encounter initiated by her husband. After several years of being a model hippie woman—consenting to open marriage, experimenting with drugs, helping run a food co-op, and joining with friends to establish a shelter for runaway youth and a free school—she joined the emerging women's culture and moved in with her female lover.

Mara Devine had a similar awakening. After her son's father fled to Canada to escape the draft, she joined a San Francisco Bay Area commune called the Transoceanic Egg. "And when the Egg broke up, that was when I had my first full-blown affair with a woman, and I was really freaked out. I didn't know what it meant, and I decided to run away and go to India." After returning home, she joined the Lime Saddle commune and participated in its transformation into an all-women enclave. Other women took off for newly established separatist communes such as WomanShare, Cabbage Lane, Dragonwagon, Rootworks, and A Woman's Place. Some of these communes published magazines and newsletters geared toward rural self-sufficiency, feminist spirituality, holistic healing, and ecofeminism. They also hosted "gatherings" where, as reported in *Womanspirit*, they "sowed the seeds of a new matriarchal vortex of spiritual energy" through music, dance, chanting, ritual, and workshops on astrology, tarot, palmistry, nutrition, yoga, massage, and herbal remedies.[11]

It is interesting to note that one hip commune preempted the feminist revolt before it hit full force by adopting a modified, almost nineteenth-century version of cultural feminism. Stephen Gaskin and his followers, who established the Farm in rural Tennessee, rendered heterosexual sex, as a means of harmonizing male and female energies, sacred. According to Stephen, women's nurturing energy was particularly important in tempering the male's aggressiveness and propensity for dominance—traits that threatened communal harmony. In 1970, as commune members caravanned across country in search of land, Stephen announced that sexual intimacy between couples signified "betrothal" and pregnancy a commitment to wed as soon as possible.

Once established, the Farm adopted a highly traditional division of labor where men worked in various communal enterprises and women tended to domestic chores. Women's work—at least rhetorically—was imbued, however, with moral significance. Their nurturing, life-sustaining "juice," expressed through the sex act and their household labor, was deemed essential to the communal enterprise. "Ladies," Stephen asserted in *Hey Beatnik,*

are supposed to take it upon themselves to create a field around them as far as their influence can reach that's nice and smells good and is clean and a good place to be. Any lady who wants to can just insist on it being that way as far as she can see. And men are supposed to be really chivalrous and really knightly and help out to do that. How's that for a Noble Idea?

Given the counterculture's general acceptance of gender duality, this emphasis on the value of women's work, the importance of female energy, and male responsibility helped avert the type of cultural feminist coups that were occurring elsewhere.[12]

Although a majority of hippie women gravitated toward difference-oriented or cultural feminism, a small minority chose other options. Constance Trouble, for example, "never accepted the Yin/Yang gender duality stuff. I just intuited that men and women weren't different." She went on to reflect, "I pretty much decided to live outside of the category 'woman' even if no one else was. I thought that was really countercultural." Jan Camp, an artist, also rejected difference-oriented feminism, a particularly brave position given that most of her female peers began producing "women's" art in response to the cultural feminist awakening. After she joined the counterculture and moved out to the country, she encountered "a community of dykes and they wanted me to be in their camp. But I didn't feel that the way they viewed men would be a good thing for my son who was going to be a man." At that point she decided that "woman" was a construct—a social or political identity that one could either choose or reject. "And I decided that what position you wanted to take as a 'woman' was a choice that didn't pertain to me. That being an artist, it didn't really matter whether you were a woman or not. It mattered that you make life an art form—and that transcends gender." She went on to reflect, "Making the choice to be an artist is making the choice to go under the wire, go under the radar of a lot of the restrictions and norms that people who choose other identities have to cope with—relationships to gender, to authority become something totally different, because, from the artist's vantage point everything is material, is content, stuff to be used rather than something to be conformed to."[13]

Despite such critiques of difference, the majority of hippie women— regardless of sexual orientation—ascribed to cultural feminism. Moreover, they configured themselves as the true bearers of counterculture values. Their new power and authority, which derived from this conviction, found full expression in New Age spiritual and self-help movements. As described in an earlier chapter, counterculture women sought spiritual enlightenment and self-realization through a wide variety of drugs, nonconventional therapies, practices, and traditions. Although encompassing a dizzying array of alternatives, women's spiritual journeys shared common features: rejection of dominant religious authority and emphasis on recovering an authentic self that is "aligned with natural, vital, and cosmic forces" and capable of intuiting and manifesting what is good, true, and right for the individual. Moreover, many women gravitated toward alternatives that accepted, as given, gender duality—masculine and feminine energies that could be harmonized, balanced, or channeled for individual and collective benefit.[14]

Well before the cultural feminist awakening, spiritual and self-realization alternatives created small, but relatively significant, openings for female participation and influence. Many were loosely organized, nonhierarchical, and experimental, which afforded women greater leadership opportunities. Many also enjoined followers to "be here now," develop their intuitive powers, and get in touch with their bodies, feelings, and nature—all of which women did "naturally." Finally, many acknowledged the importance of female energy or even the "divine feminine," a significant improvement over many established religious traditions. By the mid-1970s, hippie women, armed with the certainty that they were more in tune with cosmic and creative forces than men, enlarged these openings and essentially stormed the gates of the temple.

Women's expanding influence was most evident in neopagan, Wiccan, and Native American traditions, in the occult and mystical arts, and in self-realization and self-improvement therapies. Hippie women not only assumed leadership roles as priestesses, witches, shamans, seers, oracles, guides, and therapists; they eventually monopolized entire fields or specializations by virtue of their superior "natural" powers. Moreover, many women channeled their unique powers into successful business ventures. Hippie alternatives, far from dying out after the 1960s, became mainstream, middle-class lifestyle choices—consumer options—that paid handsome dividends well into the 1990s.[15]

The Church of All Worlds (CAW), arguably one of the most influential forces behind the U.S. pagan revival, illustrates the growing influence of hippie women in counterculture–turned–New Age spiritual movements. In the early 1960s Tim Zell, a student at Missouri's Westminster College, started a science fiction club after reading Robert Heinlein's *Stranger in a Strange Land.* His off-campus residence soon became a site of interpersonal and sexual experimentation, modeled on the book's central character, Michael Valentine Smith (the man from Mars). Zell and his friends were particularly impressed with Smith's lack of physical inhibition; open, trusting, and intuitive mode of communication; and conviction that human interaction (including sexual congress) was an expression of the divine. Hence, they greeted each other by saying, "Thou art God," later expanded to include "Thou art Goddess."[16]

In 1968, having attracted a growing hippie following, they incorporated as CAW. Shortly thereafter, CAW adopted an environmental platform, emphasizing the divinity of both humans and nature. Like Feraferia, a neopagan, countercultural organization founded around the same time, CAW placed "increasing emphasis on ecology and eco-psychic reverent identification with Nature as a means of teaching man to love his Earth, his mother, his home in a hostile universe," according to a 1970 issue of "Green Egg." This new focus on earth as the Divine Mother, the ultimate expression of the female principle, created an opening for women to claim greater authority within the organization by virtue of their closer affinity with nature. In 1972, for example, CAW's newsletter, "Green Egg," carried an article by W. Holman Keith that urged neopagan organizations to initiate an earth-reverent, matrifocal-matriarchal renaissance as well as a critical letter from H.R.M. to the editor complaining that CAW was indeed shifting toward an emphasis on the goddess as opposed to the gods.[17]

By 1973, the drift toward the goddess and feminine values was even more apparent. In the mid-summer issue of "Green Egg," Tim Zell wrote, "All so-called 'Great Religions' of the modern world are essentially patrist, and there is no true place in them for women, while nearly all Pagan religions are matrist by their very nature, and the Priestess of the Goddess is the highest possible honor." An accompanying article by W. Holman Keith criticized radical feminists for trying to "out-man the men in a man's world" and encouraged women readers to take the more radical position of affecting social change by embracing the divine feminine and their inherent power as women. Later that year, Tim announced to CAW members that his wife had left him and that he had met a new woman at the September 1973 Gnostic Aquarian Festival. Morning Glory, a self-described "hippie witch," had recently left her husband and daughter in Eugene, Oregon, to follow the pagan path. Now, as Tim's "total mate," she, her daughter Rainbow, and her eight-foot boa constrictor, Ophelia, would be joining him at CAW headquarters in St. Louis.[18]

The following year, Morning Glory was listed as coeditor of the "Green Egg" and ordained as a priestess in CAW. From 1974 on, she and CAW championed difference-based feminist spirituality that privileged "Holy Mother Nature" and the divine feminine. Despite its cultural feminist slant, however, CAW never embraced a separatist model. As Morning Glory maintained, masculine and feminine energy—a balance of yin and yang—were necessary to complete each individual and preserve harmony in the universe. In emphasizing the feminine, CAW was merely restoring balance that had been lost when pagan traditions had been suppressed by patriarchal, monotheistic religions.[19]

From CAW and Feraferia, neopaganism spread outward, attracting a large following among counterculture women with its emphasis on the divine feminine. In its August 1, 1974, newsletter, CAW published a directory of North American pagan organizations, listing twelve associations and councils, twenty-three initiatory cult orders, and twenty-three neopagan religious orders. By the mid-1980s, there were hundreds. CAW, alone, had become an international organization with thousands of "nests" worldwide. Mirroring the cleavage within the cultural feminist movement, some of these neopagan organizations adopted a separatist orientation, maintaining that pure feminine energy was not only essential to women's spiritual growth and empowerment but also necessary for the health of the planet. For a brief time, separatists and nonseparatists were at odds, each arguing that their position had the greater historical and ethical legitimacy. But by the mid-1980s, as nonseparatist organizations became thoroughly feminized and dedicated to celebrating the divine feminine, the division subsided. Together they brought neopagan feminist spirituality into the mainstream. As Margot Adler observed in 1987, "workshops, classes, and lectures on women's spirituality and the power of the ancient goddesses are everywhere, at adult education centers, at feminist bookstores, at new age institutes."[20]

Other counterculture spiritual alternatives—magic, Native American and shamanist traditions, astrology, psychic imaging, yoga, creative visualization, and various self-realization therapies—underwent a similar process of feminization. For example, according to *The Sixties Spiritual Awakening*, witchcraft, and the occult more generally, were part and parcel of how "the counterculture refined its awareness of non-rational realities." Initially both men and women practiced the occult sciences and ceremonial magic, but by the early 1970s women's growing awareness of their "difference" gave them a decided advantage. As Susan Greenwald noted, "women are culturally conceived as being closer to nature than men, and in magical practices femininity is also associated with the magical otherworld and intuition, while masculinity is connected to rationality, patriarchy and the wider non-magical culture." Once again, women parlayed counterculture values and gender constructs into a source of power and authority. CAW's June 1974 pagan directory listed eighty-eight witches and covens in North America. Its September newsletter carried an article, "Witch" (Women's International Conspiracy from Hell), in which the author asserted, "Your power comes from your own self as a woman, and it's activated by working in concert with your sisters. You are a witch by being female, untamed, angry, joyous, and immortal."[21]

From the start Wicca shared an affinity with neopaganism. Both were defined as revivals of pre-Christian, nature, and goddess-venerating traditions of Europe, and both—according to Margot Adler—were "based on the use of male-female polarity . . . to produce psychic energy." Both also produced separatist or "Dianic" cults that excluded men and functioned solely on female energy. In Wicca, however, female dominance, and even separatism, met with less resistance because of witchcraft's historical identification with women. When Z. Budapest, founder of a separatist coven in southern California, was arrested in 1975 for violating a municipal code that prohibited "advertising to tell fortunes," fellow witches and neopagans—male and female—rallied to her defense. Lee Walker, writing for CAW's "Green Egg," remarked, "Z's case involves issues basic to women's liberation. Women's spirituality and freedom of religion are at stake. This is so because women are the primary practitioners of those illegal acts, which derive from intuitively-based, women-centered religious faiths." It is interesting that those who objected to the feminization of both Wicca and neopaganism had very little to fall back on. Chris Carmines, a critic of the "pronounced movement" toward women-centeredness, argued that "magick," practiced properly, balances and harmonizes the feminine principles of intuition, "receptivity and stillness," with masculine traits of "spontaneous drive and immediate action." As stated in *Woman of Power*, the fusion of cultural feminism and counterculture values convinced most women and many men, however, "that if we are to survive as a species, it is necessary for women to come into power, and for feminist principles to rebuild the foundations of our culture."[22]

The counterculture was also fascinated with Native American and shamanistic ritual practices, imagining them as more natural, authentic, visionary, self-transforming, and earth-friendly than Western traditions. During the 1960s more men were "into" playing Indian than women, probably because the western warrior or renegade fantasy meshed so neatly with the bad-boy, counterculture rebel. To that end, men built sweat lodges, organized peyote rituals, chanted and drummed around campfires, went on vision quests, and immersed themselves in the wisdom of mostly male purveyors of Indian wisdom: John Neihardt's *Black Elk Speaks*, John Fire Lame Deer's *Lame Deer, Seeker of Visions*, Hyemeyohsts Storm's *Seven Arrows*, and Carlos Castaneda's *Teachings of Don Juan*. Counterculture women, although on the sidelines of male Indian play, were also drawn to hippie interpretations of indigenous traditions. They read themselves into the adventures of male spiritual seekers such as Castaneda, identified with Mother Earth, and emulated the "natural" ways of Indian women.[23]

With the rise of cultural feminism in the mid-1970s, women obtained new power as practitioners of Native American traditions by virtue of their superior intuitive powers and closeness to nature. This emboldened them to seek their own role models in female spiritual figures, acquire "women's wisdom," and fashion themselves into "wise women." Skyhawk, for example, began to explore spiritual alternatives in the late 1960s. In a series of dreams, spirit guides encouraged her to "move out of the city to be closer to the earth." Once in nature, a "tall medicine man" appeared to her in a dream and initiated her as a medicine woman. In the early 1980s, her dream guide appeared in the form of a real man, Swift Turtle, a "Miwok-Seneca elder," who instructed her to share her wisdom with others. By the time Skyhawk became a medicine woman, the field was already crowded. Hundreds of women, mostly white, had transformed themselves into transmitters of native wisdom. Although they undoubtedly meant well and were responding to deep spiritual longings, according to Noel Sturgeon in *Ecofeminist Natures*, they—like the counterculture as a whole—tended to view indigenous peoples as "natural resources for the betterment of white people."

Understandably, many American Indian activists were offended by the often piecemeal appropriation of their sacred sites, objects, and ceremonies and by the removal of indigenous wisdom from its cultural and historical context.[24]

Similarly, counterculture women's growing awareness of their supposedly superior intuitive powers and their connection to nature, the body, emotions, and the present gave them an advantage in other counterculture–turned–New Age spiritual practices and self-realization therapies. Again, the confluence of cultural feminism and counterculture gender duality worked in women's favor. As an article in *The Witches' Almanac* noted, "The female tends to accept both logic and irrationality as equal forces. Her body, by being more of an emotional instrument than the male's, allows such flashes without hindering their passage. . . . Statistics show that women make better professional mediums, . . . [and] have stronger psychic abilities . . . than men." Not surprisingly, the *National New Age Yellow Pages*, first issued in 1987, indicated that women monopolized psychic counseling, astrology, past-life channeling and regression, and personal transformation counseling. Women also outnumbered men as yoga students and instructors. The 1980 "National Yoga Teachers' Directory," for example, listed 290 women and forty-seven men.[25]

Yoga, with its emphasis on mind-body-spirit integration, overlapped with holistic healing, another New Age movement that counterculture women came to dominate. Again, their supposed intuitive powers and deeper connection to nature and the body gave them an advantage. As Diane Mariechild, "mother, teacher, healer, author of Mother Wit," noted, "Woman's power is the power to give birth, whether we are birthing children or ideas. Our power is the power to nurture, to nourish, to take care and protect all of life. Woman's power is the power of the heart, the compassionate action that comes from caring and sensing the interrelatedness of all life." Women's interest in holistic healing began during the 1960s. Not only were communards and back-to-the-land householders often isolated from institutional medical facilities; their preference for all things "natural" drew them to nonconventional alternatives. Moreover, their spiritual practices and travels acquainted them with non-Western traditions and the notion that physical, emotional, and spiritual health was interconnected.

For example, at Wheeler's Ranch, as described in *Home Free Home*, with professional medical treatment unavailable, people turned to folk and Indian remedies: sulfur for scabies, radishes and ginseng for hepatitis, Aloe Vera for herpes, bay leaf tea and arrowroot starch for dysentery, golden seal for skin infections. And garlic for warding off colds, expelling worms and aiding the body in fighting viruses passing through. Studying Miwok tribal customs brought the ranch another wonderful way to cure winter ailments. A sweat lodge was built out of bent branches covered with plastic behind the barn on the side of the West Canyon.

In a similar fashion, New Buffalo residents relied on Joyce Robinson, referred to by Iris Keltz in *Scrapbook of a Taos Hippie as* "the unacknowledged leader of the women," who consulted *Back to Eden* (the "bible of herbal cures") to heal a wide variety of ailments. Anne MacNaughton, who lived at Libre, recalled how women possessed "female knowledge," including "herbal information, child care, childbirth, physical information like that." As Anne mentioned, women's interest and expertise in nonconventional healing also extended to childbirth. She assisted in several home births, maintaining "I was convinced that because it had no chemicals that it was wiser." Another woman, after having her own baby using the *Chicago Policeman's Handbook*, helped other women at Wheeler's Ranch give birth on the land. Farm women, such as Pamela Hunt, not only helped women give birth; they ran the commune's clinic.[26]

By the early 1980s counterculture women dominated the New Age holistic healing movement, outnumbering male practitioners in every field from massage, aroma therapy, natural childbirth, and biofeedback to non-Western "wisdom traditions," Jungian analysis, creative visualization, and feng shui. Drawing upon the "feminine principle," wisdom gleaned from their various spiritual paths, and practical experience within the counterculture, women deftly crafted new economic niches that allowed them to pursue personal growth lifestyles while facilitating the "wellness" of others. And their activities extended beyond private practices to include organizing and participating in workshops, franchises, mail order sales and services, seminars, festivals, and extensive networks for sharing marketing, clients, skills, and information. Indeed, holistic healing, like New Age spirituality and self-realization, became a multi-million-dollar business and a significant feature of a major, middle-class lifestyle shift that occurred in the 1980s—a shift away from traditional sources of expertise and authority to finding, truth, power, and "wholeness" through self-actualization.[27]

Home birth and natural mothering, for example, emerged in conjunction with the counterculture's getting back to nature philosophy. With the rise of cultural feminism, women not only claimed exclusive authority and control but also added new meaning to both processes. Birth and "mothering" became conduits of expressive femininity, the sites where women's spiritual values, "innate wisdom," and practical skills merged. Women then took their "private" knowledge public, establishing practices as midwives, doulas, and childbirth coaches and creating networks, advocacy and support groups, mail-order businesses, Web sites, magazines, and retail establishments. Today their services and products are advertised everywhere, found in *Mothering* and *Nurturing Parent* magazines and in *The Natural Baby, Doctor Possum, Babyworks, Back to Basics, Motherwear, Whole Child,* and *Natural Resources* product catalogs. Home birth, nursing, the family bed, home schooling, and "attachment parenting," once confined to the counterculture, are now mainstream practices.[28]

Misgivings about capitalism's compatibility with counterculture values obviously fell by the wayside during the New Age. As women translated their newfound confidence in their spiritual and healing powers into business ventures, they developed a complex rationale that effectively countered charges that they had "sold out." Some drew upon feminist assertions that they, as women, had been socialized to devalue their own contributions. Their personal empowerment, in other words, hinged on rejecting gender norms that stressed female modesty, self-sacrifice, and self-deprecation. This, however, was tantamount to acknowledging that gender was socially constructed. According to cultural feminists, women, by nature, were generous, noncompetitive, cooperative, and unconcerned with recognition, status, and compensation. In other words, women simultaneously denied and affirmed difference, claiming to be innately purer than men while casting themselves as victims of gender roles and expectations that prevented them from being all that they could be. And it wasn't necessarily dishonest; they unconsciously slipped in and out of feminisms as it suited their self-interests. Indeed, hippie women who remained wedded to the cultural feminist model of kind, gentle, and nurturing precapitalist social and economic relations sacrificed the opportunities and security associated with participation in the New Age marketplace.

A far more common rationale was that women humanized capitalism, bringing it into alignment with countercultural and feminine principles. As Louise Lacey noted,

> There isn't only one way to play the competition game. The sports/ military model isn't the only possibility. Competition doesn't have to be ruthless, sneaky or single minded. But there is still a qualitative leap to be made. It seems to me that what is missing in the New Age model is precisely what women are the most characteristically qualified to provide: An intuitive grasp of the interrelationship between people within systems, combined with corollary appreciation of the process of the whole game.

The bottom line was that hippie women were aging. They needed to support families, pay mortgages, and save for retirement. The trick was to make a living without compromising their basic values. Women's priorities thus underwent a shift. During the heyday of the counterculture, women placed emphasis on social transformation. They most certainly valued individual growth and self-realization, but this was but one means of achieving their broader goal of social and cultural change. In the New Age, their priorities shifted. Personal growth or the transformation of self became an end unto itself; take care of the self and, according to Louise Lacey, the "corollary process of the whole could be realized."

In actual practice, the majority of counterculture women didn't make very good entrepreneurs. First, dropping out of school and the job market, often for extended periods of time, placed them at a disadvantage later in life. Second, they tended to find niches that were compatible with their values (yoga, meditation, holistic healing, etc.) but not always that lucrative. Most important, they had difficulty reconciling their "feminine" natures with the competitive realities of the marketplace. Indeed, by the 1980s, the New Age field had become very crowded. Virginia Logan, for example, moved her astrology–psychic reading practice to Amsterdam for half of the year because there was too much competition in the San Francisco Bay Area. But even there she had difficulty maintaining and expanding her client base. Selling her services wasn't a skill that "felt right."[29]

Peace and environmental activism were two other arenas where cultural feminism and counterculture gender constructs and values converged to heighten women's authority and power. By the mid-1970s hippie women were asserting that they naturally possessed the temperament and values necessary to counter the destructive "masculine energies" of the martial Piscean age. A few years later, when activists launched a joint assault against nuclear power and the nuclear arms race, this philosophy permeated their organizations and shaped their strategies and tactics. Indeed, the movement's most prominent spokesperson, Dr. Helen Caldicott, asserted, "A lot of the women who gain power give up their feminine principle and become like men. That's not what the world needs. It needs women who are powerful and intelligent in their own right, who maintain their feminine principle and teach men how to get in touch with theirs." Kathleen Duffy, an organizer of the 1983 International Day of Nuclear Disarmament, went one step further, asserting that "it's not the women of this planet who are responsible for this mess. We have been brought to this precipice by a way of thinking that is only scientific and sterile. Women would never, could never conceive of an idea like the Pentagon." She went on to reflect that women "strive to conjure up better and better ways of living and loving. We work real hard at it. We are making do. We tend our homes and hearths and at the same time wage combat against that band of men who traverse the globe dispensing death, destruction, and disease wherever they step."[30]

This notion, as stated in "Women of Wisdom" — "that women really think from their wombs" and are thus "connected to life and the concept of peace" — birthed a series of women's affinity groups, actions, and peace encampments. And hippie women, as New Age mothers, pagans, witches, and healers, took the lead. Marylyn Motherbear Scott, for example, joined the 1986 cross-country March for Global Disarmament from Los Angeles to Washington, D.C. Already a practicing pagan and a member of the Church of All Worlds, she was appointed priestess of the All Women's Circle and presided over a series of full moon rituals during which she invoked the goddess and the female ancestors of participants. Following the march she continued to lead women's peace actions at the Nevada test site and Concord Naval Weapons Station, introducing a younger generation of women to the power of the feminine. In a similar fashion, Constance Trouble recalled, "the anti-nuke movement was pretty diverse, and although most of us were former hippies or New Left radicals, we weren't all essentialists. But cultural feminism was definitely a dominant theme and provided a powerful rationale for women's leadership." Indeed, hippie women, including many who were tied to Wiccan or goddess-centered affinity groups, asserted their authority by connecting militarism to masculinity and emphasizing their "inherently" peaceful natures. According to Constance Trouble, even women who rejected such claims to power found the argument "potent and seductive. That women were at the forefront of the movement, organizing Mother's Day actions, neo-pagan affinity groups like Witches Weaving Webs, and women-only peace encampments, was really fresh and exciting." Essentialism, in fact, wasn't limited to the United States. It undergirded the international peace movement throughout the 1980s and still informs women's activism in organizations such as Code Pink and Mothers for Peace.[31]

In the environmental arena, hippie women spearheaded the ecofeminist and voluntary simplicity–simple living movements. Getting back to nature and living lightly on the land were central features of the counterculture's utopian vision. Nancy Nesbit, in 1970, reflected that "our struggle to become more and more civilized in the past two thousand years has pushed us away from Nature. Yet we are basically dependent on her for our food and general well-being." For her, and other hippie women, the answer was to "plant a garden, get up and watch the sun rise, open your head to what Nature has to say. Create a new life and home where a truly peaceful existence is possible for yourself and a few friends." For Marylyn Motherbear Scott, one of thousands who heeded this call, living on the land made real the abstract connection to nature. "In being in communion with nature, I was being taught, I understood in a really intimate way that my body was one with the earth."[32]

Neopagan, Wiccan, and Native American spirituality, combined with cultural feminism, strengthened and deepened this connection during the late 1970s and 1980s. Shoshana Schwimmer worked with the Diggers, lived at Morning Star Ranch from 1967 to 1968, and then joined a rural women's community after embracing cultural feminism. There

> we gather on solstices, equinoxes, and other earth holidays to sweat, circle a fire, dance, chant, feast, hug, and say blessings. . . . We are making a great pact, as we recognize each other and the need for it. It was men who tried to 'conquer' nature and in the process made us all

into endangered species. Women have long been the outsiders, privy to greater perspective but little power. We gain in power. We are the healers. We know it is we who must preserve what we can of chi, "elan vital," the greater life-force—Nature.

Sharon Doubiago similarly observed that ecological consciousness grew out of the 1960s counterculture but was initially dominated by "young males taking on traditional female values and consciousness . . . who, in turn, demanded that women remain in the lesser aspects of the realm—as menial servants, as custodial mothers only." But she, like Shoshana, discovered the "feminine principle" and concluded that "women have always thought like mountains, to allude to Aldo Leopold's paradigm for ecological thinking. (There's nothing like the experience of one's belly growing into a mountain to teach you this)."[33]

This essentialist and spiritually based identification with nature, arguably the central strand of ecofeminism, was formulated and dominated by counterculture women. It also propelled them to action and into leadership positions within the environmental movement. According to Michael D'Antonio in *Heaven on Earth*, Ayisha Homolka was an example of this development. She joined the counterculture at eighteen, took psychedelics, studied philosophy, and traveled across Europe and North Africa. She eventually studied Wicca, joined the Church of All Worlds, and embraced cultural feminism. She said that her neopagan, "earth-based spirituality . . . helps me enjoy life here and now. It makes me enjoy life here and now. It makes me feel more connected to the earth, the water, the elements that keep me alive. And I feel like I'm also part of a tribal kind of community with the rituals that make me feel alive." This ecofeminist and ecospiritualist orientation led her to help found Forests Forever, a northern California–based organization dedicated to preserving old-growth forests. Judy Goldhaft, a former core member of the Diggers, cofounded the Planet Drum Foundation, an organization that pioneered and promoted the concept of bioregionalism—an approach to living within the limits of local ecological systems.

Similarly, Morning Glory Zell, hippie-turned-neopagan and partner of Church of All Worlds founder Oberon (Tim) Zell, devoted her time in the 1980s to saving endangered species, wildlife rescue efforts, and the Council of All Beings, an organization that fosters ecological consciousness. Marylyn Motherbear Scott, also a member of the Church of

All Worlds, moved from antinuclear activism into ecofeminism. Following her cross-country peace march, "the overlay of environmentalism came along and I got active at the environmental center in Ukiah. And then I started being active in the same way for the environment with Judi Bari. Of course, we were non-violent and spiritual, and some of the other Earth Firsters didn't have that background." The women of Mateel in northern Humboldt County also became ardent ecofeminists, as did Constance Trouble, who helped found an appropriate technology demonstration project that promoted sustainable agriculture, renewable energy, and voluntary simplicity.[34]

As Constance suggested, voluntary simplicity was part of the counterculture's response to the perceived environmental crisis, a response that gained broader cultural acceptance by the 1980s. Indeed, by that time voluntary simplicity had become the simple living movement, supported by a host of publications, networks, and eventually Web sites. During the 1960s women were the primary provisioners of households and communes, making daily decisions about how to secure, allocate, and stretch basic necessities. At the same time, they were breadwinners, contributing resources through their scavenging activities, odd jobs, crafts production, and welfare checks. In their capacity of provisioners and providers, women often determined the extent to which they and others adhered to the voluntary simplicity ideal. Their power to regulate consumption increased in the 1970s when women concluded that "hippie men do not generally provide many of the things that men 'normally' provide in contexts where their dominance is routine" and that "their welfare checks gave them considerable leverage to increase their power vis-à-vis the men."[35]

The new simple living movement was spearheaded by former hippies, but attracted a younger, middle-class following concerned about environmental degradation and the stress associated with high consumption, dual-career lifestyles. Like its parent, the simple living movement is sustained by women whose moral commitment and compensatory labor translates the ideal into reality. Anna Marie Daniels, for example, noted that "men just don't realize what it takes to run a household—all the labor that's involved. John is a good man, and very committed to environmental ethics, but he's just too preoccupied to manage the day-to-day work involved in sustaining a green lifestyle." Constance Trouble made a similar observation: "We're both members of Reverend Billy's

Church of No Shopping, but I'm the one who always draws the line at purchases, always asks 'do we really need this?'"[36]

Moreover, many female advocates, young and older, view voluntary simplicity or simple living as a core element of their identities as women — an outgrowth of their nurturing, healing, earth-connected natures. It is not surprising that women are among the movement's most prominent and vocal advocates. In 1981 Doris Longacre wrote *Living More With Less.* This was followed by Sue Bender's *Plain and Simple* (1989); Amy Dacyczyen's *The Tightwad Gazette* (1993); Elaine St. James' *Simplify Your Life* (1994), *Inner Simplicity* (1995), and *Living the Simple Life* (1996); Janet Luhr's *The Simple Living Guide* (1997); and Cecile Andrews's *The Circle of Simplicity* (2000). Thus, a movement once confined to the hippie subculture is now a major lifestyle trend that has captured the attention of corporate entities such as Honda, Nordstrom, Proctor and Gamble, Ethan Allen, Kraft, Nabisco, General Motors, Clorox, and Toyota.[37]

The organic foods–sustainable agriculture movement is the final arena in which counterculture women's influence extended beyond the 1960s. As noted in Chapter Four, hippie women assumed major responsibility for food production, procurement, and preparation and imbued their food-related labor with moral significance. Marylyn Motherbear Scott, for example, was experimenting with macrobiotics as early as 1965, growing an organic, French-intensive biodynamic garden by 1967, and feeding her growing family off "every kind of seed, every kind of bean, and every kind of vegetable" throughout the 1970s. Similarly, Wendy Johnson, after becoming a Buddhist, pioneered organic gardening at the Green Gulch Farm Zen Center north of San Francisco. The garden, which she has worked for almost thirty years, supplies produce for the center's restaurant, Greens. The author of *Gardening at the Dragon's Gate: At Work in the Wild and Cultivated World,* Johnson is also a consultant with the Edible Schoolyard project, an organic garden at Berkeley's Martin Luther King Jr. Middle School that is funded by Alice Waters's Chez Panisse Foundation. Other women grew up on farms and returned to their roots with a new appreciation of the land. For example, Nancy MacNamara, after leaving her parent's farm in Newburgh, New York, "to roam the world and be a wild hippie," came home to cultivate organic fruits and vegetables. Her timing, she noted in "Women Find Their Place in the Field" in the *New York Times,* was perfect. "We had the rise of feminism at the same time as the rise of organic agriculture and the 'back to the land' movement. . . . People—especially mothers—started to want to know where their food is coming from."[38]

These and other women inspired a new generation of female farmers. By 2002, 11 percent of U.S. farms were operated principally by women, up from 5 percent in 1978. Moreover, a 2001 study conducted by Pennsylvania State University concluded that female farmers were far more likely to use sustainable practices. In some areas, such as Washington state, women comprised the majority of organic growers. Marcia Ostrom, associate professor and director of Washington State's Small Farms Program, observed that women outnumbered men in her department's Cultivating Success apprenticeship program and in Evergreen State's Ecological Agricultural Program. "Women enjoy nurturing life in both plants and in the people they're feeding. That's a very strong value for them. . . . They really want to grow good food and see themselves producing healthy food that will . . . nourish people and build community."[39]

Elaine Lipson noted in "Food, Farming . . . Feminism?" that women were also more likely "to engage in marketing strategies that build relationships with consumers" through community-supported agriculture associations, local farmers markets, and cooperative distribution centers. Veritable Vegetable, for example, is a woman-owned and -managed organic produce distributer that was founded in 1974 to supply local food co-ops and buyers clubs. Now a multi-million-dollar enterprise, it is still guided by its early philosophy and says, according to Lipson, that "the people we want to do business with are those who embrace the feminine part of themselves. . . . Those people are cooperative, creative, nurturing, and not dominating." Finally, women, as Katherine Di Matteo, executive director of the Organic Trade Association observed, are the primary purchasers of organic foods. She went on to note in "Food, Farming . . . Feminism?" that it all began in the 1960s. "The food co-op movement was all women around the table, looking for ways to find out more about the food they were purchasing and how they could have more control over the amount of money they were spending on their food and influencing the types of products they were able to purchase in bulk." By the 1990s these women's preferences had gone mainstream, supporting a host of contemporary food movements and corporate brands such as Safeway's Organics. In essence, counterculture women changed how the United States eats.[40]

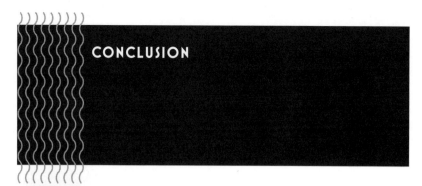

ultural feminism, despite its specious claims and strategic weaknesses, was more than a temporary, marginal, or unfortunate offshoot of radical and political feminism. Indeed, it undergirded many post-1960s social movements and lifestyle shifts, informing everything from natural childbirth and mothering to New Age spiritual beliefs, ecofeminism, holistic health, and sustainable agriculture. Hippie women, as its coarchitects, if not the primary architects, have long been ignored and marginalized, relegated to the sidelines of both the counterculture and the women's movement. In contrast to popular stereotypes, they engaged in a formidable and sustained rebellion against mainstream gender and class norms. Rejecting the suburban domesticity of their mothers, hippie women adopted roles in keeping with an older agrarian tradition—roles that, although essentialist and heteronormative, were enacted outside the privatized confines of the nuclear family. Their labor, although gendered, was not only visible, creative, challenging, and vested with political meaning; it sustained many of hippiedom's families, communities, and alternative institutions. Women's growing awareness and appreciation of their contributions was, in turn, reinforced by the counterculture's emphasis on "feminine" traits—traits that women, within an essentialist framework, "naturally" possessed.

By the mid-1970s, hippie women articulated a feminist vision that emphasized the dignity, if not superiority, of female values and labor. Armed with the certainty that they were the "true Aquarians," they used their "innate" qualities and talents to move counterculture values and practices into the mainstream. Thus, their influence extended well beyond the 1960s, profoundly altering the social, political, economic, and cultural landscape of the United States.

Hippiedom has long been associated with sex, drugs, and rock and roll. Although historians have offered a more complex and nuanced portrait of the counterculture in recent years, the myths and stereotypes still prevail. This is particularly the case with hippie women. As noted in the Introduction, women's experience and contributions have been woefully neglected by scholars of the 1960s. To some extent the counterculture *was* self-indulgent, hedonistic, and impossibly utopian in its vision. It also failed to realize many of its goals. Indeed, much of the counterculture agenda was co-opted, commercialized, and sold to mainstream consumers by hip and not so hip entrepreneurs. And yes, some counterculture women were part of this project. Many, perhaps the majority, stayed the course, however. And even if they hadn't done so, we should not lose sight of their original vision. They helped break the consensus that all was right with the United States. Behind the neat and tidy facade of postwar suburbia, they uncovered and rejected a world of pain—lives governed, as they saw it, by racial and class phobias, unyielding and unsatisfying gender roles, impersonal technologies and institutions, "mindless" consumption, "dehumanizing" labor, loneliness, isolation, environmental devastation, and fear of nonconforming, "deviant" others. More important, they took action, exercising the power of imagination to affect change.

Their example, and that of other 1960s activists, reminds us that collective action—far from being outmoded, futile, and, as some have claimed, counterproductive—has the power to reshape and even transform society. They also left us with a "usable past," a store of practical skills and knowledge that can help us address current issues and problems. Renewable energy alternatives, voluntary simplicity, recycling, "green" buildings, cohousing, organic gardening, composting, community-supported agriculture, farmers' markets, preventive and holistic medicine, bioregionalism, ecofeminism, and earth-creation reverent spirituality all have their roots in the counterculture, and all hold out hope for a more sustainable future. In closing, I want to encourage you to take another look at the book's photographs. The people who brought us these alternatives were kids. It's not General Electric, Exxon, Toyota, or Safeway that invented green alternatives; it was these heartbreakingly young daughters and sons of Aqarius.

 **NOTES**

INTRODUCTION

1. Denise Kaufman, "Denise's Story," available at http://www.theaceof cups.com.

2. Ibid.; Martin Hughes, "Denise Kaufman," *Yogi Times*, Los Angeles edition, no. 32, May 2005; Mary Gannon, "Mary's Story," available at http://www.theaceofcups.com.

3. The term *territory of men* is taken from Joelle Fraser's memoir of growing up in the counterculture: Joelle Fraser, *The Territory of Men: A Memoir* (New York: Villard, 2002).

4. Alice Echols, in *Shaky Ground: The Sixties and Its Aftershocks* (New York: Columbia University Press, 2002), pp. 109–115, argues that cultural feminism was a product of lesbian disaffection with New Left–derived radical feminism. Those who argue that feminism bypassed the counterculture include Sara Evans in *Personal Politics: The Roots of Women's Liberation in the Civil Rights Movement and the New Left* (New York: Vintage, 1980), p. 177, and *Born for Liberty* (New York: Free Press/Simon and Schuster, 1997), p. 281; and Ruth Rosen, *The World Split Open: How the Women's Movement Changed America* (New York: Viking, 2000), p. 126. Other women's historians link the counterculture to the sexual revolution and various lifestyle alternatives but reinforce the notion that women's liberation was confined to activist circles. See, for example, Nancy Cott, *No Small Courage* (New York: Oxford University Press, 2000), p. 551; and Ellen Carol Dubois and Lynn Dunmenil, *Through Women's Eyes* (New York: Bedford/St. Martin's, 2005). It is interesting to note that Debra Michals argues that the counterculture's emphasis on self-transformation and realization provided the foundation for radical feminists' experiments with consciousness-raising groups. But she, like the others, ignores the fact that hippie women were engaged in their own gender rebellion. See Debra Michals, "From 'Consciousness Expansion' to 'Consciousness Raising': Feminism and the Countercultural Politics of the Self," in Peter Braunstein and Michael William Doyle, eds., *Imagine Nation: The American Counterculture of the 1960s and 1970s* (New York: Routledge, 2002), pp. 41–68.

5. Marla Hanson, "Marla's Story," available at http://www.theaceofcups .com.

CHAPTER ONE. GODDESSES, CHICKS, EARTH MOTHERS, AND GROUPIES

1. Philip Slater, *The Pursuit of Loneliness* (Boston: Beacon Press, 1970), p. 100; Gilbert Zicklin, *Countercultural Communes: A Sociological Perspective* (Westport, CT: Greenwood Press, 1983), pp. 3–30; Timothy Miller, *The Hippies and American Values* (Knoxville: University of Tennessee Press, 1991), pp. 6–8, 103–121.

2. Timothy Leary, quoted in "Changes," *San Francisco Oracle* 1, no. 7, February 1967, p. 3; Miller, *The Hippies and American Values*, pp. 4–13, 15; Margot Adler, *Heretic's Heart: A Journey through Spirit and Revolution* (Boston: Beacon Press, 1997), p. 298; Leonard Wolf, ed., *Voices of the Love Generation* (Boston: Little, Brown, 1968), pp. 92–93.

3. Barbara Ehrenreich, *Fear of Falling: The Inner Life of the Middle Class* (New York: Pantheon Books, 1989), pp. 64–74; J. Anthony Lukas, "The Two Worlds of Linda Fitzpatrick," *New York Times*, October 16, 1967, pp. 1, 33; J. Anthony Lukas, "Police Inquiry in Hippie Killings Leaves Family of Girl 'Puzzled': Full Story Sought," *New York Times*, October 17, 1967, pp. 1, 40; J. Anthony Lukas, "Police Hopeful of Easing Hippie Problems Here," *New York Times*, October 18, 1967, pp. 1, 36; Readers Respond, "A Story of Girl Slain in Village Arouses Wide Concern," *New York Times*, October 29, 1967, p. 57.

4. Aniko Bodroghkozy, *Groove Tube: Sixties Television and the Youth Rebellion* (Durham, NC: Duke University Press, 2001), pp. 82–84.

5. Ibid., pp. 90–91, 136–138, 175–176.

6. David McBride, "On the Fault Line of Mass Culture and the Counterculture: A Social History of the Hippie Counterculture in 1960s Los Angeles" (Ph.D. diss., University of California, Los Angeles, 1998), p. 73; Charles Perry, *The Haight Ashbury: A History* (New York: Random House, 1984), p. 221.

7. Joan Didion, *Slouching toward Bethlehem* (New York: Farrar, Straus and Giroux, 1990), pp. 90–92, 96–97, 101, 113, 127–128; Tom Wolfe, *Electric Kool-Aid Acid Test* (New York: Bantam, 1999), pp. 64, 71, 86–86, 177.

8. Valerie Solanas, "SCUM Manifesto," quoted in Keith Melville, *Communes in the Counterculture: Origins, Theories, Styles of Life* (New York: William Morrow, 1972), p. 188; Vivian Estellachild, "2 Hip Communes: A Personal Experience," in Richard Fairfield, ed., *The Modern Utopian: Utopia*

U.S.A. (San Francisco: Alternatives Foundation, 1972), p. 189; Robin Morgan, "Goodbye to All That," reprinted in Rosalyn Braxandall and Linda Gordon, *Dear Sisters: Dispatches from the Women's Liberation Movement* (New York: Basic Books, 2000), pp. 53–57.

9. Sara Evans, *Personal Politics: The Roots of Women's Liberation in the Civil Rights Movement and the New Left* (New York: Vintage, 1980), p. 177; Sara Evans, *Born for Liberty* (New York: Free Press/Simon and Schuster, 1997), p. 281; Ruth Rosen, *The World Split Open: How the Women's Movement Changed America* (New York: Viking, 2000), p. 126. Please refer to Note 4 of the Introduction for commentary on these works.

10. Peter Braunstein and Michael William Doyle, "Historicizing the Counterculture of the 1960s and 1970s," in Peter Braunstein and Michael William Doyle, eds., *Imagine Nation: The American Counterculture of the 1960s and 1970s* (New York: Routledge, 2002), pp. 167–182; Barbara Ehrenreich, Elizabeth Hess, and Gloria Jacobs, "The Politics of Promiscuity," *New Age*, November/December, 1986, p. 28.

11. Robert J. Glessing, *The Underground Press in America* (Bloomington: Indiana University Press, 1970), p. 41; Beth Bailey, "Sex as a Weapon: Underground Comix and the Paradox of Liberation," in Peter Braunstein and Michael William Doyle, *Imagine Nation: The American Counterculture of the 1960s and 1970s* (New York: Routledge, 2002), p. 307; Arthur Seeger, *The Berkeley Barb: Social Control of an Underground Newsroom* (New York: Irvington Publishers, 1983), p. 34.

12. Bodroghkozy, *Groove Tube*, p. 13; Bailey, "Sex as a Weapon," pp. 308–310; Glessing, *The Underground Press in America*, pp. 92, 103, 115; "Aquarian Woman" graphic, *San Francisco Oracle* 1, no. 6, January 1967, back cover; "Madonna" photograph, *San Francisco Oracle* 1, no. 7, February 1967, p. 4.

13. Trina Robbins, "Underground Cartoonist: Wimmen's Comix, Wet Stain," in Monte Beauchamp, ed., *The Life and Times of R. Crumb: Comments from Contemporaries* (New York: St. Martin's Griffin, 1998), pp. 39–42; Bailey, "Sex as a Weapon," pp. 305–324; additional information on Trina Robbins and other female comix artists of the 1960s is available at http://imaginingourselves.imow.org; Bodroghkozy, *Groove Tube*, p. 13; Roger Streitmatter, *Voices of Revolution: The Dissident Press in America* (New York: Columbia University Press, 1991), pp. 258–274; Marilyn S. Webb, "Off Our Backs and the Feminist Dream," in Ken Wachsberger, ed., *Voices from the Underground: Inside Histories of the Vietnam Era Underground* (Tempe, AZ: Mica's Press, 1993), vol. 1, pp. 124–125. Examples of male-generated comic art can be viewed

in R. Crumb, *The Complete R. Crumb Comics* (Seattle: Fantagraphic, 1992), and Gilbert Shelton, *The Fabulous Furry Freak Brothers Omnibus* (London: Knockabout Books, 2008).

14. Perry, *The Haight Ashbury*, p. 200; W. J. Rorabaugh, *Berkeley at War* (New York: Oxford University Press, 1989), pp. 140–141; Gillian G. Gaar, *She's a Rebel: The History of Women in Rock and Roll* (Seattle: Seal Press, 1992), pp. 111–113.

15. Sheila Whiteley, *Women and Popular Music: Sexuality, Identity, and Subjectivity* (New York: Routledge, 2000), pp. 23, 25, 33–40.

16. Ariel Swartly, "Red Blue Jeans: Wanda Jackson and Grace Slick," in Barbara O'Dair, ed., *Trouble Girls: The Rolling Stone Book of Women in Rock* (New York: Rolling Stone Press, 1997), p. 148; Joel Selvin, *Summer of Love: The Inside Story of LSD, Rock and Roll, Free Love, and High Times in the Wild West* (New York: Cooper Square Press, 1994), pp. 185–187, 134, 102, 253, 277–279; Gaar, *She's a Rebel*, p. 106.

17. Perry, *The Haight Ashbury*, pp. 28–60; Denise Kaufman, "Denise's Story," available at http://www.theaceofcups.com; Mary Gannon, "Mary's Story," available at http://www.theaceofcups.com; Marla Hanson, "Marla's Story," available at http://www.theaceofcups.com; Diane Vitalich, "Diane's Story," available at http://www.theaceofcups.com; Mary Ellen Simpson, "Mary Ellen's Story," available at http://www.theaceofcups.com; June and Jean quoted in Lauren Kessler, *After All These Years: Sixties Ideals in a Different World* (New York: Thunder's Mouth Press, 1990), pp. 184, 185, and 186.

18. Avital H. Bloch, "Joan Baez: A Singer and Activist," in Avital H. Bloch and Lauri Umanski, eds., *Impossible to Hold: Women and Culture in the 1960s* (New York: New York University Press, 2005), pp. 129–130; Lisa Kennedy, "Joni Mitchell," in Barbara O'Dair, ed., *Trouble Girls: The Rolling Stone Book of Women in Rock* (New York: Rolling Stone Press, 1997), pp. 171–179; Patricia Romanowski, "Bonnie Raitt," in Barbara O'Dair, *Trouble Girls*, pp. 191–196; Karen Schoemer, "Linda Ronstadt," in Barbara O'Dair, *Trouble Girls*, pp. 197–203; Gillian Gaar, *She's a Rebel*, pp. 188–193.

19. John Burks, Jerry Hopkins, and Paul Nelson, "The Groupies and Other Girls," *Rolling Stone* 27, February 15, 1969; Ann Powers, "The Love You Make: Fans and Groupies," in Barbara O'Dair, ed., *Trouble Girls: The Rolling Stone Book of Women in Rock* (New York: Rolling Stone Press, 1997), pp. 184, 186; Roger Greenspun, "Screen Girls (and Boys) in Pursuit of Rock Stars," *New York Times*, November 9, 1970, p. 54; Katheryn Kerr Fenn, "Daughters

of the Counterculture: Rock and Roll Groupies in the 1960s and 1970s (Ph.D. diss., Duke University, 2002); Lisa Rhodes, *In Electric Ladyland: Women and Rock Culture* (Philadelphia: University of Pennsylvania Press, 2005).

20. Powers, "The Love You Make," p. 185, Constance Trouble, interviewed by author, Berkeley, CA, August 6, 2007; Mary Gannon, "Mary's Story"; Kathleen Taylor, interviewed by author, Berkeley, CA, August 15, 2007.

21. Ehrenreich, *Fear of Falling*, p. 61.

22. Marylyn Motherbear Scott, interviewed by author, Albion, CA, June 5, 2007; Trouble, interview; Ramon Sender Barayon, Gwen Leeds, Near Morningstar, Bill Wheeler, and many others, "Home Free Home: A History of Two Open-Door California Communes," chap. 1, p. 4, manuscript, n.d., available at http://www.diggers.org; Roberta Price, *Huerfano: A Memoir of Life in the Counterculture* (Amherst: University of Massachusetts Press, 2004), p. 53.

CHAPTER TWO. "WE WANTED TO BREAK AWAY"

1. Hugh Gardner, *The Children of Prosperity: Thirteen Modern American Communes* (New York: St. Martin's, 1976), p. 204; Angela Aidala and Benjamin Zablocki, "The Communes of the 1970s: Who Joined and Why?" *Marriage and Family Review* 17 (1991): p. 92; Timothy Miller, *The 60s Communes: Hippies and Beyond* (New York: Syracuse University Press, 1999), pp. 170–171; Peter Braunstein and Michael William Doyle, "Historicizing the American Counterculture of the 1960s and 1970s," in Peter Braunstein and Michael William Doyle, eds., *Imagine Nation: The American Counterculture of the 1960s and 1970s* (New York: Routledge, 2002), p. 12; Angela Aidala, "Communes and Changing Family Norms: Marriage and Lifestyle Choices among Former Members of Communal Groups," *Journal of Family Issues* 10 (1989): p. 314; Timothy Miller, *The Hippies and American Values* (Knoxville: University of Tennessee Press, 1991), pp. 15–16; Elia Katz, *Armed Love* (New York: Holt, Rinehart and Winston, 1971), p. 114.

2. Wini Breines, *Young, White, and Miserable: Growing Up Female in the Fifties* (Boston: Beacon Press, 1992), pp. 150–151, 22.

3. Tim Hodgdon, *Manhood in the Age of Aquarius: Masculinity in Two Counterculture Communities, 1965–1983* (New York: Columbia University Press, 2007), chap. 2, pp. 6–12, available at www.gutenberg-e.org; Philip Deloria, "Counterculture Indians in the New Age, in Peter Braunstein and Michael William Doyle, eds., *Imagine Nation: The American Counterculture of the 1960s and 1970s* (New York: Routledge, 2002), pp. 159–188; Ramon Sender Barayon,

Gwen Leeds, Near Morningstar, Bill Wheeler, and many others, "Home Free Home: A History of Two Open-Door California Communes," manuscript, n.d., chap. 10, pp. 6–7, available at http://www.diggers.org.

4. Hodgdon, *Manhood in the Age of Aquarius,* chap. 2, p. 6; Miller, *The Hippies and American Values,* pp. 15–16; Sender et al., "Home Free Home," chap. 18, pp. 1–2.

5. William Foote Whyte, "A Slum Sex Code," in Reinhard Bendix and Seymour Martin Lipset, eds., *Class, Status, and Power: A Reader in Social Stratification* (Glencoe, IL: Free Press, 1953), pp. 308–316; Constance B. Holstein, Janice Stroud, and Norma Haam, "Alienated and Nonalienated Youth: Perceptions of Parents, Self-Evaluations, and Moral Reasoning of Hippies and College Youth," *Youth and Society* 5 (1974): p. 286; Rosaline Santangelo, interviewed by author, Berkeley, CA, May 30, 2007.

6. Barbara Ehrenreich, *Fear of Falling: The Inner Life of the Middle Class* (New York: Pantheon Books, 1989), p. 61.

7. Kenneth Keniston, *The Uncommitted: Alienated Youth in American Society* (New York: Dell Publishing, 1965), pp. 165–169; Stephanie Coontz, *The Way We Never Were: American Families and the Nostalgia Trap* (New York: Basic Books, 1992), pp. 31–32.

8. Keniston, *The Uncommitted,* pp. 169, 171; Breines, *Young, White, and Miserable,* pp. 51–59; Kenneth Keniston, *Young Radicals: Notes on Committed Youth* (New York: Harcourt, Brace & World, 1968), p. 333.

9. Breines, *Young, White, and Miserable,* pp. 62–68, 71–72; Anna Marie Daniels, interviewed by author, Santa Barbara, CA, July 26, 2007.

10. Coontz, *The Way We Never Were,* pp. 34–35.

11. Ibid., pp. 29–41.

12. Holstein, Stroud, and Haam, "Alienated and Nonalienated Youth," pp. 289–291; Jan Camp, interviewed by author, Berkeley, CA, May 29, 2007.

13. Virginia Logan, interviewed by author, Berkeley, CA, July 12, 2007.

14. Constance Trouble, interviewed by author, Berkeley, CA, August 6, 2007.

15. Nancy Jean, interviewed by author, Berkeley, CA, June 12, 2007; Coontz, *The Way We Never Were,* p. 34.

16. Cynthia Robins, "She Never Got Off the Bus: The Hard Life and High Times of Carolyn Garcia," *San Francisco Examiner,* May 25, 1997, MAG page, available at http://www.sfgate.com.

17. Leonard Wolf, ed., *Voices of the Love Generation* (Boston: Little, Brown, 1968), pp. 97–99.

18. Marylyn Motherbear Scott, interviewed by author, Albion, CA, June 5, 2007; Kathleen Taylor, interviewed by author, Berkeley, CA, August 15, 2007.

19. Breines, *Young, White, and Miserable*, pp. 133–141.

20. Camp, interview; Robins, "She Never Got Off the Bus."

21. Logan, interview; Trouble, interview.

22. Jean, interview; Wolf, *Voices of the Love Generation*, p. 102; Scott, interview.

23. Pam Tent, *Midnight at the Palace: My Life as a Fabulous Cockette* (Los Angeles: Alyson Books, 2004), p. 3; Jodi Mitchell, "Jodi Mitchell's Wheeler Story," "MOST Newsletter" 6, no. 1, Spring 1999, pp. 3–4, available at http://laurelrose.com.

24. Wolf, ed., *Voices of the Love Generation*, pp. 21–33; Margaret Helwig, "Diane Di Prima Biography," available at http://www.womenofthebeat.org; Diane Di Prima, *Memoirs of a Beatnik* (San Francisco: Last Gasp of San Francisco, 1988), p. 51.

25. Robins, "She Never Got Off the Bus."

26. Scott, interview; Marylyn Motherbear Scott, interviewed by Deborah Altus, 60s Communes Project, May 28, 1996.

27. Charles Perry, *The Haight Ashbury: A History* (New York: Random House, 1974), pp. 22–24; Barayon et al., *Home Free Home*, chap. 2, p. 2.

28. Trouble, interview; Tent, *Midnight at the Palace*, pp. 3–5; Wolf, *Voices of the Love Generation*, pp. 99–107; Lelain Lorenzen, interviewed by Deborah Altus, 60s Communes Project, March 15, 1997.

29. Roberta Price, *Huerfano: A Memoir of Life in the Counterculture* (Amherst: University of Massachusetts Press, 2004), pp. 5–7, 23; Logan, interview.

30. Ellen Winner, "Doubting Shaman: An American Apprenticeship in Nepali Shamanism," *Shaman's Drum*, no. 32, Summer 1993, p. 25; Mara Devine, interviewed by Deborah Altus, 60s Communes Project, November 12, 1995; Vivian Gotters, interviewed by Timothy Miller, 60s Communes Project, March 23, 1996.

31. Nancy Nina, interviewed by Deborah Altus, 60s Communes Project, March 26, 1997; Mary Siler Anderson, interviewed by Deborah Altus, 60s Communes Project, November 11, 1995; Camp, interview; Jean, interview.

32. Andrew Kopkind, untitled article, *Rolling Stone*, September 20, 1969; Miller, *The Hippies and American Values*, pp. 6–8; "Affirming Humanness," *San Francisco Oracle* 1, no. 1, September 20, 1966, p. 2.

33. Tent, *Midnight at the Palace*, pp. 6–7; Logan, interview.

34. Barayon et al., *Home Free Home*, chap. 2, p. 3; Camp, interview.

35. Tent, *Midnight at the Palace*, p. 6; Pamela Hunt, interviewed by Deborah Altus, 60s Communes Project, October 19, 1995; Kay Hayward, interviewed by Deborah Altus, 60s Communes Project, May 28, 1996; Gotters, interview.

36. Matie Bell Lakish, interviewed by Deborah Altus, 60s Communes Project, August 15, 1997; Hayward, interview; Lorenzen, interview.

37. Barayon et al., *Home Free Home*, chap. 2, p. 3; Judson Jerome, *Families of Eden: Communes and the New Anarchism* (New York: Seabury Press, 1974), pp. 92–93.

CHAPTER THREE. IN HARMONIOUS INTERCOURSE

1. Leonard Wolf, ed., *Voices of the Love Generation* (Boston: Little, Brown, 1968), p. 90.

2. Ibid., p. 34.

3. Jane and Michael Stern, *Sixties People* (New York: Alfred Knopf, 1990), p. 156; Peter Coyote, *Sleeping Where I Fall* (Washington, DC: Counterpoint, 1998), pp. 7–9, 132–133, 289.

4. Jon Wagner, "Sex Roles in American Communal Utopias," in Jon Wagner, ed., *Sex Roles in Contemporary American Communes* (Bloomington: Indiana University Press, 1982), pp. 33–35; Bill Grant, "Commune Tripping," in Richard Fairfield, ed., *The Modern Utopian: Utopia U.S.A.* (San Francisco: Alternatives Foundation, 1972), p. 24; Ron E. Roberts, *The New Communes: Coming Together in America* (Englewood Cliffs, NJ: Prentice Hall, 1972), p. 89; Sara Davidson, "Hippie Families on Open Land," in Rosabeth Moss Kanter, ed., *Communes: Creating and Managing the Collective Life* (New York: Harper and Row, 1973), p. 348.

5. Wolf, *Voices of the Love Generation*, p. 90; Iris Keltz, *Scrapbook of a Taos Hippie* (El Paso, Texas: Cinco Puntos Press, 2000), p. 43.

6. David Allyn, *Make Love Not War: The Sexual Revolution, An Unfettered History* (Boston: Little, Brown, 2000), pp. 10–18.

7. Ibid., pp. 140, 180–181, 247; Constance Trouble, interviewed by author, Berkeley, CA, August 6, 2007.

8. Wini Breines, *Young, White, and Miserable* (Boston: Beacon Press, 1992), p. 86; Beth L. Bailey, *From Front Porch to Back Seat: Courtship in Twentieth-Century America* (Baltimore: Johns Hopkins University Press, 1989), pp. 55–56.

9. Allyn, *Make Love Not War*, pp. 17–26, 40.

10. Ibid., p. 46, pp. 41–53; W. J. Rorabaugh, *Berkeley at War* (New York: Oxford University Press, 1989), pp. 131–132.

11. Timothy Miller, *The Hippies and American Values* (Knoxville: University of Tennessee Press, 1991), p. 55; Leah Fritz, "Female Sexuality and the Liberated Orgasm," *The Berkeley Tribe*, October 1970, pp. 16–23.

12. Coyote, *Sleeping Where I Fall*, p. 85; Miller, *Hippies and American Values*, p. 54; Wolf, *Voices of the Love Generation*, p. 34; David E. Smith and Alan J. Rose, "Health Problems in Urban and Rural 'Crash Pad' Communes," *Clinical Pediatrics* 9, no. 9 (September 1970): pp. 534–537.

13. Barbara Ehrenreich, Elizabeth Hess, and Gloria Jacobs, "The Politics of Promiscuity," *New Age*, November/December 1986, p. 28; Angela Aidala, "Communes and Changing Family Norms: Marriage and Lifestyle Choices among Former Members of Communal Groups," *Journal of Family Issues* 10 (1989): pp. 322, 326.

14. Jan Camp, interviewed by author, Berkeley, CA, May 29, 2007; Trouble, interview; Ramon Sender Barayon, Gwen Leeds, Near Morningstar, Bill Wheeler, and many others, "Home Free Home: A History of Two Open-Door California Communes," manuscript, n.d., chap. 8, p. 1, available at http://www.diggers.org; Wolf, *Voices of the Love Generation*, p. 37.

15. Pam Hanna (Read), "Infinite Points of Time: Morningstar Chronicles," Part I (California), Digger Archives, p. 8, available at http://www.diggers.org; Barayon et al., "Home Free Home," chap. 3, p. 8, chap. 8, pp. 7–8; Marylyn Motherbear Scott, interviewed by author, Albion, CA, June 5, 2007; Roberta Price, *Huerfano: A Memoir of the Counterculture* (Amherst: University of Massachusetts Press, 2004), pp. 294, 335; Vivian Gotters, interviewed by Timothy Miller, 60s Communes Project, March 23, 1996.

16. Richard Fairfield, ed., *The Modern Utopian: Communes U.S.A.* (San Francisco: Alternatives Foundation, 1971), p. 149; Keith Melville, *Communes in the Counterculture: Origins, Theories, Styles of Life* (New York: William Morrow, 1972), p. 192; Stephen Gaskin, *Monday Night Class* (Santa Rosa, CA: Book Farm), pp. 93–94, 109–111; Louis J. Kern, "Pronatalism, Midwifery, and Synergistic Marriage: Spiritual Enlightenment and Sexual Ideology on the Farm (Tennessee)," in Wendy E. Chmielewski, Louis J. Kern, and Marlyn Klee-Hartzell, eds., *Women in Spiritual and Communitarian Societies in the United States* (Syracuse, NY: Syracuse University Press, 1993), p. 203.

17. Allyn, *Make Love Not War*, pp. 46–53, 75–84, 100–104, 207–208; Robert H. Rimmer, *The Harrad Experiment* (New York: Bantam, 1967); Robert A. Heinlein, *Stranger in a Strange Land* (New York: Putnam, 1961).

18. Pam Tent, *Midnight at the Palace: My Life as a Fabulous Cockette* (Los Angeles: Alison Books, 2004), pp. 6–7, introduction, p. 136; David McBride, "On the Fault Line of Mass Culture and the Counterculture: A Social History of the Hippie Counterculture in 1960s Los Angeles" (Ph.D. diss., University of California, Los Angeles, 1998), pp. 387–388.

19. Berkeley chapter president quoted in Richard Fairfield, ed., *Modern Utopian Magazine* 2, no. 2 (October/November 1967): 10–11; Price, *Huerfano: A Memoir of the Counterculture*, p. 90; Fairfield, *The Modern Utopian: Communes U.S.A.*, p. 164.

20. Price, *Huerfano: A Memoir of the Counterculture*, p. 176; Allyn, *Make Love Not War*, pp. 246–247; Barayon et al., "Home Free Home," chap. 20, p. 4.

21. Nancy Jean, interviewed by author, Berkeley, CA, June 12, 2007; Mara Devine, interviewed by Deborah Altus, 60s Communes Project, November 12, 1995.

22. Timothy Miller, *The 60s Communes: Hippies and Beyond* (Syracuse, NY: Syracuse University Press, 1999), pp. 138–139, 213; Robert McRuer, "Gay Gatherings: Remembering the Counterculture," in Peter Braunstein and Michael William Doyle, eds., *Imagine Nation: The American Counterculture of the 1960s and 1970s* (New York: Routledge, 2002), pp. 216–217.

23. Delia Moon and Salli Raspberry, interviewed by Timothy Miller, 60s Communes Project, September 12, 1996; Barayon et al., "Home Free Home," chap. 2, p. 9, chap. 3, p. 5; William George Thieman, "Haight Ashbury: Birth of the Counterculture" (Ph.D. diss., Miami University, 1998), pp. 101–102; Margot Adler, *Heretic's Heart: A Journey through Spirit and Revolution* (Boston: Beacon Press, 1997), pp. 161–165.

24. Tent, *Midnight at The Palace*, pp. 6–7; Helen Swick Perry, *The Human Be-In* (New York: Basic Books, 1969), pp. 199–208; Trouble, interview.

25. Coyote, *Sleeping Where I Fall*, p. 85.

26. Nancy Nina, interviewed by Deborah Altus, 60s Communes Project, March 26, 1997; Barayon et al., "Home Free Home," chap. 18, pp. 3–4, chap. 20, p. 4.

27. Price, *Huerfano*, p. 188; Anna Marie Daniels, interviewed by author, Santa Barbara, CA, July 26, 2007.

28. Nina, interview; Elaine Sundancer, *Celery Wine: A Story of a Country Commune* (Yellow Springs, OH: Community Publications Cooperative, 1973), p. 22.

29. Price, *Huerfano*, pp. 193, 238–240; Virginia Logan, interviewed by author, July 12, 2007; Camp, interview; Trouble, interview; Aidala, "Communes and Changing Family Norms," p. 316.

30. Ina May Gaskin, interviewed by Deborah Altus, 60s Communes Project, October 18, 1995; Aidala, "Communes and Changing Family Norms," pp. 322, 326.

31. Marylyn Motherbear Scott, interviewed by Deborah Altus, 60s Communes Project, May 28, 1996; Price, *Huerfano*, pp. 20–26; Wolf, *Voices of the Love Generation* p. 84.

32. Jodi Mitchell, "Jodi Mitchell's Wheeler Story," "MOST Newsletter" 6, no. 1, Spring 1999, p. 5, available at http://laurelrose.com; Price, *Huerfano*, p. 214; Elia Katz, *Armed Love* (New York: Holt, Rinehart and Winston, 1971), p. 141; Gaskin, Altus interview; Scott, author interview.

33. Tent, *Midnight at the Palace*, p. 151; Barayon et al., "Home Free Home," chap. 12, p. 2, chap. 18, pp. 3–4; Hanna (Read), "Infinite Points of Time," Part 1, pp. 13–14.

34. Davidson, "Hippie Families on Open Land," p. 340; Keltz, *Scrapbook of a Taos Hippie*, p. 182.

35. Barayon et al., "Home Free Home," chap. 20, pp. 5–6, chap. 18, p. 7.

36. Keltz, *Scrapbook*, p. 91; Hanna (Read), "Infinite Points of Time," Part 1, p. 23; Ruby Tuesday, interviewed by Timothy Miller, 60s Communes Project, March 21, 1996; Wavy Gravy, *The Hog Farm and Friends* (New York: Links Books, 1974), p. 42.

37. Hanna (Read), "Infinite Points of Time," pt. 2, p. 2; Keltz, *Scrapbook*, p. 182; Nina, interview; Gaskin, interview.

CHAPTER FOUR. "IT NEVER SEEMED LIKE DRUDGERY"

1. Peter Coyote, *Sleeping Where I Fall* (Washington, DC: Counterpoint, 1998), p. 35; Judson Jerome, *Families of Eden: Communes and the New Anarchism* (New York: Seabury Press, 1974), pp. 77–132; Timothy Miller, *The 60s Communes: Hippies and Beyond* (Syracuse, NY: Syracuse University Press, 1999), pp. 149–166; Sam Binkley, "Everybody's Life Is Like a Spiral: Narrating Post-Fordism in the Lifestyle Movement of the 1970s," *Cultural Studies-Critical Methodologies* 4 (2004): pp. 74–79; Timothy Miller, *The Hippies and American Values* (Knoxville: University of Tennessee Press, 1991), pp. 103–121.

2. Wini Breines, *Young, White, and Miserable: Growing Up Female in the Fifties* (Boston: Beacon Press, 1992), p. 53; Stephanie Coontz, *The Way We Never Were: American Families and the Nostalgia Trap* (New York: Basic Books, 1992), p. 31.

3. Richard Fairfield, ed., *The Modern Utopian: Communes U.S.A.* (San

Francisco: Alternatives Foundation, 1971), pp. 8, 10, 121, 131, 141, 144; Ron E. Roberts, *The New Communes: Coming Together in America* (Englewood Cliffs, NJ: Prentice Hall, 1972), p. 89; Jon Wagner, ed., *Sex Roles in Contemporary American Communes* (Bloomington: Indiana University Press, 1982), pp. 33–35; Miller, *The 60s Communes*, p. 155.

4. Helen McKenna, "Are You Ready for Revolution?" in *Visions of the Underground Press* (Sebastopol, CA: Alternatives Foundation, 1970), p. 3; Mary Siler Anderson, *Whatever Happened to the Hippies* (San Pedro, CA: R & E Miles, 1990), p. 121; Jerome, *Families of Eden*, pp. 85–86, 87–88.

5. John Browson, "Anarchy 66, Provo," *San Francisco Oracle* 1, no. 1, September 20, 1966, p. 3; Miller, *The 60s Communes*, p. 165; Jerome, *Families of Eden*, pp. 102–107.

6. Constance Trouble, interviewed by author, Berkeley, CA, August 6, 2007; Coyote, *Sleeping Where I Fall*, pp. 132–133; Miller, *The 60s Communes*, p. 213; John A. MacDonald, *House of Acts* (Carol Stream, IL: Creation House Press, 1970), p. 88.

7. Laura and Barb, "Harmony House," in Richard Fairfield, ed., *The Modern Utopian: Utopia U.S.A.* (San Francisco: Alternative Foundation, 1972), p. 50; Elaine Sundancer, *Celery Wine: Story of a Country Commune* (Yellow Springs, OH: Community Publications Cooperative, 1973), p. 134; Else Gidlow, "Sounds from the Seedpower Sitar: Notes on Organic Gardening," *San Francisco Oracle* 1, no. 7, February 1967, p. 20.

8. Craig Cox, *Storefront Revolution: Food Co-ops and the Counterculture* (New Brunswick, NJ: Rutgers University Press, 1994), pp. 30–32, 43; Warren J. Belasco, *Appetite for Change: How the Counterculture Took on the Food Industry, 1966–1988* (New York: Pantheon Books, 1989), pp. 88, 103.

9. Anderson, *Whatever Happened to the Hippies*, pp. 85–87; Thomas McNamee, *Alice Waters and Chez Panisse* (New York: Penguin Press, 2007), pp. 40–42; Belasco, *Appetite for Change*, pp. 94–95.

10. Belasco, *Appetite for Change*, pp. 92–95; Elyse Friedman, "The Hippie Kitchen's Long Strange Trip . . . into Your Local Supermarket," special to the *Chicago Tribune*, January 7, 2004; Kathleen Taylor, interview conducted by author, Berkeley, CA, August, 15, 2007; Kathy Dinaburg (Taylor) and D'Ann Akel, *Nutrition Survival Kit: A Natural Foods Recipe and Reference Guide* (San Francisco: Panjandrum Press, 1976), pp. 3–4.

11. Laurel Robertson, Carol Flinders, and Bronwen Godfrey, *Laurel's Kitchen: A Handbook for Vegetarian Cookery and Nutrition* (New York: Bantam, 1981), pp. 38–43, 48–50.

12. Sherri Cavan, "The Class Structure of Hippie Society," *Journal of Contemporary Ethnography* 1 (1972): p. 214.

13. Anderson, *Whatever Happened to the Hippies*, pp. 33–35; Vivian Gotters, interviewed by Timothy Miller, 60s Communes Project, March 23, 1996.

14. Lelain Lorenzen, interviewed by Deborah Altus, 60s Communes Project, March 15, 1997; Cavan, "The Class Structure of Hippie Society," pp. 221, 219, 217; Karen Lee Robins, "Karen Lee Robins: Sculptor of Goddess Images," *Woman of Power*, no. 6 (Spring 1987): p. 63.

15. Melissa Hill, interviewed by Deborah Altus, 60s Communes Project, August 6, 1996; Cavan, "The Class Structure of Hippie Society," p. 219; Alexandra [Rain] Jacopetti and Warren Wainwright, photographer, *Native Funk and Flash: An Emerging Folk Art* (San Francisco: Scrimshaw Press, 1974).

16. Susan Lydon, "A Few Folksy Fashions," *Rolling Stone*, May 25, 1968, p. 12; Jeanne Rose, "Jeanne Rose, the Herbal Queen," *Yoga Journal*, no. 46 (October 1982): p. 8; information on Trina Robbins's fashion-related business can be found at http://imaginingourselves.imow.org; Joel Selvin, *Summer of Love: The Inside Story of LSD, Rock and Roll, Free Love, and High Times in the Wild West* (New York: Cooper Square Press, 1994), pp. 167, 356; Ami Magill quoted in Martin Torgoff, *Can't Find My Way Home: America in the Great Stoned Age, 1945–2000* (New York: Simon and Schuster, 2004), pp. 196–197; Kathleen Taylor, interview conducted by author, Berkeley, CA, August, 15, 2007.

17. Trouble, interview; Anderson, *Whatever Happened to the Hippies*, pp. 75–76; Carolyn Adams quoted in Torgoff, *Can't Find My Way Home*, pp. 253–254, 287–293.

18. Trouble, interview.

19. Crescent Dragonwagon, *The Commune Cookbook* (New York: Simon and Schuster, 1972), pp. 154, 156; Jerome, *Families of Eden*, p. 114; Miller, *The 60s Communes*, pp. 162–164; Roberta Price, *Huerfano: A Memoir of Life in the Counterculture* (Amherst: University of Massachusetts Press, 2004), pp. 85, 87.

20. Fairfield, *The Modern Utopian: Communes U.S.A.*, p. 124.

21. Terry Klein, interviewed by Timothy Miller, 60s Communes Project, August 6, 1996; Anderson, *Whatever Happened to the Hippies*, pp. 13, 16; Jodi Mitchell, "Jodi Mitchell's Wheeler Story," "MOST Newsletter" 6, no. 1, Spring 1999, p. 5, available at http://laurelrose.com.

22. Bennett Berger, *The Survival of a Counterculture: Ideological Work and Everyday Life among Rural Communards* (Berkeley: University of California

Press, 1981), pp. 152–153; Jentri Anders, *Beyond Counterculture: The Community of Mateel* (Pullman: Washington State University Press, 1990), pp. 204–205.

23. Keith Melville, *Communes in the Counterculture: Origins, Theories, Styles of Life* (New York: William Morrow, 1972), p. 169.

24. Miller, *The 60s Communes*, pp. 41–148; Wagner, *Sex Roles in Contemporary American Communes*, pp. 33–35; Bill Grant, "Commune Tripping," in Richard Fairfield, ed., *The Modern Utopian: Utopia U.S.A.* (San Francisco: Alternatives Foundation, 1972), p. 24; Roberts, *The New Communes*, p. 89.

25. "Interview with Bob Carey, Member, Family of Mystic Arts," in Richard Fairfield, ed., *The Modern Utopian: Communes U.S.A.* (San Francisco: Alternatives Foundation, 1971), p. 10; Coyote, *Sleeping Where I Fall*, p. 289.

26. Richard Atcheson, *The Bearded Lady: Going on the Commune Trip and Beyond* (New York: John Day Company, 1971), pp. 323–324; Vivian Estellachild, "2 Hip Communes: A Personal Experience," in Richard Fairfield, *The Modern Utopian: Utopia U.S.A.* (San Francisco: Alternative Foundation, 1972), pp. 189–190.

27. Iris Keltz, *Scrapbook of a Taos Hippie* (El Paso, TX: Cinco Puntos Press, 2000), p. 43.

28. Name withheld, interviewed by Deborah Altus, 60s Communes Project, August 17, 1996; Ramon Sender Barayon, Gwen Leeds, Near Morningstar, Bill Wheeler, and many others, "Home Free Home: A History of Two Open-Door California Communes," chap. 16, pp. 1–2, n.d., available at http://diggers.org.

29. Barayon et al., "Home Free Home," chap. 12, p. 3, chap. 22, pp. 7–8; Alicia Bay Laurel's story is available at http://www.aliciabaylaurel.com, pp. 1–2.

30. Sundancer, *Celery Wine: The Story of a Country Commune*, pp. 35, 45–48; Lelain Lorenzen, interviewed by Deborah Altus, 60s Communes Project, March 15, 1997.

31. Noelle and Sandra Barton, interviewed by Timothy Miller, 60s Communes Project, September 15, 1996; Pamela Hunt, interviewed by Deborah Altus, 60s Communes Project, October 19, 1995; Anne MacNaughton, interviewed by Timothy Miller, 60s Communes Project, August 4, 1996.

32. Price, *Huerfano, a Memoir of Life in the Counterculture*, pp. 352, 345.

33. David E. Smith and Alan J. Rose, "Health Problems in Urban and Rural 'Crash Pad' Communes," *Clinical Perspectives* 9, no. 9 (September 1970): pp. 535–537; Miller, *The 60s Communes*, pp. 208–210.

34. Ayala Talpai, interviewed by Timothy Miller, 60s Communes Project, July 19, 1995.

35. Anderson, *Whatever Happened to the Hippies*, pp. 119–124.

36. Marylyn Motherbear Scott, interviewed by author, Albion, CA, June 5, 2007.

37. Anderson, *Whatever Happened to the Hippies*, pp. 28–31.

38. Ibid., p. 5.

39. Ibid., pp. 22–26, 149, 71–74, 146, 130, 150.

40. Melville, *Communes in the Counterculture*, pp. 134–135.

CHAPTER FIVE. "I WAS OPENING UP LIKE A TENDER FLOWER"

1. Timothy Miller, *The 60s Communes: Hippies and Beyond* (Syracuse, NY: Syracuse University Press, 1999), pp. 205–207; Martin Torgoff, *Can't Find My Way Home: America in the Great Stoned Age, 1945–2000* (New York: Simon and Schuster, 2004), p. 254.

2. Tim Hodgdon, *Manhood in the Age of Aquarius: Masculinity in Two Counterculture Communities, 1965–1983* (New York: Columbia University Press, 2007), chap. 4, pp. 6–11, available at http://www.gutenberg-e.org.

3. Aniko Bodroghkozy, *Groove Tube: Sixties Television and the Youth Rebellion* (Durham, NC: Duke University Press, 2001), pp. 82–85.

4. Ibid., pp. 136–138.

5. Tom Wolfe, *Electric Kool-Aid Acid Test* (New York: Bantam, 1999), pp. 86–87, 177.

6. Joan Didion, *Slouching toward Bethlehem* (New York: Ferrar, Straus and Giroux, 1990), pp. 90–92, 96–97, 101, 127–128.

7. John C. Ball and Frida G. Surawicz, "A Trip to San Francisco's Hippieland: Glorification of Delinquency and Irresponsibility," *International Journal of Criminology* 12 (December 1968): pp. 66–68.

8. David E. Smith and Alan J. Rose, "Observations in the Haight-Ashbury Medical Clinic of San Francisco: Health Problems in a 'Hippie' Subculture," *Clinical Pediatrics* 7, no. 6 (June 1968): p. 315; David E. Smith and Alan J. Rose, "Health Problems in Urban and Rural 'Crash Pad' Communes," *Clinical Pediatrics* 9, no. 9 (September 1970): p. 535; Torgoff, *Can't Find My Way Home*, pp. 217, 211–218.

9. Charles Hayes, ed., *Trip: An Anthology of True-Life Psychedelic Adventures* (New York: Penguin Books, 2000), p. 357.

10. Leonard Wolf, ed., *Voices of the Love Generation* (Boston: Little, Brown, 1968), pp. 199, 203.

11. Constance B. Holstein, Janice Stroud, and Norma Haan, "Alienated and Nonalienated Youth: Perceptions of Parents, Self-Evaluations, and Moral Reasoning of Hippies and College Youth," *Youth and Society* 5 (May 1974): pp. 280–281.

12. Jim Baumohl and Henry Miller, *Down and Out in Berkeley* (Berkeley: University of California School of Social Welfare, 1974), p. 46.

13. Aggregate responses from oral interviews conducted by author.

14. Ibid.

15. Judson Jerome, *Families of Eden: Communes and the New Anarchism* (New York: Seabury Press, 1974), p. 259; Keith Melville, *Communes in the Counterculture: Origins, Theories, Styles of Life* (New York: William Morrow, 1972), p. 159.

16. Mary Siler Anderson, interviewed by Deborah Altus, 60s Communes Project, November 11, 1995.

17. Hayes, *Trip*, pp. 223, 229.

18. Virginia Logan, interviewed by author, Berkeley, CA, July 12, 2007.

19. Ibid.

20. Hayes, *Trip*, pp. 68–71.

21. "Carlos Casteneda and His Followers: Finding Life's Meaning in Your Local Bookstore," *Journal of Popular Culture* 39, no. 4 (2004): pp. 584–586.

22. Wolf, *Voices of the Love Generation*, pp. 82–83.

23. Ramon Sender Barayon, Gwen Leeds, Near Morningstar, Bill Wheeler, and many others, "Home Free Home, A History of Two Open-Door California Communes," chap. 2, pp. 2–4, manuscript, n.d., available at http://www.dig gers.org; Charles Perry, *The Haight Ashbury: A History* (New York: Random House, 1984), p. 295.

24. Hayes, *Trip*, pp. 359–360.

25. Jerome, *Families of Eden*, p. 259.

26. Barayon et al., "Home Free Home," chap. 4, p. 4.

27. Nancy Nina, interviewed by Deborah Altus, 60s Communes Project, March 26, 1997.

28. Jentri Anders, *Beyond Counterculture: The Community of Manteel* (Pullman: Washington State University Press, 1990), pp. 229–320.

29. Jan Camp, interviewed by author, Berkeley, CA, May 29, 2007.

30. Wolf, *Voices of the Love Generation*, pp. 148–151.

31. Hayes, *Trip*, pp. 231–234.

32. Camp, interview.

33. Marylyn Motherbear Scott, interviewed by author, Albion, CA, June 5, 2007.

34. Ibid.

35. Barayon et al., "Home Free Home," chap. 2, p. 3.

36. Torgoff, *Can't Find My Way Home*, p. 251.

37. Guy Redden, "The New Agents: Personal Transfiguration and Radical Privatization in New Age Self-Help," *Journal of Consumer Culture* 2 (February 2002): pp. 36–38; Sam Binkley, "Everybody's Life Is Like a Spiral: Narrating Post-Fordism in the Lifestyle Movement of the 1970s," *Cultural Studies-Critical Methodologies* 4 (April 2004): pp. 76–78; John P. Bloch, *New Spirituality, Self, and Belonging: How New Agers and Neo-Pagans Talk about Themselves* (Westport, CT: Praeger, 1988), pp. 1–2; Robert S. Ellwood, *The Sixties Spiritual Awakening* (New Brunswick, NJ: Rutgers University Press, 1994), pp. 32–33, 312; Sherri Cavan, *Hippies of the Haight* (Saint Louis, MO: New Critics Press, 1972), pp. 182–183.

38. Pelican, "Birth of a New Age," *Womanspirit,* Winter Solstice, 1974: p. 3.

39. B. Holstein, Stroud, and Haan, "Alienated and Nonalienated Youth," p. 286; Bennett M. Berger, *The Survival of a Counterculture: Ideological Work and Everyday Life among Rural Communards* (Berkeley: University of California Press, 1981), p. 151; Miller, *The 60s Communes*, pp. 93–94, 104.

40. Camp, interview.

41. Logan, interview.

42. Shakti Gawain's story is available at http://shaktigawain.wwwhubs.com; Benjamin Shield and Richard Carlson, eds., *For the Love of God: New Writings on Spiritual and Psychological Leaders* (San Rafael, CA: New World Library, 1990), pp. 121–124.

43. Ellen Winner, "Doubting Shaman: An American's Apprenticeship in Nepali Shamanism," *Shaman's Drum*, no. 32, Summer 1993, pp. 25–31.

44. Redden, "The New Agents," p. 35; Bloch, *New Spirituality, Self, and Belonging*, p. 2; Anders, *Beyond Counterculture*, p. 215; Kathleen Taylor, interviewed by author, Berkeley, CA, August 15, 2007; Nancy Jean, interviewed by author, Berkeley, CA, June 12, 2007.

45. Anna Marie Daniels, interviewed by author, Santa Barbara, CA, July 26, 2007; Lisa Aldred, "Plastic Shamans and Astroturf Sun Dances: New Age Commercialization of Native American Spirituality," *American Indian Quarterly* 24, no. 3 (Summer 2000): pp. 329–352; Philip Deloria, "Counterculture

Indians and the New Age," in Peter Braunstein and Michael William Doyle, eds., *Imagine Nation: The American Counterculture of the 1960s and 1970s* (New York: Routledge, 2002), p. 174.

46. Constance Trouble, interviewed by author, Berkeley, CA, August 6, 2007; Robert N. Bellah et al., *Habits of the Heart: Individualism and Commitment in American Life* (New York: Harper and Row, 1985), p. 84.

47. Erik Cohen, "Nomads from Affluence: Notes on the Phenomenon of Drifter-Tourism," *International Journal of Comparative Sociology* 14 (1973): pp. 14, 89, 92, 95.

48. Ibid., p. 94–95; Trouble, interview.

49. Cohen, "Nomads from Affluence," p. 96.

50. Ibid., pp. 97, 102, 103.

51. Agnieszka Sobocinska, "The Ultimate Trip," "National Library of Australia Newsletter" 16, no. 11, August 2006, p. 3.

52. Roberta Price, *Huerfano: A Memoir of Life in the Counterculture* (Amherst: University of Massachusetts Press, 2004), p. 55.

53. Cohen, "Nomads from Affluence," p. 93; Marilyn Stablein, *Sleeping in Caves: A Sixties Himalayan Memoir* (Rhinebeck, NY: Monkfish Book Publishing Company, 2003), pp. xi–xiv, 76, 80–81, 89, 102, 108.

54. Cherie Lemke, fifty-three letters dated May 12, 1965–September 18, 1985, in possession of author.

55. Daniels, interview.

56. Ladybear's story is available at http://www.snowcrest.net; Mara Devine, interviewed by Deborah Altus, 60s Communes Project, November 12, 1995.

57. Terry Klein, interviewed by Timothy Miller, 60s Communes Project, August 6, 1996; Sylvia Anderson, interviewed by Deborah Altus, 60s Communes Project, August 3, 1996; Jodi Mitchell, "Jodi Mitchell's Wheeler's Story," "MOST Newsletter" 6, no. 1, Spring 1999, available at http://laurel rose.com/MORN/SP993.html.

CHAPTER SIX. LITTLE SISTERS

1. Ken Libertoff, "The Runaway Child in America: A Social History," *Journal of Family Issues* 1, no. 2 (June 1980): pp. 151–160; Karen M. Staller, *Runaways: How the Sixties Counterculture Shaped Today's Practices and Policies* (New York: Columbia University Press, 2006), pp. 29, 32–34.

2. California State Legislature, Senate, Select Committee on Children and Youth, *The Runaway Child: Hearing before the California State Legislature,*

December 18, 1973, pp. 111–113; Jeffrey D. Blum and Judith E. Smith, *Nothing Left to Lose: Studies of Street People* (Boston: Beacon Press, 1972), p. 15; Libertoff, "The Runaway Child in America," p. 161.

3. Staller, *Runaways*, pp. 29; 39–40; Blum and Smith, *Nothing Left to Lose*, p. 18; California State Legislature, *The Runaway Child*, pp. 111–113, 154–158.

4. Libertoff, "The Runaway Child in America," p. 161; Staller, *Runaways*, pp. 29, 39–40.

5. Kristine Olson Rogers, "'For Her Own Protection . . . ': Conditions of Incarceration for Female Juvenile Offenders in the State of Connecticut," *Law and Society Review* (Winter 1972): pp. 223–226, 237.

6. Blum and Smith, *Nothing Left to Lose*, p. 14, pp. 14–18.

7. Constance Trouble, interviewed by author, Berkeley, CA, August 6, 2007.

8. Richard Bock and Abigail English, *Got Me on the Run: A Study of Runaways* (Boston: Beacon Press, 1973), pp. 147–148, 155–156.

9. Robert Houriet, "Life and Death of a Commune Called Oz," in Rosabeth Moss Kanter, ed., *Communes: Creating and Managing the Collective Life* (New York: Harper and Row, 1973), p. 480.

10. Jim Baumohl and Henry Miller, *Down and Out in Berkeley* (Berkeley: University of California, Berkeley School of Social Welfare, 1974), pp. 12–13, 31, 41, 43.

11. Staller, *Runaways*, pp. 73–98; Blum and Smith, *Nothing Left to Lose*, pp. 2–8.

12. Baumohl and Miller, *Down and Out in Berkeley*, pp. 12–13, 15, 50.

13. Trouble, interview.

14. Jodi Mitchell, "Jodi Mitchell," "MOST Newsletter" 6, no. 1, Spring 1999, pp. 2, 4–5, 7–8, available at http://laurelrose.com.

15. Shannon Perry, interviewed by Deborah Altus, 60s Communes Project, March 25, 1997.

16. Joel Selvin, *Summer of Love: The Inside Story of LSD, Rock and Roll, Free Love and High Times in the Wild West* (New York: Cooper Square Press, 1994), pp. 32, 272, 127, 169, 57.

17. Karen M. Staller, "Runaway and Homeless Youth," in Gerald P. Mallon and Peg McCartt Hess, eds., *Child Welfare for the 21st Century: A Handbook of Practices, Policies, and Programs* (New York: Columbia University Press, 2005); California State Legislature, *The Runaway Child*, pp. 154–158; Peter Coyote, *Sleeping Where I Fall* (Washington, DC: Counterpoint, 1998), p. 93; Trouble, interview.

18. Jentri Anders, *Beyond Counterculture: The Community of Mateel* (Pullman: Washington State University Press, 1990), pp. 91, 253–256.

19. Gilbert Zicklin, *Countercultural Communes: A Sociological Perspective* (Westport, CT: Greenwood Press, 1983), p. 98; John Rothchild and Susan Berns Wolf, *The Children of the Counterculture* (New York: Doubleday, 1976), pp. 9, 71–72, 81–82; Timothy Miller, *The 60s Communes: Hippies and Beyond* (Syracuse, NY: Syracuse University Press, 1999), pp. 184–185.

20. Zicklin, *Countercultural Communes*, pp. 101–111.

21. Chelsea Cain, ed., *Wild Child: Girlhoods in the Counterculture* (Seattle: Seal Press, 1999), pp. xxiv, xvii, 173; Rothchild and Wolf, *Children of the Counterculture*, pp. 15, 193.

22. Zicklin, *Countercultural Communes*, p. 100; Francesca Fortunato, "The Hippie Mom and Others Respond," August 31, 2001, p. 2, available at http://archive.salon.com.

23. Cain, *Wild Child*, p. 100; Adriana Barton, "Growing Up Hippie," *Utne Reader,* November/December 2003; Whiz Perry, "I Survived a Hippie Mom," *Wire Tap Magazine,* May 17, 2000, available at http://www.wiretapmag.org.;

24. Cain, *Wild Child*, pp. 68–70, 78–79.

25. Ibid., pp. 93–94, 96–97.

26. Lisa Michaels, *Split: A Countercultural Childhood* (Boston: Houghton Mifflin, 1998), pp. 18–45; Joelle Fraser, *The Territory of Men: A Memoir* (New York: Villard Books, 2002), pp. 96–98, 180–184;

27. Herbert Marcuse, *Eros and Civilization: A Philosophical Inquiry into Freud* (Boston: Beacon, 1966), pp. 46, 92–93, 199, 201; David Allyn, *Make Love Not War: The Sexual Revolution, an Unfettered History* (New York: Little, Brown, 2000), pp. 196–205.

28. Zicklin, *Countercultural Communes*, pp. 101–107; Rothchild and Wolf, *Children of the Counterculture*, pp. 193–194; Fraser, *Territory of Men*, pp. 23–24, 45–48; Bennett M. Berger, *The Survival of a Counterculture: Ideological Work and Everyday Life among Rural Communards* (Berkeley: University of California Press, 1981), pp. 69–71.

29. Cain, *Wild Child*, pp. 59, 62; Francesca Fortunato, "The Hippie Mom and Others Respond," August 31, 2001, p. 2, available at http://archive.salon.com; Allyn, *Make Love Not War*, pp. 298–299.

30. Perry, "I Survived a Hippie Mom."

31. Fraser, *Territory of Men*, pp. 19–20; Berger, *Survival of a Counterculture*, pp. 64–66; Ben Schwabe, "The Hippie Mom and Others Respond," August 31, 2001, p. 1, available at http://archive.salon.com.

32. Perry, "I Survived a Hippie Mom"; Gabriel Golden and Francesca Fortunato, "The Hippie Mom and Others Respond," August 31, 2001, p. 2, available at http://archive.salon.com; Fraser, *Territory of Men*, p. 29.

33. Patrick Sullivan, "The Kids Are All Right," *Metro Santa Cruz*, December 5–12, 2001, book section, pp. 4–5, available at http:// www. metroactice .com; Alan Sailer, "The Hippie Mom and Others Respond," August 31, 2001, p. 1, available at http://archive.salon.com.

34. Jan Camp, interviewed by author, Berkeley, CA, October 3, 2005; Anna Marie Daniels, interviewed by author, Santa Barbara, CA, July 26, 2007; Angela A. Aidala, "Communes and Changing Family Norms: Marriage and Lifestyle Choices among Former Members of Communal Groups," *Journal of Family Issues* 10 (1989): pp. 316–317; Chris Bobel, *The Paradox of Natural Mothering* (Philadelphia: Temple University Press, 2002), pp. 48–66, 165–168.

CHAPTER SEVEN. "WE WERE THE TRUE AQUARIANS"

1. See, for example, Sam Binkley, "The Seers of Menlo Park: The Discourse of Heroic Consumption in the 'Whole Earth Catalog,'" *Journal of Consumer Culture* 3 (2003): pp. 283–313.

2. Alice Echols, *Daring to be Bad: Radical Feminism in America* (Minneapolis: University of Minnesota Press, 1989), p. 6; Alice Echols, *The Sixties and Its Aftershocks* (New York: Columbia University Press, 2002), pp. 109–112; Bennett Berger, *The Survival of a Counterculture: Ideological Work and Everyday Life among Rural Communards* (Berkeley: University of California Press, 1981), pp. 152–153; Richard Fairfield, ed., *The Modern Utopian: Utopia U.S.A* (San Francisco: Alternatives Foundation, 1972), pp. 24, 172–178, 184–187, 189–194; Ron E. Roberts, *The New Communes: Coming Together in America* (Englewood Cliffs, NJ: Prentice Hall, 1972), p. 89.

3. Richard Atcheson, *The Bearded Lady: Going on the Commune Trip and Beyond* (New York: John Day, 1971), p. 76; Peter Coyote, *Sleeping Where I Fall* (Washington, DC: Counterpoint, 1998), p. 289; Jentri Anders, *Beyond Counterculture: The Community of Mateel* (Pullman: Washington State University Press, 1990), pp. 204–205; Berger, *The Survival of a Counterculture*, pp. 152–154.

4. Ginsberg quoted in Morris Dickstein, *Gates of Eden: American Culture in the Sixties* (New York: Basic Books), p. 21; Herbert Marcuse, *Eros and Civilization* (Boston: Beacon Press, 1966), pp. 159, 161, 212, 223–224; Nancy Tuana, *The Less Noble Sex: Scientific, Religious, and Philosophical Conceptions*

of Woman's Nature (Bloomington: Indiana University Press, 1993), pp. 49, 63, 79–92, 155, 166, 171.

5. Marylyn Motherbear Scott, interviewed by author, Albion, CA, June 5, 2007.

6. Mildred Loomis, "Editorial," *Green Revolution* 33, no. 1 (January 1976): p. 1; Doris Simonis, "Mother's Day," *Green Revolution* 33, no. 1 (January 1976): p. 14.

7. Anders, *Beyond Counterculture*, p. 205.

8. Karen Lee Robins, "Sculptor of Goddess Images, *Woman of Power*, Spring 1987, p. 63.

9. Mimi Albert, "Women of Wisdom," *Yoga Journal*, May/June 1986, p. 27; Pelican, "Birth of a New Age," *Womanspirit* 1, no. 2, Winter Solstice, 1974, p. 3; Patricia Mische, "Women and Power," *New Age* 4, no. 6, November 1978, p. 80.

10. Kenoli Oleari, interviewed by Tim Miller, 60s Communes Project, September 16, 1996; Berger, *The Survival of a Counterculture*, pp. 152–153; Mara Devine, interviewed by Deborah Altus, 60s Communes Project, November 12, 1995.

11. Berger, *The Survival of a Counterculture*, pp. 152–153; Nancy Jean, interviewed by author, Berkeley, CA, June 12, 12, 2007; Devine, interview; *Womanspirit* 1, no. 1, Fall 1974, index, pp. 32–33; Timothy Miller, *The 60s Communes: Hippies and Beyond* (Syracuse, NY: Syracuse University Press, 1999), pp. 138–139.

12. Bryan Pfaffenberger, "A World of Husbands and Mothers: Sex Roles and Their Ideological Context in the Formation of the Farm," in Jon Wagner, ed., *Sex Roles in Contemporary American Communes* (Bloomington: Indiana University Press, 1982), p. 204; Louis J. Kern, "Pronatalism, Midwifery, and Synergistic Marriage: Spiritual Enlightenment and Sexual Ideology on the Farm (Tennessee)," in Wendy Chmielewski, Louis J. Kern, and Marylyn Hartzell, eds., *Women in Spiritual and Communitarian Societies in the United States* (Syracuse, NY: Syracuse University Press, 1993), pp. 217–218; Stephen Gaskin, *Hey Beatnik: This Is the Farm Book* (Summertown, TN: Book Publishing Company, 1974), n.p.

13. Constance Trouble, interviewed by author, Berkeley, CA, August 6, 2007; Jan Camp, interviewed by author, Berkeley, CA, October 3, 2005.

14. Guy Redden, "The New Agents: Personal Transfiguration and Radical Privatization in New Age Self-Help," *Journal of Consumer Culture* 2 (February 2002): p. 39.

15. Sam Binkley, "Everybody's Life Is Like a Spiral: Narrating Post-Fordism in the Lifestyle Movement of the 1970s," *Cultural Studies-Critical Methodologies* 4 (April 2004): pp. 71–95; Redden, "The New Agents," pp. 33–52.

16. David Allyn, *Make Love Not War: The Sexual Revolution, an Unfettered History* (New York: Little, Brown, 2000), p. 79; Robert S. Ellwood, *The Sixties Spiritual Awakening* (New Brunswick, NJ: Rutgers University Press, 1994), p. 184; Iacchus, Priest, "What Is the Church of All Worlds?" available at http://www.caw.org.

17. Ellwood, *The Sixties Spiritual Awakening*, pp. 183–184; Tim Zell, "Editorial," "Green Egg" 3, no. 23, March 18, 1970, p. 1; W. Holman Keith, "Pagan and Neo Pagan Ethics," and H.R.M., letter to the editor, "Green Egg" 5, no. 46, 1972.

18. Arlene Meyers, letter to the editor, and Tim Zell's response, "Green Egg" 6., no. 55, Midsummer 1973, p. 30; W. Holman Keith, "Venus Proserpina: The Feminine Mystique," "Green Egg" 6, no 55, Midsummer 1973, p. 8; Allyn, *Make Love Not War*, p. 3; Tim Zell, "Editorial Giggles," "Green Egg" 6, no. 58, November 1973, p. 3.

19. "Green Egg" 7, no. 64, August 1, 1974; "Green Egg" 7, no. 65, September 21, 1974, p. 1; "Green Egg" 7, no. 62, May 1974, p. 39; W. Holman Keith, "Paganism: Trends and Traditions," "Green Egg" 7, no. 62, May 1974, p. 9.

20. "Green Egg" 7, no. 64, August 1974, p. 30; "Green Egg" 8, no. 73, September 1975, pp. 38–45; Margot Adler, *Drawing Down the Moon* (New York: Penguin, 1986), pp. 217, 228.

21. Ellwood, *The Sixties Spiritual Awakening*, p. 312; Susan Greenwood, "Gender and Power in Magical Practices," in Steven Sutcliffe and Marion Bowman, eds., *Beyond the New Age: Exploring Alternative Spirituality* (Edinburgh: Edinburgh University Press, 2000), p. 138; "Green Egg" 7, no. 64, August 1, 1974, p. 30; "Green Egg" 7, no. 65, September 21, 1974, p. 18.

22. Adler, *Drawing Down the Moon*, p. 217; Rosemary Radford Ruether, "The Normalization of Goddess Religion," *Feminist Theology* 13 (2005): pp. 151–154; Lee Walker, "Heresy Trial of Z. Budapest," "Green Egg" 8, no. 72, August 1, 1975, pp. 6–8; Chris Carmines, "Women, Intellectualism, and Magic," *Magical Blend* 8, 1983, pp. 44–45; *Woman of Power*, Premier Issue, Spring 1984, p. 1.

23. Philip Delora, "Counterculture Indians and the New Age," in Peter Braunstein and Michael William Doyle, eds., *Imagine Nation: The American Counterculture of the 1960s and 1970s* (New York: Routledge, 2002), pp.

159–188; Susan Starr Sered, *Priestess Mother Sacred Sister* (New York: Oxford University Press, 1994), p. 199.

24. Skyhawk, "Receiving the Sacred Pipe," *Shaman's Drum*, no. 3, Winter 1985, pp. 45–46; *Shaman's Drum*, no. 4, Spring 1986, workshop announcements, pp. 11–13, 56, 58; Lisa Aldred, "Plastic Shaman and Astroturf Sun Dances: New Age Commercialization of Native American Spirituality," *American Indian Quarterly* 24, no. 3 (Summer 2000): pp. 331–333; Noel Sturgeon, *Ecofeminist Natures: Race, Gender, Feminist Theory, and Political Action* (New York: Routledge, 1997), p. 130.

25. James A. Beckford, "Holistic Imagery and Ethics in New Age Religious and Healing Movements," *Social Compass* 31 (1984): pp. 331–333; Hans Holzen, "Sex and Psychic Awareness," in Elizabeth Pepper and John Wilcock, eds., *The Witches' Almanac* (New York: Grosset and Dunlap, 1978), p. 43; Marcia Gerrase Ingenito, ed., *National New Age Yellow Pages* (Fullerton, CA: National New Age Yellow Pages, 1987); "National Yoga Teachers' Directory," *Yoga Journal* 33, August 1980, pp. 62–75; "Light of Yoga Society," *Yoga Journal* 20, May/June 1978, p. 52.

26. Beckford, "Holistic Imagery and Ethics," p. 266; Ellie Hedges and James Beckford, "Holism, Healing, and the New Age," in Steven Sutcliffe and Marion Bowman, eds., *Beyond the New Age: Exploring Alternative Spirituality* (Edinburgh: Edinburgh University Press, 2000), p. 182; Diane Mariechild, "Mother, Teacher, Healer, Author of Mother Wit," *Woman of Power*, Spring 1984, p. 21; Barbara Stevens Barnum, "Healers in Complementary Medicine," *Alternative Health Practitioner* 5, no. 3 (Winter 1999): pp. 217–224; Ramon Sender Barayon, Gwen Leeds, Near Morningstar, Bill Wheeler, and many others, "Home Free Home: A History of Two Open-Door California Communes," chap. 12, p. 4, manuscript, n.d., available at http://www.dig gers.org; Iris Keltz, *Scrapbook of a Taos Hippie* (El Paso, TX: Cinco Puntos Press, 2000), pp. 41, 36; Anne MacNaughton, interviewed by Tim Miller, 60s Communes Project, August 4, 1996; name withheld, interviewed by Deborah Altus, 60s Communes Project, August 7, 1996; Pamela Hunt, interviewed by Deborah Altus, 60s Communes Project, October 19, 1995.

27. Hedges and Beckford, "Holism, Healing, and the New Age," pp. 177, 182, 191; Ingenito, *National New Age Yellow Pages;* Victoras Kulvinskas, *New Age Directory* (Wethersford, CT: Omangod Press, 1978), pp. 34–38; Dana Uhlman, "Holistic Health," *Briarpatch Review* 11 (1980): pp. 13–14; Beckford, "Holistic Imagery and Ethics," pp. 264–266; Binkley, "Everybody's Life Is Like a Spiral," pp. 84–89.

28. Chris Bobel, *The Paradox of Natural Mothering* (Philadelphia: Temple University Press, 2002); Debra L. Kirkley, "Is Motherhood Good for Women?" *Journal of Obstetric, Gynecologic, and Neonatal Nursing* 29, no. 5 (September/October 2000): p. 461; Elizabeth Bryant Merrill, "Learning How to Mother: An Ethnographic Investigation of an Urban Breastfeeding Group," *Anthropology and Education Quarterly* 18, no. 3 (September 1987): pp. 222–240; Thomas S. Weisner, Mary Bausano, and Madeleine Karnfein, "Putting Family Ideals into Practice: Pronaturalism in Conventional and Nonconventional California Families," *Ethos* 11, no. 4 (Winter 1983): pp. 278–304.

29. Malcolm Hamilton, "An Analysis of the Festival for Mind-Body-Spirit," in Steven Sutcliffe and Marion Bowman, eds., *Beyond the New Age: Exploring Alternative Spirituality* (Edinburgh: Edinburgh University Press, 2000), p. 191; Binkley, "Everybody's Life Is Like a Spiral," p. 86; Louise Lacey, "Competition," *Briarpatch Review* 11 (1980): p. 29; Virginia Logan, interviewed by author, Berkeley, CA, July 12, 2007.

30. Pelican, "Birth of a New Age," p. 3 ; Helen Caldicott, "Notes from an Interview on Womanpower," *Woman of Power*, Spring 1984, p. 17; Kathleen Duffy, "Women and Disarmament," in Livermore Action Group, *International Day of Disarmament Handbook* (Berkeley, CA: Livermore Action Group Handbook Collective, 1983), p. 92.

31. Albert, "Women of Wisdom," p. 28; Sturgeon, *Ecofeminist Natures*, p. 69; Scott, interview; Trouble, interview.

32. Adam Rome, "Give Earth a Chance: The Environmental Movement and the Sixties," *Journal of American History* 4 (September 2003): pp. 541–544; Nancy Nesbit, "Get Back to Where You Belong," *The Modern Utopian* 4, nos. 3 and 4 (Summer/Fall 1970): p. 15; Scott, interview.

33. Shoshanna Schwimmer, "Let a Thousand Flowers Bloom," *Woman of Power*, Winter 1987, pp. 78–79; Sharon Doubiago, "Mama Coyote Talks to the Boys," in Judith Plant, ed., *Healing the Wounds: The Promise of Ecofeminism* (Philadelphia: New Society Publishers, 1989), pp. 41–42.

34. A. K. Salleh, "Deeper Than Deep Ecology: The Ecofeminist Connection," *Environmental Ethics* 6, no. 1 (1984): p. 340; Michael D'Antonio, *Heaven on Earth* (New York: Crown Publishers, 1992), pp. 160–163, 206; Martin Torgoff, *Can't Find My Way Home: America in the Great Stoned Age, 1945–2000* (New York: Simon and Schuster, 2000), pp. 252–253; "Caw Clergy–Morning Glory Zell–Raven Heart," available at http://www.caw.org; Scott, interview; Mary Siler Anderson, *Whatever Happened to the Hippies* (San Pedro, CA: R & E Miles, 1990), pp. 74–75, 130, 146; Trouble, interview.

35. Berger, *The Survival of a Counterculture*, pp. 152–153.

36. Chris Bobel, *The Paradox of Natural Mothering*, pp. 48–60; Anna Marie Daniels, interviewed by author, Santa Barbara, CA, July 26, 2007; Trouble, interview.

37. Binkley, "Everybody's Life Is Like a Spiral," pp. 85–89; Bobel, *The Paradox of Natural Mothering*, pp. 48–60.

38. Scott, interview; Patricia Leigh Brown, "Dharma in the Dirt," *New York Times*, Home and Garden, May 8, 2008, pp. 1–3, available at NYTimes. com.; Julia Moskin, "Women Find Their Place in the Field," *New York Times*, June 1, 2005, pp. 2–3, available at NYTimes.com.

39. Pat Tanumihardja, "Women at the Forefront of Organic and Sustainable Farming, *Seattle Woman*, May 7, 2007, p. 2–3, available at http//:www .seattlewomanmagazine.com.

40. Elaine Lipson, "Food, Farming . . . Feminism? Why Going Organic Makes Good Sense," *Ms. Magazine*, Summer, 2004, p. 5, available at http:// www.msmagazine.com; Elyse Friedman, "The Hippie Kitchen's Long Strange Trip . . . into Your Local Supermarket," special to the *Chicago Tribune*, January 7, 2004; Warren Belasco, *Appetite for Change: How the Counterculture Took on the Food Industry, 1966–1988* (New York: Pantheon, 1989), pp. 94–95; Craig Cox, *Storefront Revolution: Food Co-ops and the Counterculture* (New Brunswick, NJ: Rutgers University Press, 1994), pp. 30–32, 43; Thomas McNamee, *Alice Waters and Chez Panisse: The Romantic, Impractical, Often Eccentric, Ultimately Brilliant Making of a Food Revolution* (New York: Penguin, 2007), pp. 267, 282–285; John Birdsall, "Ripe for Change," *Contra Costa Times*, October 10, 2007, sec. C, pp. 1, 6, 8.

SELECTED BIBLIOGRAPHY

The following bibliography lists the central sources used in this work. For other citations in the text see the endnotes.

Adler, Margot. *Drawing Down the Moon.* New York: Penguin, 1986.

———. *Heretic's Heart: A Journey through Spirit and Revolution.* Boston: Beacon Press, 1997.

Aidala, Angela. "Communes and Changing Family Norms: Marriage and Lifestyle Choices among Former Members of Communal Groups." *Journal of Family Issues* 10 (1989): 311–338.

Aidala, Angela, and Benjamin Zablocki. "The Communes of the 1970s: Who Joined and Why?" *Marriage and Family Review* 17 (1991): 87–116.

Aldred, Lisa. "Plastic Shamans and Astroturf Sun Dances: New Age Commercialization of Native American Spirituality." *American Indian Quarterly* 24, no. 3 (Summer 2000): 329–352.

Allyn, David. *Make Love Not War: The Sexual Revolution, an Unfettered History.* Boston: Little, Brown, 2000.

Anders, Jentri. *Beyond Counterculture: The Community of Mateel.* Pullman: Washington State University Press, 1990.

Anderson, Mary Siler. *Whatever Happened to the Hippies?* San Pedro, CA: R & E Miles, 1990.

Atchenson, Richard. *The Bearded Lady: Going on the Commune Trip and Beyond.* New York: John Day Company, 1971.

Barayon, Ramon Sender, Gwen Leeds, Near Morningstar, Bill Wheeler, and many others. "Home Free Home: A History of Two Open-Door California Communes." Manuscript, n.d. Available at http://www.diggers.org/homefree/hfh_int.html.

Bailey, Beth. "Sex as a Weapon: Underground Comix and the Paradox of Liberation." In *Imagine Nation: The American Counterculture of the 1960s and 1970s,* edited by Peter Braunstein and Michael William Doyle, 305–324. New York: Routledge, 2002.

Beauchamp, Monte, ed. *The Life and Times of R. Crumb: Comments from Contemporaries.* New York: St. Martin's Griffin, 1998.

Beckford, James A. "Holistic Imagery and Ethics in New Religious and Healing Movements." *Social Compass* 31 (1984): 259–272.

Belasco, Warren. *Appetite for Change: How the Counterculture Took on the Food Industry, 1966–1988.* New York: Pantheon Books, 1989.

Berger, Bennett. *The Survival of a Counterculture: Ideological Work and Everyday Life among Rural Communards.* Berkeley: University of California Press, 1981.

Binkley, Sam. "Everybody's Life Is Like a Spiral: Narrating Post-Fordism in the Lifestyle Movement of the 1970s." *Cultural Studies-Critical Methodologies* 4 (2004): 71–95.

———. "The Seers of Menlo Park: The Discourse of Heroic Consumption in the 'Whole Earth Catalog.'" *Journal of Consumer Culture* 3 (2003): 283–313.

Bloch, Avital H., and Lauri Umanski, eds. *Impossible to Hold: Women and Culture in the 1960s.* New York: New York University Press, 2005.

Bloch, John P. *New Spirituality, Self, and Belonging: How New Agers and Neo-Pagans Talk about Themselves.* Westport, CT: Praeger, 1988.

Blum, Jeffery D., and Judith E. Smith. *Nothing Left to Lose: Studies of Street People.* Boston: Beacon Press, 1972.

Bobel, Chris. *The Paradox of Natural Mothering.* Philadelphia: Temple University Press, 2002.

Bock, Richard, and Abigail English. *Got Me on the Run: A Study of Runaways.* Boston: Beacon Press, 1973.

Bodroghkozy, Aniko. *Groove Tube: Sixties Television and the Youth Rebellion.* Durham, NC: Duke University Press, 2001.

Breines, Wini. *Young, White, and Miserable: Growing Up Female in the Fifties.* Boston: Beacon Press, 1992.

Cain, Chelsea, ed. *Wild Child: Girlhoods in the Counterculture.* Seattle: Seal Press, 1999.

Cavan, Sherri. "The Class Structure of Hippie Society." *Journal of Contemporary Ethnography* 1 (1972): 211–238.

———. *Hippies of the Haight.* Saint Louis: New Critics Press, 1972.

Chmielewski, Wendy, Louis J. Kern, and Marylyn Hartzell, eds. *Women in Spiritual and Communitarian Societies in the United States.* Syracuse, NY: Syracuse University Press, 1993.

Cohen, Erik. "Nomads from Affluence: Notes on the Phenomenon of Drifter-Tourism." *International Journal of Comparative Sociology* 14 (1973): 89–103.

Coontz, Stephanie. *The Way We Never Were: American Families and the Nostalgia Trap.* New York: Basic Books, 1992.

Cox, Craig. *Storefront Revolution: Food Co-ops and the Counterculture.* New Brunswick, NJ: Rutgers University Press, 1994.

Coyote, Peter. *Sleeping Where I Fall.* Washington, DC: Counterpoint, 1998.

Davidson, Sara. "Hippie Families on Open Land." In *Communes: Creating and Managing the Collective Life*, edited by Rosabeth Moss Kanter, 334–350. New York: Harper and Row, 1973.

———. "Open Land: Getting Back to the Communal Garden." *Harpers* 240, June 1970: 91–100.

Deloria, Philip. "Counterculture Indians and the New Age." In *Imagine Nation: The American Counterculture of the 1960s and 1970s*, edited by Peter Braunstein and Michael William Doyle, 159–188. New York: Routledge, 2002.

Didion, Joan. *Slouching toward Bethlehem.* New York: Farrar, Straus and Giroux, 1990.

Dragonwagon, Crescent. *The Commune Cookbook.* New York: Simon and Schuster, 1972.

Echols, Alice. *Daring to Be Bad: Radical Feminism in America.* Minneapolis: University of Minnesota Press, 1989.

———. *Shaky Ground: The Sixties and Its Aftershocks.* New York: Columbia University Press, 2002.

Ehrenreich, Barbara. *Fear of Falling: The Inner Life of the Middle Class.* New York: Pantheon Books, 1989.

Ehrenreich, Barbara, Elizabeth Hess, and Gloria Jacobs. "The Politics of Promiscuity." *New Age*, November/December 1986, 28–31, 57–58, 60–62.

Ellwood, Robert S. *The Sixties Spiritual Awakening.* New Brunswick, NJ: Rutgers University Press, 1994.

Evans, Sarah. *Personal Politics: The Roots of Women's Liberation in the Civil Rights Movement and the New Left.* New York: Vintage, 1980.

Fairfield, Richard, ed. *The Modern Utopian: Communes U.S.A.* San Francisco: Alternatives Foundation, 1971.

———, ed. *The Modern Utopian: Utopia U.S.A.* San Francisco: Alternatives Foundation, 1972.

Fenn, Katheryn Kerr. "Daughters of the Counterculture: Rock and Roll Groupies in the 1960s and 1970s." Ph.D. diss., Duke University, 2002.

Fraser, Joelle. *The Territory of Men: A Memoir.* New York: Villard, 2002.

Gaar, Gillian G. *She's a Rebel: The History of Women in Rock and Roll.* Seattle: Seal Press, 1992.

Gardner, Hugh. *The Children of Prosperity: Thirteen Modern American Communes.* New York: St. Martin's, 1976.

Gaskin, Stephen. *Hey Beatnik: This Is the Farm Book.* Summertown, TN: Book Publishing Company, 1974.

Glessing, Robert J. *The Underground Press in America.* Bloomington: Indiana University Press, 1970.

Gravy, Wavy. *The Hog Farm and Friends.* New York: Links, 1974.

Greenwood, Susan. "Gender and Power in Magical Practices." In *Beyond the New Age: Exploring Alternative Spirituality,* edited by Steven Surcliff and Marion Bowman, 137–154. Edinburgh: Edinburgh University Press, 2000.

Hayes, Charles, ed. *Trip: An Anthology of True-Life Psychedelic Adventures.* New York: Penguin, 2000.

Hedgepeth, William, and Dennis Stock. *The Alternative: Communal Life in New America.* New York: Macmillan, 1970.

Hodgdon, Tim. *Manhood in the Age of Aquarius: Masculinity in Two Counterculture Communities, 1965–1983.* New York: Columbia University Press, 2007. Available at http://www.gutenberg-e.org/hodgdon.

Holstein, Constance, Janice Stroud, and Norma Haam. "Alienated and Nonalienated Youth: Perceptions of Parents, Self-Evaluations, and Moral Reasoning of Hippies and College Youth." *Youth and Society* 5 (1974): 279–302.

Horton, Lucy. *Country Commune Cooking.* New York: Coward, McCann, and Geoghegan, 1972.

Jerome, Judson. *Families of Eden: Communes and the New Anarchism.* New York: Seabury Press, 1974.

Johnston, Charley M., and Robert W. Deisher. "Contemporary Communal Childrearing: A First Analysis." *Pediatrics* 52, no. 3 (1973): 319–326.

Kanter, Rosabeth Moss. *Commitment and Community: Communes and Utopias in Sociological Perspective.* Cambridge: Harvard University Press, 1972.

———, ed. *Communes: Creating and Managing the Collective Life.* New York: Harper and Row, 1973.

Katz, Elia. *Armed Love.* New York: Holt, Rinehart and Winston, 1971.

Keltz, Iris. *Scrapbook of a Taos Hippie.* El Paso, TX: Cinco Puntos Press, 2000.

Keniston, Kenneth. *The Uncommitted: Alienated Youth in American Society.*
New York: Dell, 1965.

―――. *Young Radicals: Notes on Committed Youth.* New York: Harcourt,
Brace and World, 1968.

Kern, Louis J. "Pronatalism, Midwifery, and Synergistic Marriage: Spiritual
Enlightenment and Sexual Ideology on the Farm (Tennessee)." In *Women
in Spiritual and Communitarian Societies in the United States,* edited by
Wendy E. Chmielewski, Louis J. Kern, and Marylyn Klee-Hartzell,
201–220. Syracuse: Syracuse University Press, 1993.

Kessler, Lauren. *After All These Years: Sixties Ideals in a Different World.*
New York: Thunder's Mouth Press, 1990.

Laurel, Alicia Bay. *Living on the Earth.* New York: Random House, 1971.

Leder, Kit. "Women in Communes." *WIN* 6 (1970): 14–16.

Libertoff, Ken. "The Runaway Child in America: A Social History." *Journal
of Family Issues* 1, no. 2 (June 1980): 151–164.

McBride, David. "On the Fault Line of Mass Culture and the
Counterculture: A Social History of the Hippie Counterculture in 1960s
Los Angeles." Ph.D. diss., University of California, Los Angeles, 1998.

McNamee, Thomas. *Alice Waters and Chez Panisse: The Romantic,
Impractical, Often Eccentric, Ultimately Brilliant Making of a Food
Revolution.* New York: Penguin Press, 2007.

Melville, Keith. *Communes in the Counterculture: Origins, Theories, Styles of
Life.* New York: William Morrow, 1972.

Michaels, Lisa. *Split: A Countercultural Childhood.* Boston: Houghton
Mifflin, 1998.

Michals, Debra. "From 'Consciousness Expansion' to 'Consciousness
Raising': Feminism and the Countercultural Politics of the Self." In
Imagine Nation: The American Counterculture of the 1960s and 1970s,
edited by Peter Braunstein and Michael William Doyle, 41–68. New
York: Routledge, 2002.

Miller, Henry, and Jim Baumohl. *Down and Out in Berkeley.* Berkeley:
University of California School of Social Welfare, 1974.

Miller, Timothy. *The Hippies and American Values.* Knoxville: University of
Tennessee Press, 1991.

―――. *The 60s Communes: Hippies and Beyond.* New York: Syracuse
University Press, 1999.

O'Dair, Barbara, ed. *Trouble Girls: The Rolling Stone Book of Women in Rock.*
New York: Rolling Stone Press, 1997.

Perry, Charles. *The Haight Ashbury: A History*. New York: Random House, 1984.

Pfaffenberger, Bryan. "A World of Husbands and Mothers: Sex Roles and Their Ideological Context in the Formation of the Farm." In *Sex Roles in Contemporary American Communes*, edited by Jon Wagner, 172–210. Bloomington: Indiana University Press, 1982.

Price, Roberta. *Huerfano: A Memoir of Life in the Counterculture*. Amherst: University of Massachusetts Press, 2004.

Redden, Guy. "The New Agents: Personal Transfiguration and Radical Privatization in New Age Self-Help." *Journal of Consumer Culture* 2 (2002): 33–52.

Rhodes, Lisa. *In Electric Ladyland: Women and Rock Culture*. Philadelphia: University of Pennsylvania Press, 2005.

Roberts, Ron E. *The New Communes: Coming Together in America*. Englewood Cliffs, NJ: Prentice Hall, 1972.

Robertson, Laurel, Carol Flinders, and Bronwen Godfrey. *Laurel's Kitchen: A Handbook for Vegetarian Cookery and Nutrition*. New York: Bantam, 1981.

Rome, Adam. "'Give Earth a Chance': The Environmental Movement and the Sixties." *Journal of American History* 4 (September 2003): 525–554.

Rothchild, John, and Susan Berns Wolf. *The Children of the Counterculture*. New York: Doubleday, 1976.

Seegar, Arthur. *The Berkeley Barb: Social Control of an Underground Newsroom*. New York: Irvington Publishers, 1983.

Selvin, Joel. *Summer of Love: The Inside Story of LSD, Rock and Roll, Free Love, and High Times in the Wild West*. New York: Cooper Square Press, 1994.

Smith, David, and Alan J. Rose. "Health Problems in Urban and Rural 'Crash Pad' Communes." *Clinical Pediatrics* 9, no. 9 (September 1970): 534–537.

———. "Observations in the Haight Ashbury Medical Clinic of San Francisco: Health Problems in a 'Hippie' Subculture." *Clinical Pediatrics* 7, no. 6 (June 1968): 313–316.

Stablein, Marilyn. *Sleeping in Caves: A Sixties Himalayan Memoir*. Rhinebeck, NY: Monkfish Book Publishing, 2003.

Staller, Karen M. "Constructing the Runaway Youth Problem: Boy Adventurers to Girl Prostitutes, 1960–1978." *Journal of Communications* 53, no. 2 (June 2003): 330–346.

———. *Runaways: How the Sixties Counterculture Shaped Today's Practices and Policies.* New York: Columbia University Press, 2006.

Stern, Jane, and Michael Stern. *Sixties People.* New York: Alfred Knopf, 1990.

Streitmatter, Roger. *Voices of Revolution: The Dissident Press in America.* New York: Columbia University Press, 1991.

Sundancer, Elaine. *Celery Wine: A Story of a Country Commune.* Yellow Springs, OH: Community Publications Cooperative, 1973.

Tent, Pam. *Midnight at the Palace: My Life as a Fabulous Cockette.* Los Angeles: Alyson Books, 2004.

Torgoff, Martin. *Can't Find My Way Home: America in the Great Stoned Age, 1945–2000.* New York: Simon and Schuster, 2004.

Wachsberger, Ken, ed. *Voices from the Underground: Inside Histories of the Vietnam Era Underground.* Tempe, AZ: Mica's Press, 1993.

Wagner, Jon. "Sex Roles in American Communal Utopias." In *Sex Roles in Contemporary American Communes*, edited by Jon Wagner, 1–43. Bloomington: Indiana University Press, 1982.

Whiteley, Sheila. *Women and Popular Music: Sexuality, Identity, and Subjectivity.* New York: Routledge, 2000.

Wolf, Leonard, ed. *Voices of the Love Generation.* Boston: Little, Brown, 1968.

Wolfe, Tom. *Electric Kool-Aid Acid Test.* New York: Bantam, 1999.

Zablocki, Benjamin. *Alienation and Charisma: A Study of Contemporary American Communes.* New York: Free Press, 1980.

Zicklin, Gilbert. *Countercultural Communes: A Sociological Perspective.* Westport, CT: Greenwood Press, 1983.

INTERVIEWS

Interviews during the 60s Communes Project

The following interviews, conducted as part of the 60s Communes Project, are housed with Professor Timothy Miller in the Department of Religious Studies, University of Kansas.

Mary Siler Anderson, interviewed by Deborah Altus, November 11, 1995.

Sylvia Anderson, interviewed by Deborah Altus, August 3, 1996.

Noelle and Sandra Barton, interviewed by Timothy Miller, September 15, 1996.

Mara Devine, interviewed by Deborah Altus, November 12, 1995.

Ina May Gaskin, interviewed by Deborah Altus, October 18, 1995.

Vivian Gotters, interviewed by Timothy Miller, March 23, 1996.

Kay Hayward, interviewed by Deborah Altus, May 28, 1996.

Selected Bibliography

Melissa Hill, interviewed by Deborah Altus, August 6, 1996.

Pamela Hunt, interviewed by Deborah Altus, October 19, 1995.

Terry Klein, interviewed by Timothy Miller, August 6, 1996.

Matie Bell Lakish, interviewed by Deborah Altus, August 15, 1997.

Lelain Lorenzen, interviewed by Deborah Altus, March 15, 1997.

Anne MacNaughton, interviewed by Timothy Miller, August 4, 1996.

Delia Moon and Salli Raspberry, interviewed by Timothy Miller, September 12, 1996.

Nancy Nina, interviewed by Deborah Altus, March 26, 1997.

Kenoli Oleari, interviewed by Timothy Miller, September 16, 1997.

Shannon Perry, interviewed by Deborah Altus, March 25, 1997.

Marylyn Motherbear Scott, interviewed by Deborah Altus, May 28, 1996.

Ayala Talpai, interviewed by Timothy Miller, July 19, 1995.

Ruby Tuesday, interviewed by Deborah Altus, March 21, 1996.

Interviews by Author

The following interviews, conducted by the author, are in her possession.

Jan Camp, Berkeley, CA, May 29, 2007.

Anna Marie Daniels, Santa Barbara, CA, July 26, 2007.

Nancy Jean, Berkeley, CA, June 12, 2007.

Virginia Logan, Berkeley, CA, July 12, 2007.

Kathleen Taylor, Berkeley, CA, August 15, 2007.

Rosaline Santangelo, Berkeley, CA, May 30, 2007.

Marylyn Motherbear Scott, Albion, CA, June 5, 2007.

Constance Trouble, Berkeley, CA, August 6, 2007.

INDEX